THE FOUR BOOKS OF CONFUCIANISM

TRANSLATED BY JAMES LEGGE

Animus Classics edition
First published 2021
Animus Publishing
ISBN-13: 9798533501385

CONTENTS

THE GREAT LEARNING

THE GREAT LEARNING

My master, the philosopher Ch'ang, says:—"The Great Learning is a Book transmitted by the Confucian School, and forms the gate by which first learners enter into virtue. That we can now perceive the order in which the ancients pursued their learning is solely owing to the preservation of this work, the Analects and Mencius coming after it. Learners must commence their course with this, and then it may be hoped they will be kept from error."

THE TEXT OF CONFUCIUS

1. What the Great Learning teaches, is—to illustrate illustrious virtue; to renovate the people; and to rest in the highest excellence.
2. The point where to rest being known, the object of pursuit is then determined; and, that being determined, a calm unperturbedness may be attained to. To that calmness there will succeed a tranquil repose. In that repose there may be careful deliberation, and that deliberation will be followed by the attainment of the desired end.
3. Things have their root and their branches. Affairs have their end and their beginning. To know what is first and what is last will lead near to what is taught in the Great Learning.
4. The ancients who wished to illustrate illustrious virtue throughout the kingdom, first ordered well their own States. Wishing to order well their States, they first regulated their families. Wishing to regulate their families, they first cultivated their persons. Wishing to cultivate their persons, they first rectified their hearts. Wishing to rectify their hearts, they first sought to be sincere in their thoughts. Wishing to be sincere in their thoughts, they first extended to the utmost their knowledge. Such extension of knowledge lay in the investigation of things.
5. Things being investigated, knowledge became complete. Their knowledge being complete, their thoughts were sincere.

Their thoughts being sincere, their hearts were then rectified. Their hearts being rectified, their persons were cultivated. Their persons being cultivated, their families were regulated. Their families being regulated, their States were rightly governed. Their States being rightly governed, the whole kingdom was made tranquil and happy.

6. From the Son of Heaven down to the mass of the people, all must consider the cultivation of the person the root of everything besides.

7. It cannot be, when the root is neglected, that what should spring from it will be well ordered. It never has been the case that what was of great importance has been slightly cared for, and, at the same time, that what was of slight importance has been greatly cared for.

COMMENTARY OF THE PHILOSOPHER TSANG

CHAP. I. 1. In the Announcement to K'ang, it is said, "He was able to make his virtue illustrious."

2. In the Tai Chia, it is said, "He contemplated and studied the illustrious decrees of Heaven."

3. In the Canon of the emperor (Yao), it is said, "He was able to make illustrious his lofty virtue."

4. These passages all show how those sovereigns made themselves illustrious.

CHAP. II. 1. On the bathing tub of T'ang, the following words were engraved:—"If you can one day renovate yourself, do so from day to day. Yea, let there be daily renovation."

2. In the Announcement to K'ang, it is said, "To stir up the new people."

3. In the Book of Poetry, it is said, "Although Chau was an ancient State, the ordinance which lighted on it was new."

4. Therefore, the superior man in everything uses his utmost endeavours.

CHAP. III. 1. In the Book of Poetry, it is said, "The royal domain of a thousand li is where the people rest."

2. In the Book of Poetry, it is said, "The twittering yellow bird rests on a corner of the mound." The Master said, "When

it rests, it knows where to rest. Is it possible that a man should not be equal to this bird?"

3. In the Book of Poetry, it is said, "Profound was king Wan. With how bright and unceasing a feeling of reverence did he regard his resting places!" As a sovereign, he rested in benevolence. As a minister, he rested in reverence. As a son, he rested in filial piety. As a father, he rested in kindness. In communication with his subjects, he rested in good faith.

4. In the Book of Poetry, it is said, "Look at that winding course of the Ch'i, with the green bamboos so luxuriant! Here is our elegant and accomplished prince! As we cut and then file; as we chisel and then grind: so has he cultivated himself. How grave is he and dignified! How majestic and distinguished! Our elegant and accomplished prince never can be forgotten." That expression—"As we cut and then file," indicates the work of learning. "As we chisel and then grind," indicates that of self-culture. "How grave is he and dignified!" indicates the feeling of cautious reverence. "How commanding and distinguished!" indicates an awe-inspiring deportment. "Our elegant and accomplished prince never can be forgotten," indicates how, when virtue is complete and excellence extreme, the people cannot forget them.

5. In the Book of Poetry, it is said, "Ah! the former kings are not forgotten." Future princes deem worthy what they deemed worthy, and love what they loved. The common people delight in what delighted them, and are benefited by their beneficial arrangements. It is on this account that the former kings, after they have quitted the world, are not forgotten.

CHAP. IV. The Master said, "In hearing litigations, I am like any other body. What is necessary is to cause the people to have no litigations." So, those who are devoid of principle find it impossible to carry out their speeches, and a great awe would be struck into men's minds;—this is called knowing the root.

CHAP. V. 1. This is called knowing the root.

2. This is called the perfecting of knowledge.

CHAP. VI. 1. What is meant by "making the thoughts sincere," is the allowing no self-deception, as when we hate a bad smell, and as when we love what is beautiful. This is called self-enjoyment. Therefore, the superior man must be watchful over himself when he is alone.

2. There is no evil to which the mean man, dwelling retired, will not proceed, but when he sees a superior man, he instantly tries to disguise himself, concealing his evil, and displaying what is good. The other beholds him, as if he saw his heart and reins;—of what use is his disguise? This is an instance of the saying—"What truly is within will be manifested without." Therefore, the superior man must be watchful over himself when he is alone.

3. The disciple Tsang said, "What ten eyes behold, what ten hands point to, is to be regarded with reverence!"

4. Riches adorn a house, and virtue adorns the person. The mind is expanded, and the body is at ease. Therefore, the superior man must make his thoughts sincere.

CHAP. VII. 1. What is meant by, "The cultivation of the person depends on rectifying the mind," may be thus illustrated:—If a man be under the influence of passion, he will be incorrect in his conduct. He will be the same, if he is under the influence of terror, or under the influence of fond regard, or under that of sorrow and distress.

2. When the mind is not present, we look and do not see; we hear and do not understand; we eat and do not know the taste of what we eat.

3. This is what is meant by saying that the cultivation of the person depends on the rectifying of the mind.

CHAP. VIII. 1. What is meant by "The regulation of one's family depends on the cultivation of his person," is this:—men are partial where they feel affection and love; partial where they despise and dislike; partial where they stand in awe and reverence; partial where they feel sorrow and compassion; partial where they are arrogant and rude. Thus it is that there are few men in the world who love and at the same time know the bad qualities of the object of their love, or who hate and yet know the excellences of the object of their hatred.

2. Hence it is said, in the common adage, "A man does not know the wickedness of his son; he does not know the richness

of his growing corn."

3. This is what is meant by saying that if the person be not cultivated, a man cannot regulate his family.

CHAP. IX. 1. What is meant by "In order rightly to govern the State, it is necessary first to regulate the family," is this:— It is not possible for one to teach others, while he cannot teach his own family. Therefore, the ruler, without going beyond his family, completes the lessons for the State. There is filial piety:—therewith the sovereign should be served. There is fraternal submission:—therewith elders and superiors should be served. There is kindness:—therewith the multitude should be treated.

2. In the Announcement to K'ang, it is said, "Act as if you were watching over an infant." If a mother is really anxious about it, though she may not hit exactly the wants of her infant, she will not be far from doing so. There never has been a girl who learned to bring up a child, that she might afterwards marry.

3. From the loving example of one family a whole State becomes loving, and from its courtesies the whole State becomes courteous while, from the ambition and perverseness of the One man, the whole State may be led to rebellious disorder;—such is the nature of the influence. This verifies the saying, "Affairs may be ruined by a single sentence; a kingdom may be settled by its One man."

4. Yao and Shun led on the kingdom with benevolence and the people followed them. Chieh and Chau led on the kingdom with violence, and people followed them. The orders which these issued were contrary to the practices which they loved, and so the people did not follow them. On this account, the ruler must himself be possessed of the good qualities, and then he may require them in the people. He must not have the bad qualities in himself, and then he may require that they shall not be in the people. Never has there been a man, who, not having reference to his own character and wishes in dealing with others, was able effectually to instruct them.

5. Thus we see how the government of the State depends on the regulation of the family.

6. In the Book of Poetry, it is said, "That peach tree, so delicate and elegant! How luxuriant is its foliage! This girl is going to her husband's house. She will rightly order her household." Let the household be rightly ordered, and then the people of the State may be taught.

7. In the Book of Poetry, it is said, "They can discharge their duties to their elder brothers. They can discharge their duties to their younger brothers." Let the ruler discharge his duties to his elder and younger brothers, and then he may teach the people of the State.

8. In the Book of Poetry, it is said, "In his deportment there is nothing wrong; he rectifies all the people of the State." Yes; when the ruler, as a father, a son, and a brother, is a model, then the people imitate him.

9. This is what is meant by saying, "The government of his kingdom depends on his regulation of the family."

CHAP. X. 1. What is meant by "The making the whole kingdom peaceful and happy depends on the government of his State," is this:—When the sovereign behaves to his aged, as the aged should be behaved to, the people become final; when the sovereign behaves to his elders, as the elders should be behaved to, the people learn brotherly submission; when the sovereign treats compassionately the young and helpless, the people do the same. Thus the ruler has a principle with which, as with a measuring-square, he may regulate his conduct.

2. What a man dislikes in his superiors, let him not display in the treatment of his inferiors; what he dislikes in inferiors, let him not display in the service of his superiors; what he hates in those who are before him, let him not therewith precede those who are behind him; what he hates in those who are behind him, let him not bestow on the left; what he hates to receive on the left, let him not bestow on the right:—this is what is called "The principle with which, as with a measuring-square, to regulate one's conduct."

3. In the Book of Poetry, it is said, "How much to be rejoiced in are these princes, the parents of the people!" When a prince loves what the people love, and hates what the people

hate, then is he what is called the parent of the people.

4. In the Book of Poetry, it is said, "Lofty is that southern hill, with its rugged masses of rocks! Greatly distinguished are you, O grand-teacher Yin, the people all look up to you." Rulers of States may not neglect to be careful. If they deviate to a mean selfishness, they will be a disgrace in the kingdom.

5. In the Book of Poetry, it is said, "Before the sovereigns of the Yin dynasty had lost the hearts of the people, they could appear before God. Take warning from the house of Yin. The great decree is not easily preserved." This shows that, by gaining the people, the kingdom is gained, and, by losing the people, the kingdom is lost.

6. On this account, the ruler will first take pains about his own virtue. Possessing virtue will give him the people. Possessing the people will give the territory. Possessing the territory will give him its wealth. Possessing the wealth, he will have resources for expenditure.

7. Virtue is the root; wealth is the result.

8. If he make the root his secondary object, and the result his primary, he will only wrangle with his people, and teach them rapine.

9. Hence, the accumulation of wealth is the way to scatter the people; and the letting it be scattered among them is the way to collect the people.

10. And hence, the ruler's words going forth contrary to right, will come back to him in the same way, and wealth, gotten by improper ways, will take its departure by the same.

11. In the Announcement to K'ang, it is said, "The decree indeed may not always rest on us;" that is, goodness obtains the decree, and the want of goodness loses it.

12. In the Book of Ch'u, it is said, "The kingdom of Ch'u does not consider that to be valuable. It values, instead, its good men."

13. Duke Wan's uncle, Fan, said, "Our fugitive does not account that to be precious. What he considers precious is the affection due to his parent."

14. In the Declaration of the Duke of Ch'in, it is said, "Let me have but one minister, plain and sincere, not pretending to

other abilities, but with a simple, upright, mind; and possessed of generosity, regarding the talents of others as though he himself possessed them, and, where he finds accomplished and perspicacious men, loving them in his heart more than his mouth expresses, and really showing himself able to bear them and employ them:—such a minister will be able to preserve my sons and grandsons and black-haired people, and benefits likewise to the kingdom may well be looked for from him. But if it be his character, when he finds men of ability, to be jealous and hate them; and, when he finds accomplished and perspicacious men, to oppose them and not allow their advancement, showing himself really not able to bear them:— such a minister will not be able to protect my sons and grandsons and black-haired people; and may he not also be pronounced dangerous to the State?"

15. It is only the truly virtuous man who can send away such a man and banish him, driving him out among the barbarous tribes around, determined not to dwell along with him in the Middle Kingdom. This is in accordance with the saying, "It is only the truly virtuous man who can love or who can hate others."

16. To see men of worth and not be able to raise them to office; to raise them to office, but not to do so quickly:—this is disrespectful. To see bad men and not be able to remove them; to remove them, but not to do so to a distance:—this is weakness.

17. To love those whom men hate, and to hate those whom men love:—this is to outrage the natural feeling of men. Calamities cannot fail to come down on him who does so.

18. Thus we see that the sovereign has a great course to pursue. He must show entire self-devotion and sincerity to attain it, and by pride and extravagance he will fail of it.

19. There is a great course also for the production of wealth. Let the producers be many and the consumers few. Let there be activity in the production, and economy in the expenditure. Then the wealth will always be sufficient.

20. The virtuous ruler, by means of his wealth, makes himself more distinguished. The vicious ruler accumulates wealth, at the expense of his life.

21. Never has there been a case of the sovereign loving benevolence, and the people not loving righteousness. Never has there been a case where the people have loved righteousness, and the affairs of the sovereign have not been carried to completion. And never has there been a case where the wealth in such a State, collected in the treasuries and arsenals, did not continue in the sovereign's possession.

22. The officer Mang Hsien said, "He who keeps horses and a carriage does not look after fowls and pigs. The family which keeps its stores of ice does not rear cattle or sheep. So, the house which possesses a hundred chariots should not keep a minister to look out for imposts that he may lay them on the people. Than to have such a minister, it were better for that house to have one who should rob it of its revenues." This is in accordance with the saying:—"In a State, pecuniary gain is not to be considered to be prosperity, but its prosperity will be found in righteousness."

23. When he who presides over a State or a family makes his revenues his chief business, he must be under the influence of some small, mean man. He may consider this man to be good; but when such a person is employed in the administration of a State or family, calamities from Heaven, and injuries from men, will befall it together, and, though a good man may take his place, he will not be able to remedy the evil. This illustrates again the saying, "In a State, gain is not to be considered prosperity, but its prosperity will be found in righteousness."

THE DOCTRINE OF THE MEAN

THE DOCTRINE OF THE MEAN

My master, the philosopher Ch'ung, says:—"Being without inclination to either side is called CHUNG; admitting of no change is called YUNG. By CHUNG is denoted the correct course to be pursued by all under heaven; by YUNG is denoted the fixed principle regulating all under heaven. This work contains the law of the mind, which was handed down from one to another, in the Confucian school, till Tsze-sze, fearing lest in the course of time errors should arise about it, committed it to writing, and delivered it to Mencius. The Book first speaks of one principle; it next spreads this out, and embraces all things; finally, it returns and gathers them all up under the one principle. Unroll it, and it fills the universe; roll it up, and it retires and lies hid in mysteriousness. The relish of it is inexhaustible. The whole of it is solid learning. When the skilful reader has explored it with delight till he has apprehended it, he may carry it into practice all his life, and will find that it cannot be exhausted."

CHAP. I. 1. What Heaven has conferred is called THE NATURE; an accordance with this nature is called THE PATH of duty; the regulation of this path is called INSTRUCTION.

2. The path may not be left for an instant. If it could be left, it would not be the path. On this account, the superior man does not wait till he sees things, to be cautious, nor till he hears things, to be apprehensive.

3. There is nothing more visible than what is secret, and nothing more manifest than what is minute. Therefore the superior man is watchful over himself, when he is alone.

4. While there are no stirrings of pleasure, anger, sorrow, or joy, the mind may be said to be in the state of EQUILIBRIUM. When those feelings have been stirred, and they act in their due degree, there ensues what may be called the state of HARMONY. This EQUILIBRIUM is the great root from which grow all the human actings in the world, and this HARMONY is

the universal path which they all should pursue.

5. Let the states of equilibrium and harmony exist in perfection, and a happy order will prevail throughout heaven and earth, and all things will be nourished and flourish.

CHAP. II. 1. Chung-ni said, "The superior man embodies the course of the Mean; the mean man acts contrary to the course of the Mean.

2. "The superior man's embodying the course of the Mean is because he is a superior man, and so always maintains the Mean. The mean man's acting contrary to the course of the Mean is because he is a mean man, and has no caution."

CHAP. III. The Master said, "Perfect is the virtue which is according to the Mean! Rare have they long been among the people, who could practice it!"

CHAP. IV. 1. The Master said, "I know how it is that the path of the Mean is not walked in:—The knowing go beyond it, and the stupid do not come up to it. I know how it is that the path of the Mean is not understood:—The men of talents and virtue go beyond it, and the worthless do not come up to it.

2. "There is no body but eats and drinks. But they are few who can distinguish flavours."

CHAP. V. The Master said, "Alas! How is the path of the Mean untrodden!"

CHAP. VI. The Master said, "There was Shun:—He indeed was greatly wise! Shun loved to question others, and to study their words, though they might be shallow. He concealed what was bad in them and displayed what was good. He took hold of their two extremes, determined the Mean, and employed it in his government of the people. It was by this that he was Shun!"

CHAP. VII. The Master said "Men all say, 'We are wise;' but being driven forward and taken in a net, a trap, or a pitfall, they know not how to escape. Men all say, 'We are wise;' but happening to choose the course of the Mean, they are not able to keep it for a round month."

CHAP. VIII. The Master said "This was the manner of Hui:—he made choice of the Mean, and whenever he got hold of what was good, he clasped it firmly, as if wearing it on his breast, and did not lose it."

CHAP. IX. The Master said, "The kingdom, its States, and its families, may be perfectly ruled; dignities and emoluments may be declined; naked weapons may be trampled under the feet;—but the course of the Mean cannot be attained to."

CHAP. X. 1. Tsze-lu asked about energy.

2. The Master said, "Do you mean the energy of the South, the energy of the North, or the energy which you should cultivate yourself?

3. "To show forbearance and gentleness in teaching others; and not to revenge unreasonable conduct:—this is the energy of Southern regions, and the good man makes it his study.

4. "To lie under arms; and meet death without regret:—this is the energy of Northern regions, and the forceful make it their study.

5. "Therefore, the superior man cultivates a friendly harmony, without being weak.—How firm is he in his energy! He stands erect in the middle, without inclining to either side.—How firm is he in his energy! When good principles prevail in the government of his country, he does not change from what he was in retirement.—How firm is he in his energy! When bad principles prevail in the country, he maintains his course to death without changing.—How firm is he in his energy!"

CHAP. XI. 1. The Master said, "To live in obscurity, and yet practice wonders, in order to be mentioned with honour in future ages:—this is what I do not do.

2. "The good man tries to proceed according to the right path, but when he has gone halfway, he abandons it:—I am not able so to stop.

3. "The superior man accords with the course of the Mean. Though he may be all unknown, unregarded by the world, he feels no regret.—It is only the sage who is able for this."

CHAP. XII. 1. The way which the superior man pursues, reaches wide and far, and yet is secret.

2. Common men and women, however ignorant, may intermeddle with the knowledge of it; yet in its utmost reaches,

there is that which even the sage does not know. Common men and women, however much below the ordinary standard of character, can carry it into practice; yet in its utmost reaches, there is that which even the sage is not able to carry into practice. Great as heaven and earth are, men still find some things in them with which to be dissatisfied. Thus it is that, were the superior man to speak of his way in all its greatness, nothing in the world would be found able to embrace it, and were he to speak of it in its minuteness, nothing in the world would be found able to split it.

3. It is said in the Book of Poetry, "The hawk flies up to heaven; the fishes leap in the deep." This expresses how this way is seen above and below.

4. The way of the superior man may be found, in its simple elements, in the intercourse of common men and women; but in its utmost reaches, it shines brightly through heaven and earth.

CHAP. XIII. 1. The Master said "The path is not far from man. When men try to pursue a course, which is far from the common indications of consciousness, this course cannot be considered THE PATH.

2. "In the Book of Poetry, it is said, 'In hewing an ax-handle, in hewing an ax-handle, the pattern is not far off.' We grasp one ax-handle to hew the other; and yet, if we look askance from the one to the other, we may consider them as apart. Therefore, the superior man governs men, according to their nature, with what is proper to them, and as soon as they change what is wrong, he stops.

3. "When one cultivates to the utmost the principles of his nature, and exercises them on the principle of reciprocity, he is not far from the path. What you do not like when done to yourself, do not do to others.

4. "In the way of the superior man there are four things, to not one of which have I as yet attained.—To serve my father, as I would require my son to serve me: to this I have not attained; to serve my prince, as I would require my minister to serve me: to this I have not attained; to serve my elder brother, as I would require my younger brother to serve me: to this I

have not attained; to set the example in behaving to a friend, as I would require him to behave to me: to this I have not attained. Earnest in practicing the ordinary virtues, and careful in speaking about them, if, in his practice, he has anything defective, the superior man dares not but exert himself; and if, in his words, he has any excess, he dares not allow himself such license. Thus his words have respect to his actions, and his actions have respect to his words; is it not just an entire sincerity which marks the superior man?"

CHAP. XIV. 1. The superior man does what is proper to the station in which he is; he does not desire to go beyond this.

2. In a position of wealth and honour, he does what is proper to a position of wealth and honour. In a poor and low position, he does what is proper to a poor and low position. Situated among barbarous tribes, he does what is proper to a situation among barbarous tribes. In a position of sorrow and difficulty, he does what is proper to a position of sorrow and difficulty. The superior man can find himself in no situation in which he is not himself.

3. In a high situation, he does not treat with contempt his inferiors. In a low situation, he does not court the favour of his superiors. He rectifies himself, and seeks for nothing from others, so that he has no dissatisfactions. He does not murmur against Heaven, nor grumble against men.

4. Thus it is that the superior man is quiet and calm, waiting for the appointments of Heaven, while the mean man walks in dangerous paths, looking for lucky occurrences.

5. The Master said, "In archery we have something like the way of the superior man. When the archer misses the centre of the target, he turns round and seeks for the cause of his failure in himself."

CHAP. XV. 1. The way of the superior man may be compared to what takes place in traveling, when to go to a distance we must first traverse the space that is near, and in ascending a height, when we must begin from the lower ground.

2. It is said in the Book of Poetry, "Happy union with wife and children is like the music of lutes and harps. When there

is concord among brethren, the harmony is delightful and enduring. Thus may you regulate your family, and enjoy the pleasure of your wife and children."

3. The Master said, "In such a state of things, parents have entire complacence!"

CHAP. XVI. 1. The Master said, "How abundantly do spiritual beings display the powers that belong to them!

2. "We look for them, but do not see them; we listen to, but do not hear them; yet they enter into all things, and there is nothing without them.

3. "They cause all the people in the kingdom to fast and purify themselves, and array themselves in their richest dresses, in order to attend at their sacrifices. Then, like overflowing water, they seem to be over the heads, and on the right and left of their worshippers.

4. "It is said in the Book of Poetry, 'The approaches of the spirits, you cannot surmise;—and can you treat them with indifference?'

5. "Such is the manifestness of what is minute! Such is the impossibility of repressing the outgoings of sincerity!"

CHAP. XVII. 1. The Master said, "How greatly filial was Shun! His virtue was that of a sage; his dignity was the throne; his riches were all within the four seas. He offered his sacrifices in his ancestral temple, and his descendants preserved the sacrifices to himself.

2. "Therefore having such great virtue, it could not but be that he should obtain the throne, that he should obtain those riches, that he should obtain his fame, that he should attain to his long life.

3. "Thus it is that Heaven, in the production of things, is sure to be bountiful to them, according to their qualities. Hence the tree that is flourishing, it nourishes, while that which is ready to fall, it overthrows.

4. "In the Book of Poetry, it is said, 'The admirable, amiable prince displayed conspicuously his excelling virtue, adjusting his people, and adjusting his officers. Therefore, he received from Heaven his emoluments of dignity. It protected him, assisted him, decreed him the throne; sending from Heaven

these favours, as it were repeatedly.'

5. "We may say therefore that he who is greatly virtuous will be sure to receive the appointment of Heaven."

CHAP. XVIII. 1. The Master said, "It is only king Wan of whom it can be said that he had no cause for grief! His father was king Chi, and his son was king Wu. His father laid the foundations of his dignity, and his son transmitted it.

2. "King Wu continued the enterprise of king T'ai, king Chi, and king Wan. He once buckled on his armour, and got possession of the kingdom. He did not lose the distinguished personal reputation which he had throughout the kingdom. His dignity was the royal throne. His riches were the possession of all within the four seas. He offered his sacrifices in his ancestral temple, and his descendants maintained the sacrifices to himself.

3. "It was in his old age that king Wu received the appointment to the throne, and the duke of Chau completed the virtuous course of Wan and Wu. He carried up the title of king to T'ai and Chi, and sacrificed to all the former dukes above them with the royal ceremonies. And this rule he extended to the princes of the kingdom, the great officers, the scholars, and the common people. If the father were a great officer and the son a scholar, then the burial was that due to a great officer, and the sacrifice that due to a scholar. If the father were a scholar and the son a great officer, then the burial was that due to a scholar, and the sacrifice that due to a great officer. The one year's mourning was made to extend only to the great officers, but the three years' mourning extended to the Son of Heaven. In the mourning for a father or mother, he allowed no difference between the noble and the mean."

CHAP. XIX. 1. The Master said, "How far-extending was the filial piety of king Wu and the duke of Chau!

2. "Now filial piety is seen in the skillful carrying out of the wishes of our forefathers, and the skillful carrying forward of their undertakings.

3. "In spring and autumn, they repaired and beautified the temple halls of their fathers, set forth their ancestral vessels, displayed their various robes, and presented the offerings of

the several seasons.

4. "By means of the ceremonies of the ancestral temple, they distinguished the royal kindred according to their order of descent. By ordering the parties present according to their rank, they distinguished the more noble and the less. By the arrangement of the services, they made a distinction of talents and worth. In the ceremony of general pledging, the inferiors presented the cup to their superiors, and thus something was given the lowest to do. At the concluding feast, places were given according to the hair, and thus was made the distinction of years.

5. "They occupied the places of their forefathers, practiced their ceremonies, and performed their music. They reverenced those whom they honoured, and loved those whom they regarded with affection. Thus they served the dead as they would have served them alive; they served the departed as they would have served them had they been continued among them.

6. "By the ceremonies of the sacrifices to Heaven and Earth they served God, and by the ceremonies of the ancestral temple they sacrificed to their ancestors. He who understands the ceremonies of the sacrifices to Heaven and Earth, and the meaning of the several sacrifices to ancestors, would find the government of a kingdom as easy as to look into his palm!"

CHAP. XX. 1. The duke Ai asked about government.

2. The Master said, "The government of Wan and Wu is displayed in the records,—the tablets of wood and bamboo. Let there be the men and the government will flourish; but without the men, their government decays and ceases.

3. "With the right men the growth of government is rapid, just as vegetation is rapid in the earth; and, moreover, their government might be called an easily-growing rush.

4. "Therefore the administration of government lies in getting proper men. Such men are to be got by means of the ruler's own character. That character is to be cultivated by his treading in the ways of duty. And the treading those ways of duty is to be cultivated by the cherishing of benevolence.

5. "Benevolence is the characteristic element of humanity,

22

and the great exercise of it is in loving relatives. Righteousness is the accordance of actions with what is right, and the great exercise of it is in honouring the worthy. The decreasing measures of the love due to relatives, and the steps in the honour due to the worthy, are produced by the principle of propriety.

6. "When those in inferior situations do not possess the confidence of their superiors, they cannot retain the government of the people.

7. "Hence the sovereign may not neglect the cultivation of his own character. Wishing to cultivate his character, he may not neglect to serve his parents. In order to serve his parents, he may not neglect to acquire knowledge of men. In order to know men, he may not dispense with a knowledge of Heaven.

8. "The duties of universal obligation are five, and the virtues wherewith they are practiced are three. The duties are those between sovereign and minister, between father and son, between husband and wife, between elder brother and younger, and those belonging to the intercourse of friends. Those five are the duties of universal obligation. Knowledge, magnanimity, and energy, these three, are the virtues universally binding. And the means by which they carry the duties into practice is singleness.

9. "Some are born with the knowledge of those duties; some know them by study; and some acquire the knowledge after a painful feeling of their ignorance. But the knowledge being possessed, it comes to the same thing. Some practice them with a natural ease; some from a desire for their advantages; and some by strenuous effort. But the achievement being made, it comes to the same thing."

10. The Master said, "To be fond of learning is to be near to knowledge. To practice with vigor is to be near to magnanimity. To possess the feeling of shame is to be near to energy.

11. "He who knows these three things knows how to cultivate his own character. Knowing how to cultivate his own character, he knows how to govern other men. Knowing how to govern other men, he knows how to govern the kingdom

with all its states and families.

12. "All who have the government of the kingdom with its States and families have nine standard rules to follow;—viz. the cultivation of their own characters; the honouring of men of virtue and talents; affection towards their relatives; respect towards the great ministers; kind and considerate treatment of the whole body of officers; dealing with the mass of the people as children; encouraging the resort of all classes of artisans; indulgent treatment of men from a distance; and the kindly cherishing of the princes of the States.

13. "By the ruler's cultivation of his own character, the duties of universal obligation are set forth. By honouring men of virtue and talents, he is preserved from errors of judgment. By showing affection to his relatives, there is no grumbling nor resentment among his uncles and brethren. By respecting the great ministers, he is kept from errors in the practice of government. By kind and considerate treatment of the whole body of officers, they are led to make the most grateful return for his courtesies. By dealing with the mass of the people as his children, they are led to exhort one another to what is good. By encouraging the resort of all classes of artisans, his resources for expenditure are rendered ample. By indulgent treatment of men from a distance, they are brought to resort to him from all quarters. And by kindly cherishing the princes of the states, the whole kingdom is brought to revere him.

14. "Self-adjustment and purification, with careful regulation of his dress, and the not making a movement contrary to the rules of propriety:—this is the way for a ruler to cultivate his person. Discarding slanderers, and keeping himself from the seductions of beauty; making light of riches, and giving honour to virtue:—this is the way for him to encourage men of worth and talents. Giving them places of honour and large emolument. and sharing with them in their likes and dislikes:—this is the way for him to encourage his relatives to love him. Giving them numerous officers to discharge their orders and commissions:—this is the way for him to encourage the great ministers. According to them a generous confidence, and making their emoluments large:—

this is the way to encourage the body of officers. Employing them only at the proper times, and making the imposts light:—this is the way to encourage the people. By daily examinations and monthly trials, and by making their rations in accordance with their labors:—this is the way to encourage the classes of artisans. To escort them on their departure and meet them on their coming; to commend the good among them, and show compassion to the incompetent:—this is the way to treat indulgently men from a distance. To restore families whose line of succession has been broken, and to revive states that have been extinguished; to reduce to order States that are in confusion, and support those which are in peril; to have fixed times for their own reception at court, and the reception of their envoys; to send them away after liberal treatment, and welcome their coming with small contributions:—this is the way to cherish the princes of the States.

15. "All who have the government of the kingdom with its States and families have the above nine standard rules. And the means by which they are carried into practice is singleness.

16. "In all things success depends on previous preparation, and without such previous preparation there is sure to be failure. If what is to be spoken be previously determined, there will be no stumbling. If affairs be previously determined, there will be no difficulty with them. If one's actions have been previously determined, there will be no sorrow in connection with them. If principles of conduct have been previously determined, the practice of them will be inexhaustible.

17. "When those in inferior situations do not obtain the confidence of the sovereign, they cannot succeed in governing the people. There is a way to obtain the confidence of the sovereign;—if one is not trusted by his friends, he will not get the confidence of his sovereign. There is a way to being trusted by one's friends;—if one is not obedient to his parents, he will not be true to friends. There is a way to being obedient to one's parents;—if one, on turning his thoughts in upon himself, finds a want of sincerity, he will not be obedient to his parents. There is a way to the attainment of sincerity in one's self;—if a man do not understand what is good, he will not attain

sincerity in himself.

18. "Sincerity is the way of Heaven. The attainment of sincerity is the way of men. He who possesses sincerity is he who, without an effort, hits what is right, and apprehends, without the exercise of thought;—he is the sage who naturally and easily embodies the right way. He who attains to sincerity is he who chooses what is good, and firmly holds it fast.

19. "To this attainment there are requisite the extensive study of what is good, accurate inquiry about it, careful reflection on it, the clear discrimination of it, and the earnest practice of it.

20. "The superior man, while there is anything he has not studied, or while in what he has studied there is anything he cannot understand, Will not intermit his labor. While there is anything he has not inquired about, or anything in what he has inquired about which he does not know, he will not intermit his labor. While there is anything which he has not reflected on, or anything in what he has reflected on which he does not apprehend, he will not intermit his labor. While there is anything which he has not discriminated or his discrimination is not clear, he will not intermit his labor. If there be anything which he has not practiced, or his practice fails in earnestness, he will not intermit his labor. If another man succeed by one effort, he will use a hundred efforts. If another man succeed by ten efforts, he will use a thousand.

21. "Let a man proceed in this way, and, though dull, he will surely become intelligent; though weak, he will surely become strong."

CHAP. XXI. When we have intelligence resulting from sincerity, this condition is to be ascribed to nature; when we have sincerity resulting from intelligence, this condition is to be ascribed to instruction. But given the sincerity, and there shall be the intelligence; given the intelligence, and there shall be the sincerity.

CHAP. XXII. It is only he who is possessed of the most complete sincerity that can exist under heaven, who can give its fun development to his nature. Able to give its full development to his own nature, he can do the same to the nature of other men. Able to give its full development to the nature of other men, he can give their full development to the natures of animals and things. Able to give their full development to the natures of creatures and things, he can assist the transforming and nourishing powers of Heaven and Earth. Able to assist the transforming and nourishing powers of Heaven and Earth, he may with Heaven and Earth form a ternion.

CHAP. XXIII. Next to the above is he who cultivates to the utmost the shoots of goodness in him. From those he can attain to the possession of sincerity. This sincerity becomes apparent. From being apparent, it becomes manifest. From being manifest, it becomes brilliant. Brilliant, it affects others. Affecting others, they are changed by it. Changed by it, they are transformed. It is only he who is possessed of the most complete sincerity that can exist under heaven, who can transform.

CHAP. XXIV. It is characteristic of the most entire sincerity to be able to foreknow. When a nation or family is about to flourish, there are sure to be happy omens; and when it is about to perish, there are sure to be unlucky omens. Such events are seen in the milfoil and tortoise, and affect the movements of the four limbs. When calamity or happiness is about to come, the good shall certainly be foreknown by him, and the evil also. Therefore the individual possessed of the most complete sincerity is like a spirit.

CHAP. XXV. 1. Sincerity is that whereby self-completion is effected, and its way is that by which man must direct himself.

2. Sincerity is the end and beginning of things; without sincerity there would be nothing. On this account, the superior man regards the attainment of sincerity as the most excellent thing.

3. The possessor of sincerity does not merely accomplish the self-completion of himself. With this quality he completes other men and things also. The completing himself shows his perfect virtue. The completing other men and things shows his knowledge. But these are virtues belonging to the nature, and this is the way by which a union is effected of the external and

internal. Therefore, whenever he—the entirely sincere man—employs them,—that is, these virtues,—their action will be right.

CHAP. XXVI. 1. Hence to entire sincerity there belongs ceaselessness.

2. Not ceasing, it continues long. Continuing long, it evidences itself.

3. Evidencing itself, it reaches far. Reaching far, it becomes large and substantial. Large and substantial, it becomes high and brilliant.

4. Large and substantial;—this is how it contains all things. High and brilliant;—this is how it overspreads all things. Reaching far and continuing long;—this is how it perfects all things.

5. So large and substantial, the individual possessing it is the co-equal of Earth. So high and brilliant, it makes him the co-equal of Heaven. So far-reaching and long-continuing, it makes him infinite.

6. Such being its nature, without any display, it becomes manifested; without any movement, it produces changes; and without any effort, it accomplishes its ends.

7. The way of Heaven and Earth may be completely declared in one sentence.—They are without any doubleness, and so they produce things in a manner that is unfathomable.

8. The way of Heaven and Earth is large and substantial, high and brilliant, far-reaching and long-enduring.

9. The Heaven now before us is only this bright shining spot; but when viewed in its inexhaustible extent, the sun, moon, stars, and constellations of the zodiac, are suspended in it, and all things are overspread by it. The earth before us is but a handful of soil; but when regarded in its breadth and thickness, it sustains mountains like the Hwa and the Yo, without feeling their weight, and contains the rivers and seas, without their leaking away. The mountain now before us appears only a stone; but when contemplated in all the vastness of its size, we see how the grass and trees are produced on it, and birds and beasts dwell on it, and precious things which men treasure up are found on it. The water now before us

appears but a ladleful; yet extending our view to its unfathomable depths, the largest tortoises, iguanas, iguanodons, dragons, fishes, and turtles, are produced in it, articles of value and sources of wealth abound in it.

10. It is said in the Book of Poetry, "The ordinances of Heaven, how profound are they and unceasing!" The meaning is, that it is thus that Heaven is Heaven. And again, "How illustrious was it, the singleness of the virtue of king Wan!" indicating that it was thus that king Wan was what he was. Singleness likewise is unceasing.

CHAP. XXVII. 1. How great is the path proper to the Sage!

2. Like overflowing water, it sends forth and nourishes all things, and rises up to the height of heaven.

3. All-complete is its greatness! It embraces the three hundred rules of ceremony, and the three thousand rules of demeanor.

4. It waits for the proper man, and then it is trodden.

5. Hence it is said, "Only by perfect virtue can the perfect path, in all its courses, be made a fact."

6. Therefore, the superior man honours his virtuous nature, and maintains constant inquiry and study, seeking to carry it out to its breadth and greatness, so as to omit none of the more exquisite and minute points which it embraces, and to raise it to its greatest height and brilliancy, so as to pursue the course of the Mean. He cherishes his old knowledge, and is continually acquiring new. He exerts an honest, generous earnestness, in the esteem and practice of all propriety.

7. Thus, when occupying a high situation he is not proud, and in a low situation he is not insubordinate. When the kingdom is well governed, he is sure by his words to rise; and when it is ill governed, he is sure by his silence to command forbearance to himself. Is not this what we find in the Book of Poetry,—"Intelligent is he and prudent, and so preserves his person?"

CHAP. XXVIII. 1. The Master said, "Let a man who is ignorant be fond of using his own judgment; let a man without rank be fond of assuming a directing power to himself; let a man who is living in the present age go back to the ways of antiquity;—on the persons of all who act thus calamities will be sure to come."

2. To no one but the Son of Heaven does it belong to order ceremonies, to fix the measures, and to determine the written characters.

3. Now over the kingdom, carriages have all wheels, of the-same size; all writing is with the same characters; and for conduct there are the same rules.

4. One may occupy the throne, but if he have not the proper virtue, he may not dare to make ceremonies or music. One may have the virtue, but if he do not occupy the throne, he may not presume to make ceremonies or music.

5. The Master said, "I may describe the ceremonies of the Hsia dynasty, but Chi cannot sufficiently attest my words. I have learned the ceremonies of the Yin dynasty, and in Sung they still continue. I have learned the ceremonies of Chau, which are now used, and I follow Chau."

CHAP. XXIX. 1. He who attains to the sovereignty of the kingdom, having those three important things, shall be able to effect that there shall be few errors under his government.

2. However excellent may have been the regulations of those of former times, they cannot be attested. Not being attested, they cannot command credence, and not being credited, the people would not follow them. However excellent might be the regulations made by one in an inferior situation, he is not in a position to be honoured. Unhonoured, he cannot command credence, and not being credited, the people would not follow his rules.

3. Therefore the institutions of the Ruler are rooted in his own character and conduct, and sufficient attestation of them is given by the masses of the people. He examines them by comparison with those of the three kings, and finds them without mistake. He sets them up before Heaven and Earth, and finds nothing in them contrary to their mode of operation. He presents himself with them before spiritual beings, and no doubts about them arise. He is prepared to wait for the rise of a sage a hundred ages after, and has no misgivings.

4. His presenting himself with his institutions before

spiritual beings, without any doubts arising about them, shows that he knows Heaven. His being prepared, without any misgivings, to wait for the rise of a sage a hundred ages after, shows that he knows men.

5. Such being the case, the movements of such a ruler, illustrating his institutions, constitute an example to the world for ages. His acts are for ages a law to the kingdom. His words are for ages a lesson to the kingdom. Those who are far from him, look longingly for him; and those who are near him, are never wearied with him.

6. It is said in the Book of Poetry,—"Not disliked there, not tired of here, from day to day and night to night, will they perpetuate their praise." Never has there been a ruler, who did not realize this description, that obtained an early renown throughout the kingdom.

CHAP. XXX. 1. Chung-ni handed down the doctrines of Yao and Shun, as if they had been his ancestors, and elegantly displayed the regulations of Wan and Wu, taking them as his model. Above, he harmonized with the times of Heaven, and below, he was conformed to the water and land.

2. He may be compared to Heaven and Earth in their supporting and containing, their overshadowing and curtaining, all things. He may be compared to the four seasons in their alternating progress, and to the sun and moon in their successive shining.

3. All things are nourished together without their injuring one another. The courses of the seasons, and of the sun and moon, are pursued without any collision among them. The smaller energies are like river currents; the greater energies are seen in mighty transformations. It is this which makes heaven and earth so great.

CHAP. XXXI. 1. It is only he, possessed of all sagely qualities that can exist under heaven, who shows himself quick in apprehension, clear in discernment, of far-reaching intelligence, and all-embracing knowledge, fitted to exercise rule; magnanimous, generous, benign, and mild, fitted to exercise forbearance; impulsive, energetic, firm, and enduring, fitted to maintain a firm hold; self-adjusted, grave, never swerving from the Mean, and correct, fitted to command reverence; accomplished, distinctive, concentrative, and searching, fitted to exercise discrimination.

2. All-embracing is he and vast, deep and active as a fountain, sending forth in their due season his virtues.

3. All-embracing and vast, he is like Heaven. Deep and active as a fountain, he is like the abyss. He is seen, and the people all reverence him; he speaks, and the people all believe him; he acts, and the people all are pleased with him.

4. Therefore his fame overspreads the Middle Kingdom, and extends to all barbarous tribes. Wherever ships and carriages reach; wherever the strength of man penetrates; wherever the heavens overshadow and the earth sustains; wherever the sun and moon shine; wherever frosts and dews fall:—all who have blood and breath unfeignedly honour and love him. Hence it is said,—"He is the equal of Heaven."

CHAP. XXXII. 1. It is only the individual possessed of the most entire sincerity that can exist under Heaven, who can adjust the great invariable relations of mankind, establish the great fundamental virtues of humanity, and know the transforming and nurturing operations of Heaven and Earth;—shall this individual have any being or anything beyond himself on which he depends?

2. Call him man in his ideal, how earnest is he! Call him an abyss, how deep is he! Call him Heaven, how vast is he!

3. Who can know him, but he who is indeed quick in apprehension, clear in discernment, of far-reaching intelligence, and all-embracing knowledge, possessing all Heavenly virtue?

CHAP. XXXIII. 1. It is said in the Book of Poetry, "Over her embroidered robe she puts a plain single garment," intimating a dislike to the display of the elegance of the former. Just so, it is the way of the superior man to prefer the concealment of his virtue, while it daily becomes more illustrious, and it is the way of the mean man to seek notoriety, while he daily goes more and more to ruin. It is characteristic of the superior man, appearing insipid, yet never to produce satiety; while showing a simple negligence, yet to have his accomplishments recognized; while seemingly plain, yet to be discriminating. He knows how what is distant lies in what is near. He knows where the wind proceeds from. He knows how what is minute becomes manifested. Such a one, we may be sure, will enter into virtue.

2. It is said in the Book of Poetry, "Although the fish sink and lie at the bottom, it is still quite clearly seen." Therefore the superior man examines his heart, that there may be nothing wrong there, and that he may have no cause for dissatisfaction with himself. That wherein the superior man cannot be equalled is simply this,—his work which other men cannot see.

3. It is said in the Book of Poetry, "Looked at in your apartment, be there free from shame as being exposed to the light of heaven." Therefore, the superior man, even when he is not moving, has a feeling of reverence, and while he speaks not, he has the feeling of truthfulness.

4. It is said in the Book of Poetry, "In silence is the offering presented, and the spirit approached to; there is not the slightest contention." Therefore the superior man does not use rewards, and the people are stimulated to virtue. He does not show anger, and the people are awed more than by hatchets and battle-axes.

5. It is said in the Book of Poetry, "What needs no display is virtue. All the princes imitate it." Therefore, the superior man being sincere and reverential, the whole world is conducted to a state of happy tranquillity.

6. It is said in the Book of Poetry, "I regard with pleasure your brilliant virtue, making no great display of itself in sounds and appearances." The Master said, "Among the appliances to transform the people, sound and appearances are but trivial influences. It is said in another ode, 'His Virtue is light as a hair.' Still, a hair will admit of comparison as to its size. 'The doings of the supreme Heaven have neither sound nor smell.'—That is perfect virtue."

THE CONFUCIAN
ANALECTS

THE CONFUCIAN ANALECTS

BOOK I. HSIO R

CHAP. I. 1. The Master said, 'Is it not pleasant to learn with a constant perseverance and application?

2. 'Is it not delightful to have friends coming from distant quarters?'

3. 'Is he not a man of complete virtue, who feels no discomposure though men may take no note of him?'

CHAP. II. 1. The philosopher Yu said, 'They are few who, being filial and fraternal, are fond of offending against their superiors. There have been none, who, not liking to offend against their superiors, have been fond of stirring up confusion.

2. 'The superior man bends his attention to what is radical. That being established, all practical courses naturally grow up. Filial piety and fraternal submission!—are they not the root of all benevolent actions?'

CHAP. III. The Master said, 'Fine words and an insinuating appearance are seldom associated with true virtue.'

CHAP. IV. The philosopher Tsang said, 'I daily examine myself on three points:—whether, in transacting business for others, I may have been not faithful;—whether, in intercourse with friends, I may have been not sincere;—whether I may have not mastered and practised the instructions of my teacher.'

CHAP. V. The Master said, 'To rule a country of a thousand chariots, there must be reverent attention to business, and sincerity; economy in expenditure, and love for men; and the employment of the people at the proper seasons.'

CHAP. VI. The Master said, 'A youth, when at home, should be filial, and, abroad, respectful to his elders. He should be earnest and truthful. He should overflow in love to all, and cultivate the friendship of the good. When he has time and opportunity, after the performance of these things, he should employ them in polite studies.'

CHAP. VII. Tsze-hsia said, 'If a man withdraws his mind from the love of beauty, and applies it as sincerely to the love of the virtuous; if, in serving his parents, he can exert his utmost strength; if, in serving his prince, he can devote his life; if, in his intercourse with his friends, his words are sincere:— although men say that he has not learned, I will certainly say that he has.'

CHAP. VIII. 1. The Master said, 'If the scholar be not grave, he will not call forth any veneration, and his learning will not be solid.

2. 'Hold faithfulness and sincerity as first principles.

3. 'Have no friends not equal to yourself.

4. 'When you have faults, do not fear to abandon them.'

CHAP. IX. The philosopher Tsang said, 'Let there be a careful attention to perform the funeral rites to parents, and let them be followed when long gone with the ceremonies of sacrifice;—then the virtue of the people will resume its proper excellence.'

CHAP. X. 1. Tsze-ch'in asked Tsze-kung, saying, 'When our master comes to any country, he does not fail to learn all about its government. Does he ask his information? or is it given to him?'

2. Tsze-kung said, 'Our master is benign, upright, courteous, temperate, and complaisant, and thus he gets his information. The master's mode of asking information!—is it not different from that of other men?'

CHAP. XI. The Master said, 'While a man's father is alive, look at the bent of his will; when his father is dead, look at his conduct. If for three years he does not alter from the way of his father, he may be called filial.'

CHAP. XII. 1. The philosopher Yu said, 'In practising the rules of propriety, a natural ease is to be prized. In the ways prescribed by the ancient kings, this is the excellent quality, and in things small and great we follow them.

2. 'Yet it is not to be observed in all cases. If one, knowing how such ease should be prized, manifests it, without regulating it by the rules of propriety, this likewise is not to be

done.'

CHAP. XIII. The philosopher Yu said, 'When agreements are made according to what is right, what is spoken can be made good. When respect is shown according to what is proper, one keeps far from shame and disgrace. When the parties upon whom a man leans are proper persons to be intimate with, he can make them his guides and masters.'

CHAP. XIV. The Master said, 'He who aims to be a man of complete virtue in his food does not seek to gratify his appetite, nor in his dwelling place does he seek the appliances of ease; he is earnest in what he is doing, and careful in his speech; he frequents the company of men of principle that he may be rectified:—such a person may be said indeed to love to learn.'

CHAP. XV. 1. Tsze-kung said, 'What do you pronounce concerning the poor man who yet does not flatter, and the rich man who is not proud?' The Master replied, 'They will do; but they are not equal to him, who, though poor, is yet cheerful, and to him, who, though rich, loves the rules of propriety.'

2. Tsze-kung replied, 'It is said in the Book of Poetry, "As you cut and then file, as you carve and then polish."—The meaning is the same, I apprehend, as that which you have just expressed.'

3. The Master said, 'With one like Ts'ze, I can begin to talk about the odes. I told him one point, and he knew its proper sequence.'

CHAP. XVI. The Master said, 'I will not be afflicted at men's not knowing me; I will be afflicted that I do not know men.'

BOOK II. WEI CHANG

CHAP. I. The Master said, 'He who exercises government by means of his virtue may be compared to the north polar star, which keeps its place and all the stars turn towards it.'

CHAP. II. The Master said, 'In the Book of Poetry are three hundred pieces, but the design of them all may be embraced in one sentence—"Having no depraved thoughts."'

CHAP. III. 1. The Master said, 'If the people be led by laws, and uniformity sought to be given them by punishments, they will try to avoid the punishment, but have no sense of shame.

2. 'If they be led by virtue, and uniformity sought to be given them by the rules of propriety, they will have the sense of shame, and moreover will become good.'

CHAP. IV. 1. The Master said, 'At fifteen, I had my mind bent on learning.

2. 'At thirty, I stood firm.

3. 'At forty, I had no doubts.

4. 'At fifty, I knew the decrees of Heaven.

5. 'At sixty, my ear was an obedient organ for the reception of truth.

6. 'At seventy, I could follow what my heart desired, without transgressing what was right.'

CHAP. V. 1. Mang I asked what filial piety was. The Master said, 'It is not being disobedient.'

2. Soon after, as Fan Ch'ih was driving him, the Master told him, saying, 'Mang-sun asked me what filial piety was, and I answered him,—"not being disobedient."'

3. Fan Ch'ih said, 'What did you mean?' The Master replied, 'That parents, when alive, be served according to propriety; that, when dead, they should be buried according to propriety; and that they should be sacrificed to according to propriety.'

CHAP. VI. Mang Wu asked what filial piety was. The Master said, 'Parents are anxious lest their children should be sick.'

CHAP. VII. Tsze-yu asked what filial piety was. The Master said, 'The filial piety of now-a-days means the support of one's parents. But dogs and horses likewise are able to do something in the way of support;—without reverence, what is there to distinguish the one support given from the other?'

CHAP. VIII. Tsze-hsia asked what filial piety was. The Master said, 'The difficulty is with the countenance. If, when their elders have any troublesome affairs, the young take the toil of them, and if, when the young have wine and food, they set them before their elders, is THIS to be considered filial piety?'

CHAP. IX. The Master said, 'I have talked with Hui for a whole day, and he has not made any objection to anything I said;—as if he were stupid. He has retired, and I have examined his conduct when away from me, and found him able to illustrate my teachings. Hui!—He is not stupid.'

CHAP. X. 1. The Master said, 'See what a man does.

2. 'Mark his motives.

3. 'Examine in what things he rests.

4. 'How can a man conceal his character?

5. 'How can a man conceal his character?'

CHAP. XI. The Master said, 'If a man keeps cherishing his old knowledge, so as continually to be acquiring new, he may be a teacher of others.'

CHAP. XII. The Master said, 'The accomplished scholar is not a utensil.'

CHAP. XIII. Tsze-kung asked what constituted the superior man. The Master said, 'He acts before he speaks, and afterwards speaks according to his actions.'

CHAP. XIV. The Master said, 'The superior man is catholic and no partisan. The mean man is partisan and not catholic.'

CHAP. XV. The Master said, 'Learning without thought is labour lost; thought without learning is perilous.'

CHAP. XVI. The Master said, 'The study of strange doctrines is injurious indeed!'

CHAP. XVII. The Master said, 'Yu, shall I teach you what knowledge is? When you know a thing, to hold that you know it; and when you do not know a thing, to allow that you do not know it;—this is knowledge.'

CHAP. XVIII. 1. Tsze-chang was learning with a view to official emolument.

41

2. The Master said, 'Hear much and put aside the points of which you stand in doubt, while you speak cautiously at the same time of the others:—then you will afford few occasions for blame. See much and put aside the things which seem perilous, while you are cautious at the same time in carrying the others into practice:—then you will have few occasions for repentance. When one gives few occasions for blame in his words, and few occasions for repentance in his conduct, he is in the way to get emolument.'

CHAP. XIX. The Duke Ai asked, saying, 'What should be done in order to secure the submission of the people?' Confucius replied, 'Advance the upright and set aside the crooked, then the people will submit. Advance the crooked and set aside the upright, then the people will not submit.'

CHAP. XX. Chi K'ang asked how to cause the people to reverence their ruler, to be faithful to him, and to go on to nerve themselves to virtue. The Master said, 'Let him preside over them with gravity;—then they will reverence him. Let him be filial and kind to all;—then they will be faithful to him. Let him advance the good and teach the incompetent;—then they will eagerly seek to be virtuous.'

CHAP. XXI. 1. Some one addressed Confucius, saying, 'Sir, why are you not engaged in the government?'

2. The Master said, 'What does the Shu-ching say of filial piety?—"You are filial, you discharge your brotherly duties. These qualities are displayed in government." This then also constitutes the exercise of government. Why must there be THAT—making one be in the government?'

CHAP. XXII. The Master said, 'I do not know how a man without truthfulness is to get on. How can a large carriage be made to go without the cross-bar for yoking the oxen to, or a small carriage without the arrangement for yoking the horses?'

CHAP. XXIII. 1. Tsze-chang asked whether the affairs of ten ages after could be known.

2. Confucius said, 'The Yin dynasty followed the regulations of the Hsia: wherein it took from or added to them may be known. The Chau dynasty has followed the regulations of Yin: wherein it took from or added to them may be known.

Some other may follow the Chau, but though it should be at the distance of a hundred ages, its affairs may be known.'

CHAP. XXIV. 1. The Master said, 'For a man to sacrifice to a spirit which does not belong to him is flattery.

2. 'To see what is right and not to do it is want of courage.'

BOOK III. PA YIH

CHAP. I. Confucius said of the head of the Chi family, who had eight rows of pantomimes in his area, 'If he can bear to do this, what may he not bear to do?'

CHAP. II. The three families used the YUNG ode, while the vessels were being removed, at the conclusion of the sacrifice. The Master said, '"Assisting are the princes;—the son of heaven looks profound and grave:"—what application can these words have in the hall of the three families?'

CHAP. III. The Master said, 'If a man be without the virtues proper to humanity, what has he to do with the rites of propriety? If a man be without the virtues proper to humanity, what has he to do with music?'

CHAP. IV. 1. Lin Fang asked what was the first thing to be attended to in ceremonies.

2. The Master said, 'A great question indeed!

3. 'In festive ceremonies, it is better to be sparing than extravagant. In the ceremonies of mourning, it is better that there be deep sorrow than a minute attention to observances.'

CHAP. V. The Master said, 'The rude tribes of the east and north have their princes, and are not like the States of our great land which are without them.'

CHAP. VI. The chief of the Chi family was about to sacrifice to the T'ai mountain. The Master said to Zan Yu, 'Can you not save him from this?' He answered, 'I cannot.' Confucius said, 'Alas! will you say that the T'ai mountain is not so discerning as Lin Fang?'

CHAP. VII. The Master said, 'The student of virtue has no contentions. If it be said he cannot avoid them, shall this be in archery? But he bows complaisantly to his competitors; thus he ascends the hall, descends, and exacts the forfeit of drinking. In his contention, he is still the Chun-tsze.'

CHAP. VIII. 1. Tsze-hsia asked, saying, 'What is the meaning of the passage—"The pretty dimples of her artful smile! The well-defined black and white of her eye! The plain ground for the colours?"'

2. The Master said, 'The business of laying on the colours follows (the preparation of) the plain ground.'

3. 'Ceremonies then are a subsequent thing?' The Master said, 'It is Shang who can bring out my meaning. Now I can begin to talk about the odes with him.'

CHAP. IX. The Master said, 'I could describe the ceremonies of the Hsia dynasty, but Chi cannot sufficiently attest my words. I could describe the ceremonies of the Yin dynasty, but Sung cannot sufficiently attest my words. (They cannot do so) because of the insufficiency of their records and wise men. If those were sufficient, I could adduce them in support of my words.'

CHAP. X. The Master said, 'At the great sacrifice, after the pouring out of the libation, I have no wish to look on.'

CHAP. XI. Some one asked the meaning of the great sacrifice. The Master said, 'I do not know. He who knew its meaning would find it as easy to govern the kingdom as to look on this;—pointing to his palm.

CHAP. XII. 1. He sacrificed to the dead, as if they were present. He sacrificed to the spirits, as if the spirits were present.

2. The Master said, 'I consider my not being present at the sacrifice, as if I did not sacrifice.'

CHAP. XIII. 1. Wang-sun Chia asked, saying, 'What is the meaning of the saying, "It is better to pay court to the furnace than to the south-west corner?"'

2. The Master said, 'Not so. He who offends against Heaven has none to whom he can pray.'

CHAP. XIV. The Master said, 'Chau had the advantage of viewing the two past dynasties. How complete and elegant are its regulations! I follow Chau.'

CHAP. XV. The Master, when he entered the grand temple, asked about everything. Some one said, 'Who will say that the son of the man of Tsau knows the rules of propriety! He has entered the grand temple and asks about everything.' The Master heard the remark, and said, 'This is a rule of propriety.'

CHAP. XVI. The Master said, 'In archery it is not going through the leather which is the principal thing;—because people's strength is not equal. This was the old way.'

CHAP. XVII. 1. Tsze-kung wished to do away with the offering of a sheep connected with the inauguration of the first day of each month.

2. The Master said, 'Ts'ze, you love the sheep; I love the ceremony.'

CHAP. XVIII. The Master said, 'The full observance of the rules of propriety in serving one's prince is accounted by people to be flattery.'

CHAP. XIX. The Duke Ting asked how a prince should employ his ministers, and how ministers should serve their prince. Confucius replied, 'A prince should employ his minister according to according to the rules of propriety; ministers should serve their prince with faithfulness.'

CHAP. XX. The Master said, 'The Kwan Tsu is expressive of enjoyment without being licentious, and of grief without being hurtfully excessive.'

CHAP. XXI. 1. The Duke Ai asked Tsai Wo about the altars of the spirits of the land. Tsai Wo replied, 'The Hsia sovereign planted the pine tree about them; the men of the Yin planted the cypress; and the men of the Chau planted the chestnut tree, meaning thereby to cause the people to be in awe.'

2. When the Master heard it, he said, 'Things that are done, it is needless to speak about; things that have had their course, it is needless to remonstrate about; things that are past, it is needless to blame.'

CHAP. XXII. 1. The Master said, 'Small indeed was the capacity of Kwan Chung!'

2. Some one said, 'Was Kwan Chung parsimonious?' 'Kwan,' was the reply, 'had the San Kwei, and his officers performed no double duties; how can he be considered parsimonious?'

3. 'Then, did Kwan Chung know the rules of propriety?' The Master said, 'The princes of States have a screen intercepting the view at their gates. Kwan had likewise a screen at his gate. The princes of States on any friendly meeting between two of them, had a stand on which to place their inverted cups. Kwan had also such a stand. If Kwan knew the

rules of propriety, who does not know them?'

CHAP. XXIII. The Master instructing the grand music-master of Lu said, 'How to play music may be known. At the commencement of the piece, all the parts should sound together. As it proceeds, they should be in harmony while severally distinct and flowing without break, and thus on to the conclusion.'

CHAP. XXIV. The border warden at Yi requested to be introduced to the Master, saying, 'When men of superior virtue have come to this, I have never been denied the privilege of seeing them.' The followers of the sage introduced him, and when he came out from the interview, he said, 'My friends, why are you distressed by your master's loss of office? The kingdom has long been without the principles of truth and right; Heaven is going to use your master as a bell with its wooden tongue.'

CHAP. XXV. The Master said of the Shao that it was perfectly beautiful and also perfectly good. He said of the Wu that it was perfectly beautiful but not perfectly good.

CHAP. XXVI. The Master said, 'High station filled without indulgent generosity; ceremonies performed without reverence; mourning conducted without sorrow;—wherewith should I contemplate such ways?'

BOOK IV. LE JIN

CHAP. I. The Master said, 'It is virtuous manners which constitute the excellence of a neighbourhood. If a man in selecting a residence, do not fix on one where such prevail, how can he be wise?'

CHAP. II. The Master said, 'Those who are without virtue cannot abide long either in a condition of poverty and hardship, or in a condition of enjoyment. The virtuous rest in virtue; the wise desire virtue.'

CHAP. III. The Master said, 'It is only the (truly) virtuous man, who can love, or who can hate, others.'

CHAP. IV. The Master said, 'If the will be set on virtue, there will be no practice of wickedness.'

CHAP. V. 1. The Master said, 'Riches and honours are what men desire. If it cannot be obtained in the proper way, they should not be held. Poverty and meanness are what men dislike. If it cannot be avoided in the proper way, they should not be avoided.

2. 'If a superior man abandon virtue, how can he fulfil the requirements of that name?

3. 'The superior man does not, even for the space of a single meal, act contrary to virtue. In moments of haste, he cleaves to it. In seasons of danger, he cleaves to it.'

CHAP. VI. 1. The Master said, 'I have not seen a person who loved virtue, or one who hated what was not virtuous. He who loved virtue, would esteem nothing above it. He who hated what is not virtuous, would practise virtue in such a way that he would not allow anything that is not virtuous to approach his person.

2. 'Is any one able for one day to apply his strength to virtue? I have not seen the case in which his strength would be insufficient.

3. 'Should there possibly be any such case, I have not seen it.'

CHAP. VII. The Master said, 'The faults of men are characteristic of the class to which they belong. By observing a man's faults, it may be known that he is virtuous.'

CHAP. VIII. The Master said, 'If a man in the morning hear the right way, he may die in the evening without regret.'

CHAP. IX. The Master said, 'A scholar, whose mind is set on truth, and who is ashamed of bad clothes and bad food, is not fit to be discoursed with.'

CHAP. X. The Master said, 'The superior man, in the world, does not set his mind either for anything, or against anything; what is right he will follow.'

CHAP. XI. The Master said, 'The superior man thinks of virtue; the small man thinks of comfort. The superior man thinks of the sanctions of law; the small man thinks of favours which he may receive.'

CHAP. XII. The Master said: 'He who acts with a constant view to his own advantage will be much murmured against.'

CHAP. XIII. The Master said, 'If a prince is able to govern his kingdom with the complaisance proper to the rules of propriety, what difficulty will he have? If he cannot govern it with that complaisance, what has he to do with the rules of propriety?'

CHAP. XIV. The Master said, 'A man should say, I am not concerned that I have no place, I am concerned how I may fit myself for one. I am not concerned that I am not known, I seek to be worthy to be known.'

CHAP. XV. 1. The Master said, 'Shan, my doctrine is that of an all-pervading unity.' The disciple Tsang replied, 'Yes.'

2. The Master went out, and the other disciples asked, saying, 'What do his words mean?' Tsang said, 'The doctrine of our master is to be true to the principles of our nature and the benevolent exercise of them to others,—this and nothing more.'

CHAP. XVI. The Master said, 'The mind of the superior man is conversant with righteousness; the mind of the mean man is conversant with gain.'

CHAP. XVII. The Master said, 'When we see men of worth, we should think of equalling them; when we see men of a contrary character, we should turn inwards and examine ourselves.'

CHAP. XVIII. The Master said, 'In serving his parents, a son may remonstrate with them, but gently; when he sees that they do not incline to follow his advice, he shows an increased degree of reverence, but does not abandon his purpose; and should they punish him, he does not allow himself to murmur.'

CHAP. XIX. The Master said, 'While his parents are alive, the son may not go abroad to a distance. If he does go abroad, he must have a fixed place to which he goes.'

CHAP. XX. The Master said, 'If the son for three years does not alter from the way of his father, he may be called filial.'

CHAP. XXI. The Master said, 'The years of parents may by no means not be kept in the memory, as an occasion at once for joy and for fear.'

CHAP. XXII. The Master said, 'The reason why the ancients did not readily give utterance to their words, was that they feared lest their actions should not come up to them.'

CHAP. XXIII. The Master said, 'The cautious seldom err.'

CHAP. XXIV. The Master said, 'The superior man wishes to be slow in his speech and earnest in his conduct.'

CHAP. XXV. The Master said, 'Virtue is not left to stand alone. He who practises it will have neighbours.'

CHAP. XXVI. Tsze-yu said, 'In serving a prince, frequent remonstrances lead to disgrace. Between friends, frequent reproofs make the friendship distant.'

BOOK V. KUNG-YE CH'ANG

CHAP. I. 1. The Master said of Kung-ye Ch'ang that he might be wived; although he was put in bonds, he had not been guilty of any crime. Accordingly, he gave him his own daughter to wife. 2. Of Nan Yung he said that if the country were well governed he would not be out of office, and if it were ill-governed, he would escape punishment and disgrace. He gave him the daughter of his own elder brother to wife.

CHAP. II. The Master said of Tsze-chien, 'Of superior virtue indeed is such a man! If there were not virtuous men in Lu, how could this man have acquired this character?'

CHAP. III. Tsze-kung asked, 'What do you say of me, Ts'ze? The Master said, 'You are a utensil.' 'What utensil?' 'A gemmed sacrificial utensil.'

CHAP. IV. 1. Some one said, 'Yung is truly virtuous, but he is not ready with his tongue.' 2. The Master said, 'What is the good of being ready with the tongue? They who encounter men with smartnesses of speech for the most part procure themselves hatred. I know not whether he be truly virtuous, but why should he show readiness of the tongue?'

CHAP. V. The Master was wishing Ch'i-tiao K'ai to enter on official employment. He replied, 'I am not yet able to rest in the assurance of THIS.' The Master was pleased.

CHAP. VI. The Master said, 'My doctrines make no way. I will get upon a raft, and float about on the sea. He that will accompany me will be Yu, I dare say.' Tsze-lu hearing this was glad, upon which the Master said, 'Yu is fonder of daring than I am. He does not exercise his judgment upon matters.'

CHAP. VII. 1. Mang Wu asked about Tsze-lu, whether he was perfectly virtuous. The Master said, 'I do not know.' 2. He asked again, when the Master replied, 'In a kingdom of a thousand chariots, Yu might be employed to manage the military levies, but I do not know whether he be perfectly virtuous.' 3. 'And what do you say of Ch'iu?' The Master replied, 'In a city of a thousand families, or a clan of a hundred chariots, Ch'iu might be employed as governor, but I do not know whether he is perfectly virtuous.' 4. 'What do you say of Ch'ih?' The Master replied, 'With his sash girt and standing in a court, Ch'ih might be employed to converse with the visitors and guests, but I do not know whether he is perfectly virtuous.'

CHAP. VII. 1. The Master said to Tsze-kung, 'Which do you consider superior, yourself or Hui?'

2. Tsze-kung replied, 'How dare I compare myself with Hui? Hui hears one point and knows all about a subject; I hear one point, and know a second.'

3. The Master said, 'You are not equal to him. I grant you, you are not equal to him.'

CHAP. IX. 1. Tsai Yu being asleep during the daytime, the Master said, 'Rotten wood cannot be carved; a wall of dirty earth will not receive the trowel. This Yu!—what is the use of my reproving him?'

2. The Master said, 'At first, my way with men was to hear their words, and give them credit for their conduct. Now my way is to hear their words, and look at their conduct. It is from Yu that I have learned to make this change.'

CHAP. X. The Master said, 'I have not seen a firm and unbending man.' Some one replied, 'There is Shan Ch'ang.' 'Ch'ang,' said the Master, 'is under the influence of his passions; how can he be pronounced firm and unbending?'

CHAP. XI. Tsze-kung said, 'What I do not wish men to do to me, I also wish not to do to men.' The Master said, 'Ts'ze, you have not attained to that.'

CHAP. XII. Tsze-kung said, 'The Master's personal displays of his principles and ordinary descriptions of them may be heard. His discourses about man's nature, and the way of Heaven, cannot be heard.'

CHAP. XIII. When Tsze-lu heard anything, if he had not yet succeeded in carrying it into practice, he was only afraid lest he should hear something else.

CHAP. XIV. Tsze-kung asked, saying, 'On what ground did Kung-wan get that title of WAN?' The Master said, 'He was of an active nature and yet fond of learning, and he was not ashamed to ask and learn of his inferiors!—On these grounds he has been styled WAN.'

CHAP. XV. The Master said of Tsze-ch'an that he had four of the characteristics of a superior man:—in his conduct of himself, he was humble; in serving his superiors, he was respectful; in nourishing the people, he was kind; in ordering the people, he was just.'

CHAP. XVI. The Master said, 'Yen P'ing knew well how to maintain friendly intercourse. The acquaintance might be long, but he showed the same respect as at first.'

CHAP. XVII. The Master said, 'Tsang Wan kept a large tortoise in a house, on the capitals of the pillars of which he had hills made, and with representations of duckweed on the small pillars above the beams supporting the rafters.—Of what sort was his wisdom?'

CHAP. XVIII. 1. Tsze-chang asked, saying, 'The minister Tsze-wan thrice took office, and manifested no joy in his countenance. Thrice he retired from office, and manifested no displeasure. He made it a point to inform the new minister of the way in which he had conducted the government;—what do you say of him?' The Master replied. 'He was loyal.' 'Was he perfectly virtuous?' 'I do not know. How can he be pronounced perfectly virtuous?'

2. Tsze-chang proceeded, 'When the officer Ch'ui killed the prince of Ch'i, Ch'an Wan, though he was the owner of forty horses, abandoned them and left the country. Coming to another State, he said, "They are here like our great officer, Ch'ui," and left it. He came to a second State, and with the same observation left it also;—what do you say of him?' The Master replied, 'He was pure.' 'Was he perfectly virtuous?' 'I do not know. How can he be pronounced perfectly virtuous?'

CHAP. XIX. Chi Wan thought thrice, and then acted. When the Master was informed of it, he said, 'Twice may do.'

CHAP. XX. The Master said, 'When good order prevailed in his country, Ning Wu acted the part of a wise man. When his country was in disorder, he acted the part of a stupid man. Others may equal his wisdom, but they cannot equal his stupidity.'

CHAP. XXI. When the Master was in Ch'an, he said, 'Let

me return! Let me return! The little children of my school are ambitious and too hasty. They are accomplished and complete so far, but they do not know how to restrict and shape themselves.'

CHAP. XXII. The Master said, 'Po-i and Shu-ch'i did not keep the former wickednesses of men in mind, and hence the resentments directed towards them were few.'

CHAP. XXIII. The Master said, 'Who says of Wei-shang Kao that he is upright? One begged some vinegar of him, and he begged it of a neighbour and gave it to the man.'

CHAP. XXIV. The Master said, 'Fine words, an insinuating appearance, and excessive respect;—Tso Ch'iu-ming was ashamed of them. I also am ashamed of them. To conceal resentment against a person, and appear friendly with him;— Tso Ch'iu-ming was ashamed of such conduct. I also am ashamed of it.'

CHAP. XXV. 1. Yen Yuan and Chi Lu being by his side, the Master said to them, 'Come, let each of you tell his wishes.'

2. Tsze-lu said, 'I should like, having chariots and horses, and light fur dresses, to share them with my friends, and though they should spoil them, I would not be displeased.'

3. Yen Yuan said, 'I should like not to boast of my excellence, nor to make a display of my meritorious deeds.'

4. Tsze-lu then said, 'I should like, sir, to hear your wishes.' The Master said, 'They are, in regard to the aged, to give them rest; in regard to friends, to show them sincerity; in regard to the young, to treat them tenderly.'

CHAP. XXVI. The Master said, 'It is all over! I have not yet seen one who could perceive his faults, and inwardly accuse himself.'

CHAP. XXVII. The Master said, 'In a hamlet of ten families, there may be found one honourable and sincere as I am, but not so fond of learning.'

BOOK VI. YUNG YEY

CHAP. I. 1. The Master said, 'There is Yung!—He might occupy the place of a prince.'

2. Chung-kung asked about Tsze-sang Po-tsze. The Master said, 'He may pass. He does not mind small matters.'

3. Chung-kung said, 'If a man cherish in himself a reverential feeling of the necessity of attention to business, though he may be easy in small matters in his government of the people, that may be allowed. But if he cherish in himself that easy feeling, and also carry it out in his practice, is not such an easy mode of procedure excessive?'

4. The Master said, 'Yung's words are right.'

CHAP. II. The Duke Ai asked which of the disciples loved to learn. Confucius replied to him, 'There was Yen Hui; HE loved to learn. He did not transfer his anger; he did not repeat a fault. Unfortunately, his appointed time was short and he died; and now there is not such another. I have not yet heard of any one who loves to learn as he did.'

CHAP. III. 1. Tsze-hwa being employed on a mission to Ch'i, the disciple Zan requested grain for his mother. The Master said, 'Give her a fu.' Yen requested more. 'Give her an yu,' said the Master. Yen gave her five ping.

2. The Master said, 'When Ch'ih was proceeding to Ch'i, he had fat horses to his carriage, and wore light furs. I have heard that a superior man helps the distressed, but does not add to the wealth of the rich.'

3. Yuan Sze being made governor of his town by the Master, he gave him nine hundred measures of grain, but Sze declined them.

4. The Master said, 'Do not decline them. May you not give them away in the neighbourhoods, hamlets, towns, and villages?'

CHAP. IV. The Master, speaking of Chung-kung, said, 'If the calf of a brindled cow be red and horned, although men may not wish to use it, would the spirits of the mountains and rivers put it aside?'

CHAP. V. The Master said, 'Such was Hui that for three months there would be nothing in his mind contrary to perfect virtue. The others may attain to this on some days or in some months, but nothing more.'

CHAP. VI. Chi K'ang asked about Chung-yu, whether he was fit to be employed as an officer of government. The Master said, 'Yu is a man of decision; what difficulty would he find in being an officer of government?' K'ang asked, 'Is Ts'ze fit to be employed as an officer of government?' and was answered, 'Ts'ze is a man of intelligence; what difficulty would he find in being an officer of government?' And to the same question about Ch'iu the Master gave the same reply, saying, 'Ch'iu is a man of various ability.'

CHAP. VII. The chief of the Chi family sent to ask Min Tsze-ch'ien to be governor of Pi. Min Tsze-ch'ien said, 'Decline the offer for me politely. If any one come again to me with a second invitation, I shall be obliged to go and live on the banks of the Wan.'

CHAP. VIII. Po-niu being ill, the Master went to ask for him. He took hold of his hand through the window, and said, 'It is killing him. It is the appointment of Heaven, alas! That such a man should have such a sickness! That such a man should have such a sickness!'

CHAP. IX. The Master said, 'Admirable indeed was the virtue of Hui! With a single bamboo dish of rice, a single gourd dish of drink, and living in his mean narrow lane, while others could not have endured the distress, he did not allow his joy to be affected by it. Admirable indeed was the virtue of Hui!'

CHAP. X. Yen Ch'iu said, 'It is not that I do not delight in your doctrines, but my strength is insufficient.' The Master said, 'Those whose strength is insufficient give over in the middle of the way but now you limit yourself.'

CHAP. XI. The Master said to Tsze-hsia, 'Do you be a scholar after the style of the superior man, and not after that of the mean man.'

CHAP. XII. Tsze-yu being governor of Wu-ch'ang, the Master said to him, 'Have you got good men there?' He answered, 'There is Tan-t'ai Mieh-ming, who never in walking takes a short cut, and never comes to my office, excepting on public business.'

CHAP. XIII. The Master said, 'Mang Chih-fan does not boast of his merit. Being in the rear on an occasion of flight, when they were about to enter the gate, he whipped up his horse, saying, "It is not that I dare to be last. My horse would not advance."'

CHAP. XIV. The Master said, 'Without the specious speech of the litanist T'o and the beauty of the prince Chao of Sung, it is difficult to escape in the present age.'

CHAP. XV. The Master said, 'Who can go out but by the door? How is it that men will not walk according to these ways?'

CHAP. XVI. The Master said, 'Where the solid qualities are in excess of accomplishments, we have rusticity; where the accomplishments are in excess of the solid qualities, we have the manners of a clerk. When the accomplishments and solid qualities are equally blended, we then have the man of virtue.'

CHAP. XVII. The Master said, 'Man is born for uprightness. If a man lose his uprightness, and yet live, his escape from death is the effect of mere good fortune.'

CHAP. XVIII. The Master said, 'They who know the truth are not equal to those who love it, and they who love it are not equal to those who delight in it.'

CHAP. XIX. The Master said, 'To those whose talents are above mediocrity, the highest subjects may be announced. To those who are below mediocrity, the highest subjects may not be announced.'

CHAP. XX. Fan Ch'ih asked what constituted wisdom. The Master said, 'To give one's self earnestly to the duties due to men, and, while respecting spiritual beings, to keep aloof from them, may be called wisdom.' He asked about perfect virtue. The Master said, 'The man of virtue makes the difficulty to be overcome his first business, and success only a subsequent consideration;—this may be called perfect virtue.'

CHAP. XXI. The Master said, 'The wise find pleasure in water; the virtuous find pleasure in hills. The wise are active; the virtuous are tranquil. The wise are joyful; the virtuous are long-lived.'

CHAP. XXII. The Master said, 'Ch'i, by one change, would come to the State of Lu. Lu, by one change, would come to a State where true principles predominated.'

CHAP. XXIII. The Master said, 'A cornered vessel without corners.—A strange cornered vessel! A strange cornered vessel!'

CHAP. XXIV. Tsai Wo asked, saying, 'A benevolent man, though it be told him,—'There is a man in the well' will go in after him, I suppose.' Confucius said, 'Why should he do so?' A superior man may be made to go to the well, but he cannot be made to go down into it. He may be imposed upon, but he cannot be fooled.'

CHAP. XXV. The Master said, 'The superior man, extensively studying all learning, and keeping himself under the restraint of the rules of propriety, may thus likewise not overstep what is right.'

CHAP. XXVI. The Master having visited Nan-tsze, Tsze-lu was displeased, on which the Master swore, saying, 'Wherein I have done improperly, may Heaven reject me, may Heaven reject me!'

CHAP. XXVII. The Master said, 'Perfect is the virtue which is according to the Constant Mean! Rare for a long time has been its practise among the people.'

CHAP. XXVIII. 1. Tsze-kung said, 'Suppose the case of a man extensively conferring benefits on the people, and able to assist all, what would you say of him? Might he be called perfectly virtuous?' The Master said, 'Why speak only of virtue in connexion with him? Must he not have the qualities of a sage? Even Yao and Shun were still solicitous about this.

2. 'Now the man of perfect virtue, wishing to be established himself, seeks also to establish others; wishing to be enlarged himself, he seeks also to enlarge others.

3. 'To be able to judge of others by what is nigh in ourselves;—this may be called the art of virtue.'

BOOK VII. SHU R

CHAP. I. The Master said, 'A transmitter and not a maker, believing in and loving the ancients, I venture to compare myself with our old P'ang.'

CHAP. II. The Master said, 'The silent treasuring up of knowledge; learning without satiety; and instructing others without being wearied:—which one of these things belongs to me?'

CHAP. III. The Master said, 'The leaving virtue without proper cultivation; the not thoroughly discussing what is learned; not being able to move towards righteousness of which a knowledge is gained; and not being able to change what is not good:—these are the things which occasion me solicitude.'

CHAP. IV. When the Master was unoccupied with business, his manner was easy, and he looked pleased.

CHAP. V. The Master said, 'Extreme is my decay. For a long time, I have not dreamed, as I was wont to do, that I saw the duke of Chau.'

CHAP. VI. 1. The Master said, 'Let the will be set on the path of duty.

2. 'Let every attainment in what is good be firmly grasped.

3. 'Let perfect virtue be accorded with.

4. 'Let relaxation and enjoyment be found in the polite arts.'

CHAP. VII. The Master said, 'From the man bringing his bundle of dried flesh for my teaching upwards, I have never refused instruction to any one.'

CHAP. VIII. The Master said, 'I do not open up the truth to one who is not eager to get knowledge, nor help out any one who is not anxious to explain himself. When I have presented one corner of a subject to any one, and he cannot from it learn the other three, I do not repeat my lesson.'

CHAP. IX. 1. When the Master was eating by the side of a mourner, he never ate to the full.

2. He did not sing on the same day in which he had been weeping.

CHAP. X. 1. The Master said to Yen Yuan, 'When called to office, to undertake its duties; when not so called, to lie retired;—it is only I and you who have attained to this.'

2. Tsze-lu said, 'If you had the conduct of the armies of a great State, whom would you have to act with you?'

3. The Master said, 'I would not have him to act with me, who will unarmed attack a tiger, or cross a river without a boat, dying without any regret. My associate must be the man who proceeds to action full of solicitude, who is fond of adjusting his plans, and then carries them into execution.'

CHAP. XI. The Master said, 'If the search for riches is sure to be successful, though I should become a groom with whip in hand to get them, I will do so. As the search may not be successful, I will follow after that which I love.'

CHAP. XII. The things in reference to which the Master exercised the greatest caution were —fasting, war, and sickness.

CHAP. XIII. When the Master was in Ch'i, he heard the Shao, and for three months did not know the taste of flesh. 'I did not think" he said, 'that music could have been made so excellent as this.'

CHAP. XIV. 1. Yen Yu said, 'Is our Master for the ruler of Wei?' Tsze-kung said, 'Oh! I will ask him.'

2. He went in accordingly, and said, 'What sort of men were Po-i and Shu-ch'i?' 'They were ancient worthies,' said the Master. 'Did they have any repinings because of their course?' The Master again replied, 'They sought to act virtuously, and they did so; what was there for them to repine about?' On this, Tsze-kung went out and said, 'Our Master is not for him.'

CHAP. XV. The Master said, 'With coarse rice to eat, with water to drink, and my bended arm for a pillow;—I have still joy in the midst of these things. Riches and honours acquired by unrighteousness, are to me as a floating cloud.'

CHAP. XVI. The Master said, 'If some years were added to my life, I would give fifty to the study of the Yi, and then I might come to be without great faults.'

CHAP. XVII The Master's frequent themes of discourse were—the Odes, the History, and the maintenance of the

Rules of Propriety. On all these he frequently discoursed.

CHAP. XVIII. 1. The Duke of Sheh asked Tsze-lu about Confucius, and Tsze-lu did not answer him.

2. The Master said, 'Why did you not say to him,—He is simply a man, who in his eager pursuit (of knowledge) forgets his food, who in the joy of its attainment forgets his sorrows, and who does not perceive that old age is coming on?'

CHAP. XIX. The Master said, 'I am not one who was born in the possession of knowledge; I am one who is fond of antiquity, and earnest in seeking it there.'

CHAP. XX. The subjects on which the Master did not talk, were—extraordinary things, feats of strength, disorder, and spiritual beings.

CHAP. XXI. The Master said, 'When I walk along with two others, they may serve me as my teachers. I will select their good qualities and follow them, their bad qualities and avoid them.'

CHAP. XXII. The Master said, 'Heaven produced the virtue that is in me. Hwan T'ui—what can he do to me?'

CHAP. XXIII. The Master said, 'Do you think, my disciples, that I have any concealments? I conceal nothing from you. There is nothing which I do that is not shown to you, my disciples;—that is my way.'

CHAP. XXIV. There were four things which the Master taught,—letters, ethics, devotion of soul, and truthfulness.

CHAP. XXV. 1. The Master said, 'A sage it is not mine to see; could I see a man of real talent and virtue, that would satisfy me.'

2. The Master said, 'A good man it is not mine to see; could I see a man possessed of constancy, that would satisfy me.

3. 'Having not and yet affecting to have, empty and yet affecting to be full, straitened and yet affecting to be at ease:— it is difficult with such characteristics to have constancy.'

CHAP. XXVI. The Master angled,—but did not use a net. He shot,—but not at birds perching.

CHAP. XXVII. The Master said, 'There may be those who act without knowing why. I do not do so. Hearing much and selecting what is good and following it; seeing much and keeping it in memory:—this is the second style of knowledge.'

CHAP. XXVIII. 1. It was difficult to talk (profitably and reputably) with the people of Hu-hsiang, and a lad of that place having had an interview with the Master, the disciples doubted. 2. The Master said, 'I admit people's approach to me without committing myself as to what they may do when they have retired. Why must one be so severe? If a man purify himself to wait upon me, I receive him so purified, without guaranteeing his past conduct.'

CHAP. XXIX. The Master said, 'Is virtue a thing remote? I wish to be virtuous, and lo! virtue is at hand.'

CHAP. XXX. 1. The minister of crime of Ch'an asked whether the duke Chao knew propriety, and Confucius said, 'He knew propriety.'

2. Confucius having retired, the minister bowed to Wu-ma Ch'I to come forward, and said, 'I have heard that the superior man is not a partisan. May the superior man be a partisan also? The prince married a daughter of the house of Wu, of the same surname with himself, and called her,—"The elder Tsze of Wu." If the prince knew propriety, who does not know it?'

3. Wu-ma Ch'i reported these remarks, and the Master said, 'I am fortunate! If I have any errors, people are sure to know them.'

CHAP. XXXI. When the Master was in company with a person who was singing, if he sang well, he would make him repeat the song, while he accompanied it with his own voice.

CHAP. XXXII. The Master said, 'In letters I am perhaps equal to other men, but the character of the superior man, carrying out in his conduct what he professes, is what I have not yet attained to.'

CHAP. XXXIII. The Master said, 'The sage and the man of perfect virtue;—how dare I rank myself with them? It may simply be said of me, that I strive to become such without satiety, and teach others without weariness.' Kung-hsi Hwa said, 'This is just what we, the disciples, cannot imitate you in.'

CHAP. XXXIV. The Master being very sick, Tsze-lu asked leave to pray for him. He said, 'May such a thing be done?'

Tsze-lu replied, 'It may. In the Eulogies it is said, "Prayer has been made for thee to the spirits of the upper and lower worlds."' The Master said, 'My praying has been for a long time.'

CHAP. XXXV. The Master said, 'Extravagance leads to insubordination, and parsimony to meanness. It is better to be mean than to be insubordinate.'

CHAP. XXXVI. The Master said, 'The superior man is satisfied and composed; the mean man is always full of distress.'

CHAP. XXXVII. The Master was mild, and yet dignified; majestic, and yet not fierce; respectful, and yet easy.

BOOK VIII. T'AI-PO

CHAP. I. The Master said, 'T'ai-po may be said to have reached the highest point of virtuous action. Thrice he declined the kingdom, and the people in ignorance of his motives could not express their approbation of his conduct.'

CHAP. II. 1. The Master said, 'Respectfulness, without the rules of propriety, becomes laborious bustle; carefulness, without the rules of propriety, becomes timidity; boldness, without the rules of propriety, becomes insubordination; straightforwardness, without the rules of propriety, becomes rudeness.

2. 'When those who are in high stations perform well all their duties to their relations, the people are aroused to virtue. When old friends are not neglected by them, the people are preserved from meanness.'

CHAP. III. The philosopher Tsang being ill, he called to him the disciples of his school, and said, 'Uncover my feet, uncover my hands. It is said in the Book of Poetry, "We should be apprehensive and cautious, as if on the brink of a deep gulf, as if treading on thin ice," and so have I been. Now and hereafter, I know my escape from all injury to my person, O ye, my little children.'

CHAP. IV. 1. The philosopher Tsang being ill, Meng Chang went to ask how he was.

2. Tsang said to him, 'When a bird is about to die, its notes are mournful; when a man is about to die, his words are good.

3. 'There are three principles of conduct which the man of high rank should consider specially important:—that in his deportment and manner he keep from violence and heedlessness; that in regulating his countenance he keep near to sincerity; and that in his words and tones he keep far from lowness and impropriety. As to such matters as attending to the sacrificial vessels, there are the proper officers for them.'

CHAP. V. The philosopher Tsang said, 'Gifted with ability, and yet putting questions to those who were not so; possessed of much, and yet putting questions to those possessed of little;

having, as though he had not; full, and yet counting himself as empty; offended against, and yet entering into no altercation; formerly I had a friend who pursued this style of conduct.'

CHAP. VI. The philosopher Tsang said, 'Suppose that there is an individual who can be entrusted with the charge of a young orphan prince, and can be commissioned with authority over a state of a hundred li, and whom no emergency however great can drive from his principles:—is such a man a superior man? He is a superior man indeed.'

CHAP. VII. 1. The philosopher Tsang said, 'The officer may not be without breadth of mind and vigorous endurance. His burden is heavy and his course is long.

2. 'Perfect virtue is the burden which he considers it is his to sustain;—is it not heavy? Only with death does his course stop;—is it not long?

CHAP. VIII. 1. The Master said, 'It is by the Odes that the mind is aroused.

2. 'It is by the Rules of Propriety that the character is established.

3. 'It is from Music that the finish is received.'

CHAP. IX. The Master said, 'The people may be made to follow a path of action, but they may not be made to understand it.'

CHAP. X. The Master said, 'The man who is fond of daring and is dissatisfied with poverty, will proceed to insubordination. So will the man who is not virtuous, when you carry your dislike of him to an extreme.'

CHAP. XI. The Master said, 'Though a man have abilities as admirable as those of the Duke of Chau, yet if he be proud and niggardly, those other things are really not worth being looked at.'

CHAP. XII. The Master said, 'It is not easy to find a man who has learned for three years without coming to be good.'

CHAP. XIII. 1. The Master said, 'With sincere faith he unites the love of learning; holding firm to death, he is perfecting the excellence of his course.

2. 'Such an one will not enter a tottering State, nor dwell in a disorganized one. When right principles of government

prevail in the kingdom, he will show himself; when they are prostrated, he will keep concealed.

3. 'When a country is well-governed, poverty and a mean condition are things to be ashamed of. When a country is ill-governed, riches and honour are things to be ashamed of.'

CHAP. XIV. The Master said, 'He who is not in any particular office, has nothing to do with plans for the administration of its duties.'

CHAP. XV. The Master said, 'When the music master Chih first entered on his office, the finish of the Kwan Tsu was magnificent;—how it filled the ears!'

CHAP. XVI. The Master said, 'Ardent and yet not upright; stupid and yet not attentive; simple and yet not sincere:—such persons I do not understand.'

CHAP. XVII. The Master said, 'Learn as if you could not reach your object, and were always fearing also lest you should lose it.'

CHAP. XVIII. The Master said, 'How majestic was the manner in which Shun and Yu held possession of the empire, as if it were nothing to them!'

CHAP. XIX. 1. The Master said, 'Great indeed was Yao as a sovereign! How majestic was he! It is only Heaven that is grand, and only Yao corresponded to it. How vast was his virtue! The people could find no name for it.

2. 'How majestic was he in the works which he accomplished! How glorious in the elegant regulations which he instituted!'

CHAP. XX. 1. Shun had five ministers, and the empire was well-governed.

2. King Wu said, 'I have ten able ministers.'

3. Confucius said, 'Is not the saying that talents are difficult to find, true? Only when the dynasties of T'ang and Yu met, were they more abundant than in this of Chau, yet there was a woman among them. The able ministers were no more than nine men.

4. 'King Wan possessed two of the three parts of the empire, and with those he served the dynasty of Yin. The virtue of the house of Chau may be said to have reached the

66

highest point indeed.'

CHAP. XXI. The Master said, 'I can find no flaw in the character of Yu. He used himself coarse food and drink, but displayed the utmost filial piety towards the spirits. His ordinary garments were poor, but he displayed the utmost elegance in his sacrificial cap and apron. He lived in a low mean house, but expended all his strength on the ditches and water-channels. I can find nothing like a flaw in Yu.'

BOOK IX. TSZE HAN

CHAP. I. The subjects of which the Master seldom spoke were—profitableness, and also the appointments of Heaven, and perfect virtue.

CHAP. II. 1. A man of the village of Ta-hsiang said, 'Great indeed is the philosopher K'ung! His learning is extensive, and yet he does not render his name famous by any particular thing.'

2. The Master heard the observation, and said to his disciples, 'What shall I practise? Shall I practise charioteering, or shall I practise archery? I will practise charioteering.'

CHAP. III. 1. The Master said, 'The linen cap is that prescribed by the rules of ceremony, but now a silk one is worn. It is economical, and I follow the common practice.

2. 'The rules of ceremony prescribe the bowing below the hall, but now the practice is to bow only after ascending it. That is arrogant. I continue to bow below the hall, though I oppose the common practice.'

CHAP. IV. There were four things from which the Master was entirely free. He had no foregone conclusions, no arbitrary predeterminations, no obstinacy, and no egoism.

CHAP. V. 1. The Master was put in fear in K'wang.

2. He said, 'After the death of King Wan, was not the cause of truth lodged here in me?

3. 'If Heaven had wished to let this cause of truth perish, then I, a future mortal, should not have got such a relation to that cause. While Heaven does not let the cause of truth perish, what can the people of K'wang do to me?'

CHAP. VI. 1. A high officer asked Tsze-kung, saying, 'May we not say that your Master is a sage? How various is his ability!'

2. Tsze-kung said, 'Certainly Heaven has endowed him unlimitedly. He is about a sage. And, moreover, his ability is various.'

3. The Master heard of the conversation and said, 'Does the high officer know me? When I was young, my condition was

low, and therefore I acquired my ability in many things, but they were mean matters. Must the superior man have such variety of ability? He does not need variety of ability.'

4. Lao said, 'The Master said, "Having no official employment, I acquired many arts."'

CHAP. VII. The Master said, 'Am I indeed possessed of knowledge? I am not knowing. But if a mean person, who appears quite empty-like, ask anything of me, I set it forth from one end to the other, and exhaust it.'

CHAP. VIII. The Master said, 'The FANG bird does not come; the river sends forth no map:—it is all over with me!'

CHAP. IX. When the Master saw a person in a mourning dress, or any one with the cap and upper and lower garments of full dress, or a blind person, on observing them approaching, though they were younger than himself, he would rise up, and if he had to pass by them, he would do so hastily.

CHAP. X. 1. Yen Yuan, in admiration of the Master's doctrines, sighed and said, 'I looked up to them, and they seemed to become more high; I tried to penetrate them, and they seemed to become more firm; I looked at them before me, and suddenly they seemed to be behind.

2. 'The Master, by orderly method, skilfully leads men on. He enlarged my mind with learning, and taught me the restraints of propriety.

3. 'When I wish to give over the study of his doctrines, I cannot do so, and having exerted all my ability, there seems something to stand right up before me; but though I wish to follow and lay hold of it, I really find no way to do so.'

CHAP. XI. 1. The Master being very ill, Tsze-lu wished the disciples to act as ministers to him.

2. During a remission of his illness, he said, 'Long has the conduct of Yu been deceitful! By pretending to have ministers when I have them not, whom should I impose upon? Should I impose upon Heaven?

3. 'Moreover, than that I should die in the hands of ministers, is it not better that I should die in the hands of you, my disciples? And though I may not get a great burial, shall I

die upon the road?'

CHAP. XII. Tsze-kung said, 'There is a beautiful gem here. Should I lay it up in a case and keep it? or should I seek for a good price and sell it?' The Master said, 'Sell it! Sell it! But I would wait for one to offer the price.'

CHAP. XIII. 1. The Master was wishing to go and live among the nine wild tribes of the east.

2. Some one said, 'They are rude. How can you do such a thing?' The Master said, 'If a superior man dwelt among them, what rudeness would there be?'

CHAP. XIV. The Master said, 'I returned from Wei to Lu, and then the music was reformed, and the pieces in the Royal songs and Praise songs all found their proper places.'

CHAP. XV. The Master said, 'Abroad, to serve the high ministers and nobles; at home, to serve one's father and elder brothers; in all duties to the dead, not to dare not to exert one's self; and not to be overcome of wine:—which one of these things do I attain to?'

CHAP. XVI. The Master standing by a stream, said, 'It passes on just like this, not ceasing day or night!'

CHAP. XVII. The Master said, 'I have not seen one who loves virtue as he loves beauty.'

CHAP. XVIII. The Master said, 'The prosecution of learning may be compared to what may happen in raising a mound. If there want but one basket of earth to complete the work, and I stop, the stopping is my own work. It may be compared to throwing down the earth on the level ground. Though but one basketful is thrown at a time, the advancing with it is my own going forward.'

CHAP. XIX. The Master said, 'Never flagging when I set forth anything to him;—ah! that is Hui.'

CHAP. XX. The Master said of Yen Yuan, 'Alas! I saw his constant advance. I never saw him stop in his progress.'

CHAP. XXI. The Master said, 'There are cases in which the blade springs, but the plant does not go on to flower! There are cases where it flowers, but no fruit is subsequently produced!'

CHAP. XXII. The Master said, 'A youth is to be regarded

with respect. How do we know that his future will not be equal to our present? If he reach the age of forty or fifty, and has not made himself heard of, then indeed he will not be worth being regarded with respect.'

CHAP. XXIII. The Master said, 'Can men refuse to assent to the words of strict admonition? But it is reforming the conduct because of them which is valuable. Can men refuse to be pleased with words of gentle advice? But it is unfolding their aim which is valuable. If a man be pleased with these words, but does not unfold their aim, and assents to those, but does not reform his conduct, I can really do nothing with him.'

CHAP. XXIV. The Master said, 'Hold faithfulness and sincerity as first principles. Have no friends not equal to yourself. When you have faults, do not fear to abandon them.'

CHAP. XXV. The Master said, 'The commander of the forces of a large state may be carried off, but the will of even a common man cannot be taken from him.'

CHAP. XXVI. 1. The Master said, 'Dressed himself in a tattered robe quilted with hemp, yet standing by the side of men dressed in furs, and not ashamed;—ah! it is Yu who is equal to this!

2. '"He dislikes none, he covets nothing;—what can he do but what is good!"'

3. Tsze-lu kept continually repeating these words of the ode, when the Master said, 'Those things are by no means sufficient to constitute (perfect) excellence.'

CHAP. XXVII. The Master said, 'When the year becomes cold, then we know how the pine and the cypress are the last to lose their leaves.'

CHAP. XXVIII. The Master said, 'The wise are free from perplexities; the virtuous from anxiety; and the bold from fear.'

CHAP. XXIX. The Master said, 'There are some with whom we may study in common, but we shall find them unable to go along with us to principles. Perhaps we may go on with them to principles, but we shall find them unable to get established in those along with us. Or if we may get so established along with them, we shall find them unable to weigh occurring events along with us.'

CHAP. XXX. 1. How the flowers of the aspen-plum flutter and turn! Do I not think of you? But your house is distant.

2. The Master said, 'It is the want of thought about it. How is it distant?'

BOOK X. HEANG TANG

Chap. I. 1. Confucius, in his village, looked simple and sincere, and as if he were not able to speak.

2. When he was in the prince's ancestorial temple, or in the court, he spoke minutely on every point, but cautiously.

Chap II. 1. When he was waiting at court, in speaking with the great officers of the lower grade, he spake freely, but in a straightforward manner; in speaking with those of the higher grade, he did so blandly, but precisely.

2. When the ruler was present, his manner displayed respectful uneasiness; it was grave, but self-possessed.

Chap. III. 1. When the prince called him to employ him in the reception of a visitor, his countenance appeared to change, and his legs to move forward with difficulty.

2. He inclined himself to the other officers among whom he stood, moving his left or right arm, as their position required, but keeping the skirts of his robe before and behind evenly adjusted.

3. He hastened forward, with his arms like the wings of a bird.

4. When the guest had retired, he would report to the prince, 'The visitor is not turning round any more.'

Chap. IV. 1. When he entered the palace gate, he seemed to bend his body, as if it were not sufficient to admit him.

2. When he was standing, he did not occupy the middle of the gate-way; when he passed in or out, he did not tread upon the threshold.

3. When he was passing the vacant place of the prince, his countenance appeared to change, and his legs to bend under him, and his words came as if he hardly had breath to utter them.

4. He ascended the reception hall, holding up his robe with both his hands, and his body bent; holding in his breath also, as if he dared not breathe.

5. When he came out from the audience, as soon as he had descended one step, he began to relax his countenance, and

had a satisfied look. When he had got to the bottom of the steps, he advanced rapidly to his place, with his arms like wings, and on occupying it, his manner still showed respectful uneasiness.

CHAP. V. 1. When he was carrying the scepter of his ruler, he seemed to bend his body, as if he were not able to bear its weight. He did not hold it higher than the position of the hands in making a bow, nor lower than their position in giving anything to another. His countenance seemed to change, and look apprehensive, and he dragged his feet along as if they were held by something to the ground.

2. In presenting the presents with which he was charged, he wore a placid appearance.

3. At his private audience, he looked highly pleased.

CHAP. VI. 1. The superior man did not use a deep purple, or a puce colour, in the ornaments of his dress.

2. Even in his undress, he did not wear anything of a red or reddish colour.

3. In warm weather, he had a single garment either of coarse or fine texture, but he wore it displayed over an inner garment.

4. Over lamb's fur he wore a garment of black; over fawn's fur one of white; and over fox's fur one of yellow.

5. The fur robe of his undress was long, with the right sleeve short.

6. He required his sleeping dress to be half as long again as his body.

7. When staying at home, he used thick furs of the fox or the badger.

8. When he put off mourning, he wore all the appendages of the girdle.

9. His under-garment, except when it was required to be of the curtain shape, was made of silk cut narrow above and wide below.

10. He did not wear lamb's fur or a black cap, on a visit of condolence.

11. On the first day of the month he put on his court robes, and presented himself at court.

CHAP. VII. 1. When fasting, he thought it necessary to have

74

his clothes brightly clean and made of linen cloth.

2. When fasting, he thought it necessary to change his food, and also to change the place where he commonly sat in the apartment.

CHAP. VIII. 1. He did not dislike to have his rice finely cleaned, nor to have his minced meat cut quite small.

2. He did not eat rice which had been injured by heat or damp and turned sour, nor fish or flesh which was gone. He did not eat what was discoloured, or what was of a bad flavour, nor anything which was ill-cooked, or was not in season.

3. He did not eat meat which was not cut properly, nor what was served without its proper sauce.

4. Though there might be a large quantity of meat, he would not allow what he took to exceed the due proportion for the rice. It was only in wine that he laid down no limit for himself, but he did not allow himself to be confused by it.

5. He did not partake of wine and dried meat bought in the market.

6. He was never without ginger when he ate.

7. He did not eat much.

8. When he had been assisting at the prince's sacrifice, he did not keep the flesh which he received overnight. The flesh of his family sacrifice he did not keep over three days. If kept over three days, people could not eat it.

9. When eating, he did not converse. When in bed, he did not speak.

10. Although his food might be coarse rice and vegetable soup, he would offer a little of it in sacrifice with a grave, respectful air.

CHAP. IX. If his mat was not straight, he did not sit on it.

CHAP. X. 1. When the villagers were drinking together, on those who carried staffs going out, he went out immediately after.

2. When the villagers were going through their ceremonies to drive away pestilential influences, he put on his court robes and stood on the eastern steps.

CHAP. XI. 1. When he was sending complimentary inquiries to any one in another State, he bowed twice as he escorted the messenger away.

2. Chi K'ang having sent him a present of physic, he bowed and received it, saying, 'I do not know it. I dare not taste it.'

CHAP. XII. The stable being burned down, when he was at court, on his return he said, 'Has any man been hurt?' He did not ask about the horses.

CHAP. XIII. 1. When the prince sent him a gift of cooked meat, he would adjust his mat, first taste it, and then give it away to others. When the prince sent him a gift of undressed meat, he would have it cooked, and offer it to the spirits of his ancestors. When the prince sent him a gift of a living animal, he would keep it alive.

2. When he was in attendance on the prince and joining in the entertainment, the prince only sacrificed. He first tasted everything.

3. When he was ill and the prince came to visit him, he had his head to the east, made his court robes be spread over him, and drew his girdle across them.

4. When the prince's order called him, without waiting for his carriage to be yoked, he went at once.

CHAP. XIV. When he entered the ancestral temple of the State, he asked about everything.

CHAP. XV. 1. When any of his friends died, if he had no relations who could be depended on for the necessary offices, he would say, 'I will bury him.'

2. When a friend sent him a present, though it might be a carriage and horses, he did not bow.

3. The only present for which he bowed was that of the flesh of sacrifice.

CHAP. XVI. 1. In bed, he did not lie like a corpse. At home, he did not put on any formal deportment.

2. When he saw any one in a mourning dress, though it might be an acquaintance, he would change countenance; when he saw any one wearing the cap of full dress, or a blind person, though he might be in his undress, he would salute them in a ceremonious manner.

3. To any person in mourning he bowed forward to the crossbar of his carriage; he bowed in the same way to any one

bearing the tables of population.

4. When he was at an entertainment where there was an abundance of provisions set before him, he would change countenance and rise up.

5. On a sudden clap of thunder, or a violent wind, he would change countenance.

CHAP. XVII. 1. When he was about to mount his carriage, he would stand straight, holding the cord.

2. When he was in the carriage, he did not turn his head quite round, he did not talk hastily, he did not point with his hands.

CHAP. XVIII. 1. Seeing the countenance, it instantly rises. It flies round, and by and by settles.

2. The Master said, 'There is the hen-pheasant on the hill bridge. At its season! At its season!' Tsze-lu made a motion to it. Thrice it smelt him and then rose.

BOOK XI. HSIEN TSIN

CHAP. I. 1. The Master said, 'The men of former times, in the matters of ceremonies and music were rustics, it is said, while the men of these latter times, in ceremonies and music, are accomplished gentlemen.

2. 'If I have occasion to use those things, I follow the men of former times.'

CHAP. II. 1. The Master said, 'Of those who were with me in Ch'an and Ts'ai, there are none to be found to enter my door.'

2. Distinguished for their virtuous principles and practice, there were Yen Yuan, Min Tsze-ch'ien, Zan Po-niu, and Chung-kung; for their ability in speech, Tsai Wo and Tsze-kung; for their administrative talents, Zan Yu and Chi Lu; for their literary acquirements, Tsze-yu and Tsze-hsia.

CHAP. III. The Master said, 'Hui gives me no assistance. There is nothing that I say in which he does not delight.'

CHAP. IV. The Master said, 'Filial indeed is Min Tsze-ch'ien! Other people say nothing of him different from the report of his parents and brothers.'

CHAP. V. Nan Yung was frequently repeating the lines about a white scepter stone. Confucius gave him the daughter of his elder brother to wife.

CHAP. VI. Chi K'ang asked which of the disciples loved to learn. Confucius replied to him, 'There was Yen Hui; he loved to learn. Unfortunately his appointed time was short, and he died. Now there is no one who loves to learn, as he did.'

CHAP. VII. 1. When Yen Yuan died, Yen Lu begged the carriage of the Master to sell and get an outer shell for his son's coffin.

2. The Master said, 'Every one calls his son his son, whether he has talents or has not talents. There was Li; when he died, he had a coffin but no outer shell. I would not walk on foot to get a shell for him, because, having followed in the rear of the great officers, it was not proper that I should walk on foot.'

CHAP. VIII. When Yen Yuan died, the Master said, 'Alas!

Heaven is destroying me! Heaven is destroying me!'

CHAP. IX. 1. When Yen Yuan died, the Master bewailed him exceedingly, and the disciples who were with him said, 'Master, your grief is excessive?'

2. 'Is it excessive?' said he.

3. 'If I am not to mourn bitterly for this man, for whom should I mourn?'

CHAP. X. 1. When Yen Yuan died, the disciples wished to give him a great funeral, and the Master said, 'You may not do so.'

2. The disciples did bury him in great style.

3. The Master said, 'Hui behaved towards me as his father. I have not been able to treat him as my son. The fault is not mine; it belongs to you, O disciples.'

CHAP. XI. Chi Lu asked about serving the spirits of the dead. The Master said, 'While you are not able to serve men, how can you serve their spirits?' Chi Lu added, 'I venture to ask about death?' He was answered, 'While you do not know life, how can you know about death?'

CHAP. XII. 1. The disciple Min was standing by his side, looking bland and precise; Tsze-lu, looking bold and soldierly; Zan Yu and Tsze-kung, with a free and straightforward manner. The Master was pleased.

2. He said, 'Yu, there!—he will not die a natural death.'

CHAP. XIII. 1. Some parties in Lu were going to take down and rebuild the Long Treasury.

2. Min Tsze-ch'ien said, 'Suppose it were to be repaired after its old style;—why must it be altered and made anew?'

3. The Master said, 'This man seldom speaks; when he does, he is sure to hit the point.'

CHAP. XIV. 1. The Master said, 'What has the lute of Yu to do in my door?'

2. The other disciples began not to respect Tsze-lu. The Master said, 'Yu has ascended to the hall, though he has not yet passed into the inner apartments.'

CHAP. XV. 1. Tsze-kung asked which of the two, Shih or Shang, was the superior. The Master said, 'Shih goes beyond the due mean, and Shang does not come up to it.'

2. 'Then,' said Tsze-kung, 'the superiority is with Shih, I suppose.'

3. The Master said, 'To go beyond is as wrong as to fall short.'

CHAP. XVI. 1. The head of the Chi family was richer than the duke of Chau had been, and yet Ch'iu collected his imposts for him, and increased his wealth.

2. The Master said, 'He is no disciple of mine. My little children, beat the drum and assail him.'

CHAP. XVII. 1. Ch'ai is simple.

2. Shan is dull.

3. Shih is specious.

4. Yu is coarse.

CHAP. XVIII. 1. The Master said, 'There is Hui! He has nearly attained to perfect virtue. He is often in want.

2. 'Ts'ze does not acquiesce in the appointments of Heaven, and his goods are increased by him. Yet his judgments are often correct.'

CHAP. XIX. Tsze-chang asked what were the characteristics of the GOOD man. The Master said, 'He does not tread in the footsteps of others, but moreover, he does not enter the chamber of the sage.'

CHAP. XX. The Master said, 'If, because a man's discourse appears solid and sincere, we allow him to be a good man, is he really a superior man? or is his gravity only in appearance?'

CHAP. XXI. Tsze-lu asked whether he should immediately carry into practice what he heard. The Master said, 'There are your father and elder brothers to be consulted;—why should you act on that principle of immediately carrying into practice what you hear?' Zan Yu asked the same, whether he should immediately carry into practice what he heard, and the Master answered, 'Immediately carry into practice what you hear.' Kung-hsi Hwa said, 'Yu asked whether he should carry immediately into practice what he heard, and you said, "There are your father and elder brothers to be consulted." Ch'iu asked whether he should immediately carry into practice what he heard, and you said, "Carry it immediately into practice." I,

Ch'ih, am perplexed, and venture to ask you for an explanation.' The Master said, 'Ch'iu is retiring and slow; therefore, I urged him forward. Yu has more than his own share of energy; therefore I kept him back.'

CHAP. XXII. The Master was put in fear in K'wang and Yen Yuan fell behind. The Master, on his rejoining him, said, 'I thought you had died.' Hui replied, 'While you were alive, how should I presume to die?'

CHAP. XXIII. 1. Chi Tsze-zan asked whether Chung Yu and Zan Ch'iu could be called great ministers.

2. The Master said, 'I thought you would ask about some extraordinary individuals, and you only ask about Yu and Ch'iu!

3. 'What is called a great minister, is one who serves his prince according to what is right, and when he finds he cannot do so, retires.

4. 'Now, as to Yu and Ch'iu, they may be called ordinary ministers.'

5. Tsze-zan said, 'Then they will always follow their chief;— will they?'

6. The Master said, 'In an act of parricide or regicide, they would not follow him.'

CHAP. XXIV. 1. Tsze-lu got Tsze-kao appointed governor of Pi.

2. The Master said, 'You are injuring a man's son.'

3. Tsze-lu said, 'There are (there) common people and officers; there are the altars of the spirits of the land and grain. Why must one read books before he can be considered to have learned?'

4. The Master said, 'It is on this account that I hate your glib-tongued people.'

CHAP. XXV. 1. Tsze-lu, Tsang Hsi, Zan Yu, and Kung-hsi Hwa were sitting by the Master.

2. He said to them, 'Though I am a day or so older than you,
do not think of that.

3. 'From day to day you are saying, "We are not known." If some ruler were to know you, what would you like to do?'

4. Tsze-lu hastily and lightly replied, 'Suppose the case of a State of ten thousand chariots; let it be straitened between other large States; let it be suffering from invading armies; and to this let there be added a famine in corn and in all vegetables:—if I were intrusted with the government of it, in three years' time I could make the people to be bold, and to recognise the rules of righteous conduct.' The Master smiled at him.

5. Turning to Yen Yu, he said, 'Ch'iu, what are your wishes?' Ch'iu replied, 'Suppose a state of sixty or seventy li square, or one of fifty or sixty, and let me have the government of it;—in three years' time, I could make plenty to abound among the people. As to teaching them the principles of propriety, and music, I must wait for the rise of a superior man to do that.'

6. 'What are your wishes, Ch'ih,' said the Master next to Kung-hsi Hwa. Ch'ih replied, 'I do not say that my ability extends to these things, but I should wish to learn them. At the services of the ancestral temple, and at the audiences of the princes with the sovereign, I should like, dressed in the dark square-made robe and the black linen cap, to act as a small assistant.'

7. Last of all, the Master asked Tsang Hsi, 'Tien, what are your wishes?' Tien, pausing as he was playing on his lute, while it was yet twanging, laid the instrument aside, and rose. 'My wishes,' he said, 'are different from the cherished purposes of these three gentlemen.' 'What harm is there in that?' said the Master; 'do you also, as well as they, speak out your wishes.' Tien then said, 'In this, the last month of spring, with the dress of the season all complete, along with five or six young men who have assumed the cap, and six or seven boys, I would wash in the I, enjoy the breeze among the rain altars, and return home singing.' The Master heaved a sigh and said, 'I give my approval to Tien.'

8. The three others having gone out, Tsang Hsi remained behind, and said, 'What do you think of the words of these three friends?' The Master replied, 'They simply told each one his wishes.'

9. Hsi pursued, 'Master, why did you smile at Yu?'

10. He was answered, 'The management of a State demands the rules of propriety. His words were not humble; therefore I smiled at him.'

11. Hsi again said, 'But was it not a State which Ch'iu proposed for himself?' The reply was, 'Yes; did you ever see a territory of sixty or seventy li or one of fifty or sixty, which was not a State?'

12. Once more, Hsi inquired, 'And was it not a State which Ch'ih proposed for himself?' The Master again replied, 'Yes; who but princes have to do with ancestral temples, and with audiences but the sovereign? If Ch'ih were to be a small assistant in these services, who could be a great one?

BOOK XII. YEN YUAN

CHAP. I. 1. Yen Yuan asked about perfect virtue. The Master said, 'To subdue one's self and return to propriety, is perfect virtue. If a man can for one day subdue himself and return to propriety, all under heaven will ascribe perfect virtue to him. Is the practice of perfect virtue from a man himself, or is it from others?' 2. Yen Yuan said, 'I beg to ask the steps of that process.' The Master replied, 'Look not at what is contrary to propriety; listen not to what is contrary to propriety; speak not what is contrary to propriety; make no movement which is contrary to propriety.' Yen Yuan then said, 'Though I am deficient in intelligence and vigour, I will make it my business to practise this lesson.'

CHAP. II. Chung-kung asked about perfect virtue. The Master said, 'It is, when you go abroad, to behave to every one as if you were receiving a great guest; to employ the people as if you were assisting at a great sacrifice; not to do to others as you would not wish done to yourself; to have no murmuring against you in the country, and none in the family.' Chung-kung said, 'Though I am deficient in intelligence and vigour, I will make it my business to practise this lesson.'

CHAP. III. 1. Sze-ma Niu asked about perfect virtue.

2. The Master said, 'The man of perfect virtue is cautious and slow in his speech.'

3. 'Cautious and slow in his speech!' said Niu;—'is this what is meant by perfect virtue?' The Master said, 'When a man feels the difficulty of doing, can he be other than cautious and slow in speaking?'

CHAP. IV. 1. Sze-ma Niu asked about the superior man. The Master said, 'The superior man has neither anxiety nor fear.'

2. 'Being without anxiety or fear!' said Nui;—'does this constitute what we call the superior man?'

3. The Master said, 'When internal examination discovers nothing wrong, what is there to be anxious about, what is there

to fear?'

CHAP. V. 1. Sze-ma Niu, full of anxiety, said, 'Other men all have their brothers, I only have not.'

2. Tsze-hsia said to him, 'There is the following saying which I have heard:—

3. "'Death and life have their determined appointment; riches and honours depend upon Heaven."

4. 'Let the superior man never fail reverentially to order his own conduct, and let him be respectful to others and observant of propriety:—then all within the four seas will be his brothers. What has the superior man to do with being distressed because he has no brothers?'

CHAP. VI. Tsze-chang asked what constituted intelligence. The Master said, 'He with whom neither slander that gradually soaks into the mind, nor statements that startle like a wound in the flesh, are successful, may be called intelligent indeed. Yea, he with whom neither soaking slander, nor startling statements, are successful, may be called farseeing.'

CHAP. VII. 1. Tsze-kung asked about government. The Master said, 'The requisites of government are that there be sufficiency of food, sufficiency of military equipment, and the confidence of the people in their ruler.'

2. Tsze-kung said, 'If it cannot be helped, and one of these must be dispensed with, which of the three should be foregone first?' 'The military equipment,' said the Master.

3. Tsze-kung again asked, 'If it cannot be helped, and one of the remaining two must be dispensed with, which of them should be foregone?' The Master answered, 'Part with the food. From of old, death has been the lot of all men; but if the people have no faith in their rulers, there is no standing for the state.'

CHAP. VIII. 1. Chi Tsze-ch'ang said, 'In a superior man it is only the substantial qualities which are wanted;—why should we seek for ornamental accomplishments?'

2. Tsze-kung said, 'Alas! Your words, sir, show you to be a superior man, but four horses cannot overtake the tongue.

3. Ornament is as substance; substance is as ornament. The hide of a tiger or a leopard stripped of its hair, is like the hide

of a dog or a goat stripped of its hair.'

CHAP. IX. 1. The Duke Ai inquired of Yu Zo, saying, 'The year is one of scarcity, and the returns for expenditure are not sufficient;—what is to be done?'

2. Yu Zo replied to him, 'Why not simply tithe the people?'

3. 'With two tenths, said the duke, 'I find it not enough;—how could I do with that system of one tenth?'

4. Yu Zo answered, 'If the people have plenty, their prince will not be left to want alone. If the people are in want, their prince cannot enjoy plenty alone.'

CHAP. X. 1. Tsze-chang having asked how virtue was to be exalted, and delusions to be discovered, the Master said, 'Hold faithfulness and sincerity as first principles, and be moving continually to what is right;—this is the way to exalt one's virtue.

2. 'You love a man and wish him to live; you hate him and wish him to die. Having wished him to live, you also wish him to die. This is a case of delusion.

3. '"It may not be on account of her being rich, yet you come to make a difference."'

CHAP. XI. 1. The Duke Ching, of Ch'i, asked Confucius about government.

2. Confucius replied, 'There is government, when the prince is prince, and the minister is minister; when the father is father, and the son is son.'

3. 'Good!' said the duke; 'if, indeed; the prince be not prince, the minister not minister, the father not father, and the son not son, although I have my revenue, can I enjoy it?'

CHAP. XII. 1. The Master said, 'Ah! it is Yu, who could with half a word settle litigations!'

2. Tsze-lu never slept over a promise.

CHAP. XIII. The Master said, 'In hearing litigations, I am like any other body. What is necessary, however, is to cause the people to have no litigations.'

CHAP. XIV. Tsze-chang asked about government. The Master said, 'The art of governing is to keep its affairs before the mind without weariness, and to practise them with undeviating consistency.'

CHAP. XV. The Master said, 'By extensively studying all learning, and keeping himself under the restraint of the rules of propriety, one may thus likewise not err from what is right.'

CHAP. XVI. The Master said, 'The superior man seeks to perfect the admirable qualities of men, and does not seek to perfect their bad qualities. The mean man does the opposite of this.'

CHAP. XVII. Chi K'ang asked Confucius about government. Confucius replied, 'To govern means to rectify. If you lead on the people with correctness, who will dare not to be correct?'

CHAP. XVIII. Chi K'ang, distressed about the number of thieves in the state, inquired of Confucius how to do away with them. Confucius said, 'If you, sir, were not covetous, although you should reward them to do it, they would not steal.'

CHAP. XIX. Chi K'ang asked Confucius about government, saying, 'What do you say to killing the unprincipled for the good of the principled?' Confucius replied, 'Sir, in carrying on your government, why should you use killing at all? Let your evinced desires be for what is good, and the people will be good. The relation between superiors and inferiors, is like that between the wind and the grass. The grass must bend, when the wind blows across it.'

CHAP. XX. 1. Tsze-chang asked, 'What must the officer be, who may be said to be distinguished?'

2. The Master said, 'What is it you call being distinguished?'

3. Tsze-chang replied, 'It is to be heard of through the State, to be heard of throughout his clan.'

4. The Master said, 'That is notoriety, not distinction.

5. 'Now the man of distinction is solid and straightforward, and loves righteousness. He examines people's words, and looks at their countenances. He is anxious to humble himself to others. Such a man will be distinguished in the country; he will be distinguished in his clan.

6. 'As to the man of notoriety, he assumes the appearance of virtue, but his actions are opposed to it, and he rests in this character without any doubts about himself. Such a man will be heard of in the country; he will be heard of in the clan.'

CHAP. XXI. 1. Fan Ch'ih rambling with the Master under the trees about the rain altars, said, 'I venture to ask how to exalt virtue, to correct cherished evil, and to discover delusions.'

2. The Master said, 'Truly a good question!

3. 'If doing what is to be done be made the first business, and success a secondary consideration;—is not this the way to exalt virtue? To assail one's own wickedness and not assail that of others;—is not this the way to correct cherished evil? For a morning's anger to disregard one's own life, and involve that of his parents;—is not this a case of delusion?'

CHAP. XXII. 1. Fan Ch'ih asked about benevolence. The Master said, 'It is to love all men.' He asked about knowledge. The Master said, 'It is to know all men.'

2. Fan Ch'ih did not immediately understand these answers.

3. The Master said, 'Employ the upright and put aside all the crooked;—in this way the crooked can be made to be upright.'

4. Fan Ch'ih retired, and, seeing Tsze-hsia, he said to him, 'A Little while ago, I had an interview with our Master, and asked him about knowledge. He said, 'Employ the upright, and put aside all the crooked;—in this way, the crooked will be made to be upright.' What did he mean?'

5. Tsze-hsia said, 'Truly rich is his saying!

6. 'Shun, being in possession of the kingdom, selected from among all the people, and employed Kao-yao, on which all who were devoid of virtue disappeared. T'ang, being in possession of the kingdom, selected from among all the people, and employed I Yin, and all who were devoid of virtue disappeared.'

CHAP. XXIII. Tsze-kung asked about friendship. The Master said, 'Faithfully admonish your friend, and skillfully lead him on. If you find him impracticable, stop. Do not disgrace yourself.'

CHAP. XXIV. The philosopher Tsang said, 'The superior man on grounds of culture meets with his friends, and by their friendship helps his virtue.'

BOOK XIII. TSZE-LU

CHAP. I. 1. Tsze-lu asked about government. The Master said, 'Go before the people with your example, and be laborious in their affairs.'

2. He requested further instruction, and was answered, 'Be not weary (in these things).'

CHAP. II. 1. Chung-kung, being chief minister to the Head of the Chi family, asked about government. The Master said, 'Employ first the services of your various officers, pardon small faults, and raise to office men of virtue and talents.'

2. Chung-kung said, 'How shall I know the men of virtue and talent, so that I may raise them to office?' He was answered, 'Raise to office those whom you know. As to those whom you do not know, will others neglect them?'

CHAP. III. 1. Tsze-lu said, 'The ruler of Wei has been waiting for you, in order with you to administer the government. What will you consider the first thing to be done?'

2. The Master replied, 'What is necessary is to rectify names.'

3. 'So, indeed!' said Tsze-lu. 'You are wide of the mark! Why must there be such rectification?'

4. The Master said, 'How uncultivated you are, Yu! A superior man, in regard to what he does not know, shows a cautious reserve.

5. 'If names be not correct, language is not in accordance with the truth of things. If language be not in accordance with the truth of things, affairs cannot be carried on to success.

6. 'When affairs cannot be carried on to success, proprieties and music will not flourish. When proprieties and music do not flourish, punishments will not be properly awarded. When punishments are not properly awarded, the people do not know how to move hand or foot.

7. 'Therefore a superior man considers it necessary that the names he uses may be spoken appropriately, and also that what he speaks may be carried out appropriately. What the superior

man requires, is just that in his words there may be nothing incorrect.'

CHAP. IV. 1. Fan Ch'ih requested to be taught husbandry. The Master said, 'I am not so good for that as an old husbandman.' He requested also to be taught gardening, and was answered, 'I am not so good for that as an old gardener.'

2. Fan Ch'ih having gone out, the Master said, 'A small man, indeed, is Fan Hsu!

3. If a superior love propriety, the people will not dare not to be reverent. If he love righteousness, the people will not dare not to submit to his example. If he love good faith, the people will not dare not to be sincere. Now, when these things obtain, the people from all quarters will come to him, bearing their children on their backs;—what need has he of a knowledge of husbandry?'

CHAP. V. The Master said, 'Though a man may be able to recite the three hundred odes, yet if, when intrusted with a governmental charge, he knows not how to act, or if, when sent to any quarter on a mission, he cannot give his replies unassisted, notwithstanding the extent of his learning, of what practical use is it?'

CHAP. VI. The Master said, 'When a prince's personal conduct is correct, his government is effective without the issuing of orders. If his personal conduct is not correct, he may issue orders, but they will not be followed.'

CHAP. VII. The Master said, 'The governments of Lu and Wei are brothers.'

CHAP. VIII. The Master said of Ching, a scion of the ducal family of Wei, that he knew the economy of a family well. When he began to have means, he said, 'Ha! here is a collection!' When they were a little increased, he said, 'Ha! this is complete!' When he had become rich, he said, 'Ha! this is admirable!'

CHAP. IX.

1. When the Master went to Wei, Zan Yu acted as driver of his carriage.

2. The Master observed, 'How numerous are the people!'

3. Yu said, 'Since they are thus numerous, what more shall

be done for them?' 'Enrich them,' was the reply.

4. 'And when they have been enriched, what more shall be done?' The Master said, 'Teach them.'

CHAP. X. The Master said, 'If there were (any of the princes) who would employ me, in the course of twelve months, I should have done something considerable. In three years, the government would be perfected.'

CHAP. XI. The Master said, '"If good men were to govern a country in succession for a hundred years, they would be able to transform the violently bad, and dispense with capital punishments." True indeed is this saying!'

CHAP. XII. The Master said, 'If a truly royal ruler were to arise, it would still require a generation, and then virtue would prevail.'

CHAP. XIII. The Master said, 'If a minister make his own conduct correct, what difficulty will he have in assisting in government? If he cannot rectify himself, what has he to do with rectifying others?'

CHAP. XIV. The disciple Zan returning from the court, the Master said to him, 'How are you so late?' He replied, 'We had government business.' The Master said, 'It must have been family affairs. If there had been government business, though I am not now in office, I should have been consulted about it.'

CHAP. XV. 1. The Duke Ting asked whether there was a single sentence which could make a country prosperous. Confucius replied, 'Such an effect cannot be expected from one sentence.

2. 'There is a saying, however, which people have—"To be a prince is difficult; to be a minister is not easy."

3. 'If a ruler knows this,—the difficulty of being a prince,— may there not be expected from this one sentence the prosperity of his country?'

4. The duke then said, 'Is there a single sentence which can ruin a country?' Confucius replied, 'Such an effect as that cannot be expected from one sentence. There is, however, the saying which people have—"I have no pleasure in being a prince, but only in that no one can offer any opposition to what I say!"

5. 'If a ruler's words be good, is it not also good that no one oppose them? But if they are not good, and no one opposes them, may there not be expected from this one sentence the ruin of his country?'

CHAP. XVI. 1. The Duke of Sheh asked about government. 2. The Master said, 'Good government obtains, when those who are near are made happy, and those who are far off are attracted.'

CHAP. XVII. Tsze-hsia, being governor of Chu-fu, asked about government. The Master said, 'Do not be desirous to have things done quickly; do not look at small advantages. Desire to have things done quickly prevents their being done thoroughly. Looking at small advantages prevents great affairs from being accomplished.'

CHAP. XVIII. 1. The Duke of Sheh informed Confucius, saying, 'Among us here there are those who may be styled upright in their conduct. If their father have stolen a sheep, they will bear witness to the fact.'

2. Confucius said, 'Among us, in our part of the country, those who are upright are different from this. The father conceals the misconduct of the son, and the son conceals the misconduct of the father. Uprightness is to be found in this.'

CHAP. XIX. Fan Ch'ih asked about perfect virtue. The Master said, 'It is, in retirement, to be sedately grave; in the management of business, to be reverently attentive; in intercourse with others, to be strictly sincere. Though a man go among rude, uncultivated tribes, these qualities may not be neglected.'

CHAP. XX. 1. Tsze-kung asked, saying, 'What qualities must a man possess to entitle him to be called an officer? The Master said, 'He who in his conduct of himself maintains a sense of shame, and when sent to any quarter will not disgrace his prince's commission, deserves to be called an officer.'

2. Tsze-kung pursued, 'I venture to ask who may be placed in the next lower rank?' And he was told, 'He whom the circle of his relatives pronounce to be filial, whom his fellow-villagers and neighbours pronounce to be fraternal.'

3. Again the disciple asked, 'I venture to ask about the class

still next in order.' The Master said, 'They are determined to be sincere in what they say, and to carry out what they do. They are obstinate little men. Yet perhaps they may make the next class.'

4. Tsze-kung finally inquired, 'Of what sort are those of the present day, who engage in government?' The Master said 'Pooh! they are so many pecks and hampers, not worth being taken into account.'

CHAP. XXI. The Master said, 'Since I cannot get men pursuing the due medium, to whom I might communicate my instructions, I must find the ardent and the cautiously-decided. The ardent will advance and lay hold of truth; the cautiously-decided will keep themselves from what is wrong.'

CHAP. XXII. 1. The Master said, 'The people of the south have a saying—"A man without constancy cannot be either a wizard or a doctor." Good!

2. 'Inconstant in his virtue, he will be visited with disgrace.'

3. The Master said, 'This arises simply from not attending to the prognostication.'

CHAP. XXIII. The Master said, 'The superior man is affable, but not adulatory; the mean man is adulatory, but not affable.'

CHAP. XXIV. Tsze-kung asked, saying, 'What do you say of a man who is loved by all the people of his neighbourhood?' The Master replied, 'We may not for that accord our approval of him.' 'And what do you say of him who is hated by all the people of his neighbourhood?' The Master said, 'We may not for that conclude that he is bad. It is better than either of these cases that the good in the neighbourhood love him, and the bad hate him.'

CHAP. XXV. The Master said, 'The superior man is easy to serve and difficult to please. If you try to please him in any way which is not accordant with right, he will not be pleased. But in his employment of men, he uses them according to their capacity. The mean man is difficult to serve, and easy to please. If you try to please him, though it be in a way which is not accordant with right, he may be pleased. But in his employment of men, he wishes them to be equal to everything.'

CHAP. XXVI. The Master said, 'The superior man has a dignified ease without pride. The mean man has pride without a dignified ease.'

CHAP. XXVII. The Master said, 'The firm, the enduring, the simple, and the modest are near to virtue.'

CHAP. XXVIII. Tsze-lu asked, saying, 'What qualities must a man possess to entitle him to be called a scholar?' The Master said, 'He must be thus,—earnest, urgent, and bland:—among his friends, earnest and urgent; among his brethren, bland.'

CHAP. XXIX. The Master said, 'Let a good man teach the people seven years, and they may then likewise be employed in war.'

CHAP. XXX. The Master said, 'To lead an uninstructed people to war, is to throw them away.'

BOOK XIV. HSIEN WAN

CHAP. I. Hsien asked what was shameful. The Master said, 'When good government prevails in a state, to be thinking only of salary; and, when bad government prevails, to be thinking, in the same way, only of salary;—this is shameful.'

CHAP. II. 1. 'When the love of superiority, boasting, resentments, and covetousness are repressed, this may be deemed perfect virtue.'

2. The Master said, 'This may be regarded as the achievement of what is difficult. But I do not know that it is to be deemed perfect virtue.'

CHAP. III. The Master said, 'The scholar who cherishes the love of comfort is not fit to be deemed a scholar.'

CHAP. IV. The Master said, 'When good government prevails in a state, language may be lofty and bold, and actions the same. When bad government prevails, the actions may be lofty and bold, but the language may be with some reserve.'

CHAP. V. The Master said, 'The virtuous will be sure to speak correctly, but those whose speech is good may not always be virtuous. Men of principle are sure to be bold, but those who are bold may not always be men of principle.'

CHAP. VI. Nan-kung Kwo, submitting an inquiry to Confucius, said, 'I was skillful at archery, and Ao could move a boat along upon the land, but neither of them died a natural death. Yu and Chi personally wrought at the toils of husbandry, and they became possessors of the kingdom.' The Master made no reply; but when Nan-kung Kwo went out, he said, 'A superior man indeed is this! An esteemer of virtue indeed is this!'

CHAP. VII. The Master said, 'Superior men, and yet not always virtuous, there have been, alas! But there never has been a mean man, and, at the same time, virtuous.'

CHAP. VIII. The Master said, 'Can there be love which does not lead to strictness with its object? Can there be loyalty which does not lead to the instruction of its object?'

CHAP. IX. The Master said, 'In preparing the governmental

notifications, P'i Shan first made the rough draft; Shi-shu examined and discussed its contents; Tsze-yu, the manager of Foreign intercourse, then polished the style; and, finally, Tsze-ch'an of Tung-li gave it the proper elegance and finish.'

CHAP. X. 1. Some one asked about Tsze-ch'an. The Master said, 'He was a kind man.'

2. He asked about Tsze-hsi. The Master said, 'That man! That man!'

3. He asked about Kwan Chung. 'For him,' said the Master, 'the city of Pien, with three hundred families, was taken from the chief of the Po family, who did not utter a murmuring word, though, to the end of his life, he had only coarse rice to eat.'

CHAP. XI. The Master said, 'To be poor without murmuring is difficult. To be rich without being proud is easy.'

CHAP. XII. The Master said, 'Mang Kung-ch'o is more than fit to be chief officer in the families of Chao and Wei, but he is not fit to be great officer to either of the States Tang or Hsieh.'

CHAP. XIII. 1. Tsze-lu asked what constituted a COMPLETE man. The Master said, 'Suppose a man with the knowledge of Tsang Wu-chung, the freedom from covetousness of Kung-ch'o, the bravery of Chwang of Pien, and the varied talents of Zan Ch'iu; add to these the accomplishments of the rules of propriety and music:—such a one might be reckoned a COMPLETE man.'

2. He then added, 'But what is the necessity for a complete man of the present day to have all these things? The man, who in the view of gain, thinks of righteousness; who in the view of danger is prepared to give up his life; and who does not forget an old agreement however far back it extends:—such a man may be reckoned a COMPLETE man.'

CHAP. XIV. 1. The Master asked Kung-ming Chia about Kung-shu Wan, saying, 'Is it true that your master speaks not, laughs not, and takes not?'

2. Kung-ming Chia replied, 'This has arisen from the reporters going beyond the truth.—My master speaks when it is the time to speak, and so men do not get tired of his

speaking. He laughs when there is occasion to be joyful, and so men do not get tired of his laughing. He takes when it is consistent with righteousness to do so, and so men do not get tired of his taking.' The Master said, 'So! But is it so with him?'

CHAP. XV. The Master said, 'Tsang Wu-chung, keeping possession of Fang, asked of the duke of Lu to appoint a successor to him in his family. Although it may be said that he was not using force with his sovereign, I believe he was.'

CHAP. XVI. The Master said, 'The duke Wan of Tsin was crafty and not upright. The duke Hwan of Ch'i was upright and not crafty.'

CHAP. XVII. 1. Tsze-lu said, 'The Duke Hwan caused his brother Chiu to be killed, when Shao Hu died with his master, but Kwan Chung did not die. May not I say that he was wanting in virtue?'

2. The Master said, 'The Duke Hwan assembled all the princes together, and that not with weapons of war and chariots:—it was all through the influence of Kwan Chung. Whose beneficence was like his? Whose beneficence was like his?'

CHAP. XVIII. 1. Tsze-kung said, 'Kwan Chung, I apprehend, was wanting in virtue. When the Duke Hwan caused his brother Chiu to be killed, Kwan Chung was not able to die with him. Moreover, he became prime minister to Hwan.'

2. The Master said, 'Kwan Chung acted as prime minister to the Duke Hwan, made him leader of all the princes, and united and rectified the whole kingdom. Down to the present day, the people enjoy the gifts which he conferred. But for Kwan Chung, we should now be wearing our hair unbound, and the lappets of our coats buttoning on the left side.

3. 'Will you require from him the small fidelity of common men and common women, who would commit suicide in a stream or ditch, no one knowing anything about them?'

CHAP. XIX. 1. The great officer, Hsien, who had been family-minister to Kung-shu Wan, ascended to the prince's court in company with Wan.

2. The Master, having heard of it, said, 'He deserved to be

considered WAN (the accomplished).'

CHAP. XX. 1. The Master was speaking about the unprincipled course of the duke Ling of Wei, when Ch'i K'ang said, 'Since he is of such a character, how is it he does not lose his State?'

2. Confucius said, 'The Chung-shu Yu has the superintendence of his guests and of strangers; the litanist, T'o, has the management of his ancestral temple; and Wang-sun Chia has the direction of the army and forces:—with such officers as these, how should he lose his State?'

CHAP. XXI. The Master said, 'He who speaks without modesty will find it difficult to make his words good.'

CHAP. XXII. 1. Chan Ch'ang murdered the Duke Chien of Ch'i.

2. Confucius bathed, went to court, and informed the duke Ai, saying, 'Chan Hang has slain his sovereign. I beg that you will undertake to punish him.'

3. The duke said, 'Inform the chiefs of the three families of it.'

4. Confucius retired, and said, 'Following in the rear of the great officers, I did not dare not to represent such a matter, and my prince says, "Inform the chiefs of the three families of it."'

5. He went to the chiefs, and informed them, but they would not act. Confucius then said, 'Following in the rear of the great officers, I did not dare not to represent such a matter.'

CHAP. XXIII. Tsze-lu asked how a ruler should be served. The Master said, 'Do not impose on him, and, moreover, withstand him to his face.'

CHAP. XXIV. The Master said, 'The progress of the superior man is upwards; the progress of the mean man is downwards.'

CHAP. XXV. The Master said, 'In ancient times, men learned with a view to their own improvement. Now-a-days, men learn with a view to the approbation of others.'

CHAP. XXVI. 1. Chu Po-yu sent a messenger with friendly inquiries to Confucius.

2. Confucius sat with him, and questioned him. 'What,' said he, 'is your master engaged in?' The messenger replied, 'My master is anxious to make his faults few, but he has not yet succeeded.' He then went out, and the Master said, 'A messenger indeed! A messenger indeed!'

CHAP. XXVII. The Master said, 'He who is not in any particular office, has nothing to do with plans for the administration of its duties.'

CHAP. XXVIII. The philosopher Tsang said, 'The superior man, in his thoughts, does not go out of his place.'

CHAP. XXIX. The Master said, 'The superior man is modest in his speech, but exceeds in his actions.'

CHAP. XXX. 1. The Master said, 'The way of the superior man is threefold, but I am not equal to it. Virtuous, he is free from anxieties; wise, he is free from perplexities; bold, he is free from fear.

2. Tsze-kung said, 'Master, that is what you yourself say.'

CHAP. XXXI. Tsze-kung was in the habit of comparing men together. The Master said, 'Tsze must have reached a high pitch of excellence! Now, I have not leisure for this.'

CHAP. XXXII. The Master said, 'I will not be concerned at men's not knowing me; I will be concerned at my own want of ability.'

CHAP. XXXIII. The Master said, 'He who does not anticipate attempts to deceive him, nor think beforehand of his not being believed, and yet apprehends these things readily (when they occur);—is he not a man of superior worth?'

CHAP. XXXIV. 1. Wei-shang Mau said to Confucius, 'Ch'iu, how is it that you keep roosting about? Is it not that you are an insinuating talker?'

2. Confucius said, 'I do not dare to play the part of such a talker, but I hate obstinacy.'

CHAP. XXXV. The Master said, 'A horse is called a ch'i, not because of its strength, but because of its other good qualities.'

CHAP. XXXVI. 1. Some one said, 'What do you say concerning the principle that injury should be recompensed with kindness?'

2. The Master said, 'With what then will you recompense

kindness?

3. 'Recompense injury with justice, and recompense kindness with kindness.'

CHAP. XXXVII. 1. The Master said, 'Alas! there is no one that knows me.'

2. Tsze-kung said, 'What do you mean by thus saying—that no one knows you?' The Master replied, 'I do not murmur against Heaven. I do not grumble against men. My studies lie low, and my penetration rises high. But there is Heaven;—that knows me!'

CHAP. XXXVIII. 1. The Kung-po Liao, having slandered Tsze-lu to Chi-sun, Tsze-fu Ching-po informed Confucius of it, saying, 'Our master is certainly being led astray by the Kung-po Liao, but I have still power enough left to cut Liao off, and expose his corpse in the market and in the court.'

2. The Master said, 'If my principles are to advance, it is so ordered. If they are to fall to the ground, it is so ordered. What can the Kung-po Liao do where such ordering is concerned?'

CHAP. XXXIX. 1. The Master said, 'Some men of worth retire from the world.

2. Some retire from particular states.

3. Some retire because of disrespectful looks.

4. Some retire because of contradictory language.'

CHAP. XL. The Master said, 'Those who have done this are seven men.'

CHAP. XLI. Tsze-lu happening to pass the night in Shih-man, the gatekeeper said to him, 'Whom do you come from?' Tsze-lu said, 'From Mr. K'ung.' 'It is he,—is it not?'—said the other, 'who knows the impracticable nature of the times and yet will be doing in them.'

CHAP. XLII. 1. The Master was playing, one day, on a musical stone in Wei, when a man, carrying a straw basket, passed the door of the house where Confucius was, and said, 'His heart is full who so beats the musical stone.'

2. A little while after, he added, 'How contemptible is the one-ideaed obstinacy those sounds display! When one is taken no notice of, he has simply at once to give over his wish for public employment. "Deep water must be crossed with the

clothes on; shallow water may be crossed with the clothes held up.'''

3. The Master said, 'How determined is he in his purpose! But this is not difficult!'

CHAP. XLIII. 1. Tsze-chang said, 'What is meant when the Shu says that Kao-tsung, while observing the usual imperial mourning, was for three years without speaking?'

2. The Master said, 'Why must Kao-tsung be referred to as an example of this? The ancients all did so. When the sovereign died, the officers all attended to their several duties, taking instructions from the prime minister for three years.'

CHAP. XLIV. The Master said, 'When rulers love to observe the rules of propriety, the people respond readily to the calls on them for service.'

CHAP. XLV. Tsze-lu asked what constituted the superior man. The Master said, 'The cultivation of himself in reverential carefulness.' 'And is this all?' said Tsze-lu. 'He cultivates himself so as to give rest to others,' was the reply. 'And is this all?' again asked Tsze-lu. The Master said, 'He cultivates himself so as to give rest to all the people. He cultivates himself so as to give rest to all the people:—even Yao and Shun were still solicitous about this.'

CHAP. XLVI. Yuan Zang was squatting on his heels, and so waited the approach of the Master, who said to him, 'In youth not humble as befits a junior; in manhood, doing nothing worthy of being handed down; and living on to old age:—this is to be a pest.' With this he hit him on the shank with his staff.

CHAP. XLVI. 1. A youth of the village of Ch'ueh was employed by Confucius to carry the messages between him and his visitors. Some one asked about him, saying, 'I suppose he has made great progress.'

2. The Master said, 'I observe that he is fond of occupying the seat of a full-grown man; I observe that he walks shoulder to shoulder with his elders. He is not one who is seeking to make progress in learning. He wishes quickly to become a man.'

BOOK XV. WEI LING KUNG

CHAP. I. 1. The Duke Ling of Wei asked Confucius about tactics. Confucius replied, 'I have heard all about sacrificial vessels, but I have not learned military matters.' On this, he took his departure the next day.

2. When he was in Chan, their provisions were exhausted, and his followers became so ill that they were unable to rise.

3. Tsze-lu, with evident dissatisfaction, said, 'Has the superior man likewise to endure in this way?' The Master said, 'The superior man may indeed have to endure want, but the mean man, when he is in want, gives way to unbridled license.'

CHAP. II. 1. The Master said, 'Ts'ze, you think, I suppose, that I am one who learns many things and keeps them in memory?'

2. Tsze-kung replied, 'Yes,—but perhaps it is not so?'

3. 'No,' was the answer; 'I seek a unity all-pervading.'

CHAP. III. The Master said, 'Yu, those who know virtue are few.'

CHAP. IV. The Master said, 'May not Shun be instanced as having governed efficiently without exertion? What did he do? He did nothing but gravely and reverently occupy his royal seat.'

CHAP. V. 1. Tsze-chang asked how a man should conduct himself, so as to be everywhere appreciated.

2. The Master said, 'Let his words be sincere and truthful, and his actions honourable and careful;—such conduct may be practised among the rude tribes of the South or the North. If his words be not sincere and truthful and his actions not honourable and careful, will he, with such conduct, be appreciated, even in his neighbourhood?

3. 'When he is standing, let him see those two things, as it were, fronting him. When he is in a carriage, let him see them attached to the yoke. Then may he subsequently carry them into practice.'

4. Tsze-chang wrote these counsels on the end of his sash.

CHAP. VI. 1. The Master said, 'Truly straightforward was

the historiographer Yu. When good government prevailed in his State, he was like an arrow. When bad government prevailed, he was like an arrow.

2. A superior man indeed is Chu Po-yu! When good government prevails in his state, he is to be found in office. When bad government prevails, he can roll his principles up, and keep them in his breast.'

CHAP. VII. The Master said, 'When a man may be spoken with, not to speak to him is to err in reference to the man. When a man may not be spoken with, to speak to him is to err in reference to our words. The wise err neither in regard to their man nor to their words.'

CHAP. VIII. The Master said, 'The determined scholar and the man of virtue will not seek to live at the expense of injuring their virtue. They will even sacrifice their lives to preserve their virtue complete.'

CHAP. IX. Tsze-kung asked about the practice of virtue. The Master said, 'The mechanic, who wishes to do his work well, must first sharpen his tools. When you are living in any state, take service with the most worthy among its great officers, and make friends of the most virtuous among its scholars.'

CHAP. X. 1. Yen Yuan asked how the government of a country should be administered.

2. The Master said, 'Follow the seasons of Hsia.

3. 'Ride in the state carriage of Yin.

4. 'Wear the ceremonial cap of Chau.

5. 'Let the music be the Shao with its pantomimes.

6. Banish the songs of Chang, and keep far from specious talkers. The songs of Chang are licentious; specious talkers are dangerous.'

CHAP. XI. The Master said, 'If a man take no thought about what is distant, he will find sorrow near at hand.'

CHAP. XII. The Master said, 'It is all over! I have not seen one who loves virtue as he loves beauty.'

CHAP. XIII. The Master said, 'Was not Tsang Wan like one who had stolen his situation? He knew the virtue and the talents of Hui of Liu-hsia, and yet did not procure that he should stand with him in court.'

CHAP. XIV. The Master said, 'He who requires much from himself and little from others, will keep himself from being the object of resentment.'

CHAP. XV. The Master said, 'When a man is not in the habit of saying—"What shall I think of this? What shall I think of this?" I can indeed do nothing with him!'

CHAP. XVI. The Master said, 'When a number of people are together, for a whole day, without their conversation turning on righteousness, and when they are fond of carrying out the suggestions of a small shrewdness;—theirs is indeed a hard case.'

CHAP. XVII. The Master said, 'The superior man in everything considers righteousness to be essential. He performs it according to the rules of propriety. He brings it forth in humility. He completes it with sincerity. This is indeed a superior man.'

CHAP. XVIII. The Master said, 'The superior man is distressed by his want of ability. He is not distressed by men's not knowing him.'

CHAP. XIX. The Master said, 'The superior man dislikes the thought of his name not being mentioned after his death.'

CHAP. XX. The Master said, 'What the superior man seeks, is in himself. What the mean man seeks, is in others.'

CHAP. XXI. The Master said, 'The superior man is dignified, but does not wrangle. He is sociable, but not a partizan.'

CHAP. XXII. The Master said, 'The superior man does not promote a man simply on account of his words, nor does he put aside good words because of the man.'

CHAP. XXIII. Tsze-kung asked, saying, 'Is there one word which may serve as a rule of practice for all one's life?' The Master said, 'Is not RECIPROCITY such a word? What you do not want done to yourself, do not do to others.'

CHAP. XXIV. 1. The Master said, 'In my dealings with men, whose evil do I blame, whose goodness do I praise, beyond what is proper? If I do sometimes exceed in praise, there must be ground for it in my examination of the individual.

2. 'This people supplied the ground why the three dynasties pursued the path of straightforwardness.'

CHAP. XXV. The Master said, 'Even in my early days, a historiographer would leave a blank in his text, and he who had a horse would lend him to another to ride. Now, alas! there are no such things.'

CHAP. XXVI. The Master said, 'Specious words confound virtue. Want of forbearance in small matters confounds great plans.'

CHAP. XXVII. The Master said, 'When the multitude hate a man, it is necessary to examine into the case. When the multitude like a man, it is necessary to examine into the case.'

CHAP. XXVIII. The Master said, 'A man can enlarge the principles which he follows; those principles do not enlarge the man.'

CHAP. XXIX. The Master said, 'To have faults and not to reform them,—this, indeed, should be pronounced having faults.'

CHAP. XXX. The Master said, 'I have been the whole day without eating, and the whole night without sleeping:— occupied with thinking. It was of no use. The better plan is to learn.'

CHAP. XXXI. The Master said, 'The object of the superior man is truth. Food is not his object. There is plowing;—even in that there is sometimes want. So with learning;— emolument may be found in it. The superior man is anxious lest he should not get truth; he is not anxious lest poverty should come upon him.'

CHAP. XXXII. 1. The Master said, 'When a man's knowledge is sufficient to attain, and his virtue is not sufficient to enable him to hold, whatever he may have gained, he will lose again.

2. 'When his knowledge is sufficient to attain, and he has virtue enough to hold fast, if he cannot govern with dignity, the people will not respect him.

3. 'When his knowledge is sufficient to attain, and he has virtue enough to hold fast; when he governs also with dignity, yet if he try to move the people contrary to the rules of

propriety:—full excellence is not reached.'

CHAP. XXXIII. The Master said, 'The superior man cannot be known in little matters; but he may be intrusted with great concerns. The small man may not be intrusted with great concerns, but he may be known in little matters.'

CHAP. XXXIV. The Master said, 'Virtue is more to man than either water or fire. I have seen men die from treading on water and fire, but I have never seen a man die from treading the course of virtue.'

CHAP. XXXV. The Master said, 'Let every man consider virtue as what devolves on himself. He may not yield the performance of it even to his teacher.'

CHAP. XXXVI. The Master said, 'The superior man is correctly firm, and not firm merely.'

CHAP. XXXVII. The Master said, 'A minister, in serving his prince, reverently discharges his duties, and makes his emolument a secondary consideration.'

CHAP. XXXVIII. The Master said, 'In teaching there should be no distinction of classes.'

CHAP. XXXIX. The Master said, 'Those whose courses are different cannot lay plans for one another.' CHAP. XL. The Master said, 'In language it is simply required that it convey the meaning.'

CHAP. XLI. 1. The Music-master, Mien, having called upon him, when they came to the steps, the Master said, 'Here are the steps.' When they came to the mat for the guest to sit upon, he said, 'Here is the mat.' When all were seated, the Master informed him, saying, 'So and so is here; so and so is here.'

2. The Music-master, Mien, having gone out, Tsze-chang asked, saying. 'Is it the rule to tell those things to the Music-master?'

3. The Master said, 'Yes. This is certainly the rule for those who lead the blind.'

BOOK XVI. KE SHE

CHAP. I. 1. The head of the Chi family was going to attack Chwan-yu.

2. Zan Yu and Chi-lu had an interview with Confucius, and said, 'Our chief, Chi, is going to commence operations against Chwan-yu.'

3. Confucius said, 'Ch'iu, is it not you who are in fault here?

4. 'Now, in regard to Chwan-yu, long ago, a former king appointed its ruler to preside over the sacrifices to the eastern Mang; moreover, it is in the midst of the territory of our State; and its ruler is a minister in direct connexion with the sovereign:—What has your chief to do with attacking it?'

5. Zan Yu said, 'Our master wishes the thing; neither of us two ministers wishes it.'

6. Confucius said, 'Ch'iu, there are the words of Chau Zan,—"When he can put forth his ability, he takes his place in the ranks of office; when he finds himself unable to do so, he retires from it. How can he be used as a guide to a blind man, who does not support him when tottering, nor raise him up when fallen?"

7. 'And further, you speak wrongly. When a tiger or rhinoceros escapes from his cage; when a tortoise or piece of jade is injured in its repository:—whose is the fault?'

8. Zan Yu said, 'But at present, Chwan-yu is strong and near to Pi; if our chief do not now take it, it will hereafter be a sorrow to his descendants.'

9. Confucius said. 'Ch'iu, the superior man hates that declining to say—"I want such and such a thing," and framing explanations for the conduct.

10. 'I have heard that rulers of States and chiefs of families are not troubled lest their people should be few, but are troubled lest they should not keep their several places; that they are not troubled with fears of poverty, but are troubled with fears of a want of contented repose among the people in their several places. For when the people keep their several places, there will be no poverty; when harmony prevails, there

will be no scarcity of people; and when there is such a contented repose, there will be no rebellious upsettings.

11. 'So it is.—Therefore, if remoter people are not submissive, all the influences of civil culture and virtue are to be cultivated to attract them to be so; and when they have been so attracted, they must be made contented and tranquil.

12. 'Now, here are you, Yu and Ch'iu, assisting your chief. Remoter people are not submissive, and, with your help, he cannot attract them to him. In his own territory there are divisions and downfalls, leavings and separations, and, with your help, he cannot preserve it.

13. 'And yet he is planning these hostile movements within the State.—I am afraid that the sorrow of the Chi-sun family will not be on account of Chwan-yu, but will be found within the screen of their own court.'

CHAP. II. 1. Confucius said, 'When good government prevails in the empire, ceremonies, music, and punitive military expeditions proceed from the son of Heaven. When bad government prevails in the empire, ceremonies, music, and punitive military expeditions proceed from the princes. When these things proceed from the princes, as a rule, the cases will be few in which they do not lose their power in ten generations. When they proceed from the Great officers of the princes, as a rule, the cases will be few in which they do not lose their power in five generations. When the subsidiary ministers of the great officers hold in their grasp the orders of the state, as a rule, the cases will be few in which they do not lose their power in three generations.

2. 'When right principles prevail in the kingdom, government will not be in the hands of the Great officers.

3. 'When right principles prevail in the kingdom, there will be no discussions among the common people.'

CHAP. III. Confucius said, 'The revenue of the state has left the ducal House now for five generations. The government has been in the hands of the Great officers for four generations. On this account, the descendants of the three Hwan are much reduced.'

CHAP. IV. Confucius said, 'There are three friendships

which are advantageous, and three which are injurious. Friendship with the upright; friendship with the sincere; and friendship with the man of much observation:—these are advantageous. Friendship with the man of specious airs; friendship with the insinuatingly soft; and friendship with the glib-tongued:—these are injurious.'

CHAP. V. Confucius said, 'There are three things men find enjoyment in which are advantageous, and three things they find enjoyment in which are injurious. To find enjoyment in the discriminating study of ceremonies and music; to find enjoyment in speaking of the goodness of others; to find enjoyment in having many worthy friends:—these are advantageous. To find enjoyment in extravagant pleasures; to find enjoyment in idleness and sauntering; to find enjoyment in the pleasures of feasting:—these are injurious.'

CHAP. VI. Confucius said, 'There are three errors to which they who stand in the presence of a man of virtue and station are liable. They may speak when it does not come to them to speak;—this is called rashness. They may not speak when it comes to them to speak;—this is called concealment. They may speak without looking at the countenance of their superior;—this is called blindness.'

CHAP. VII. Confucius said, 'There are three things which the superior man guards against. In youth, when the physical powers are not yet settled, he guards against lust. When he is strong and the physical powers are full of vigor, he guards against quarrelsomeness. When he is old, and the animal powers are decayed, he guards against covetousness.'

CHAP. VIII. 1. Confucius said, 'There are three things of which the superior man stands in awe. He stands in awe of the ordinances of Heaven. He stands in awe of great men. He stands in awe of the words of sages.

2. 'The mean man does not know the ordinances of Heaven, and consequently does not stand in awe of them. He is disrespectful to great men. He makes sport of the words of sages.'

CHAP. IX. Confucius said, 'Those who are born with the possession of knowledge are the highest class of men. Those who learn, and so, readily, get possession of knowledge, are the next. Those who are dull and stupid, and yet compass the learning, are another class next to these. As to those who are dull and stupid and yet do not learn;—they are the lowest of the people.'

CHAP. X. Confucius said, 'The superior man has nine things which are subjects with him of thoughtful consideration. In regard to the use of his eyes, he is anxious to see clearly. In regard to the use of his ears, he is anxious to hear distinctly. In regard to his countenance, he is anxious that it should be benign. In regard to his demeanor, he is anxious that it should be respectful. In regard to his speech, he is anxious that it should be sincere. In regard to his doing of business, he is anxious that it should be reverently careful. In regard to what he doubts about, he is anxious to question others. When he is angry, he thinks of the difficulties (his anger may involve him in). When he sees gain to be got, he thinks of righteousness.'

CHAP. XI. 1. Confucius said, 'Contemplating good, and pursuing it, as if they could not reach it; contemplating evil, and shrinking from it, as they would from thrusting the hand into boiling water:—I have seen such men, as I have heard such words.

2. 'Living in retirement to study their aims, and practising righteousness to carry out their principles:—I have heard these words, but I have not seen such men.'

CHAP. XII. 1. The duke Ching of Ch'i had a thousand teams, each of four horses, but on the day of his death, the people did not praise him for a single virtue. Po-i and Shu-ch'i died of hunger at the foot of the Shau-yang mountain, and the people, down to the present time, praise them.

2. 'Is not that saying illustrated by this?'

CHAP. XIII. 1. Ch'an K'ang asked Po-yu, saying, 'Have you heard any lessons from your father different from what we have all heard?'

2. Po-yu replied, 'No. He was standing alone once, when I passed below the hall with hasty steps, and said to me, "Have you learned the Odes?" On my replying "Not yet," he added, "If you do not learn the Odes, you will not be fit to converse

with." I retired and studied the Odes.

3. 'Another day, he was in the same way standing alone, when I passed by below the hall with hasty steps, and said to me, 'Have you learned the rules of Propriety?' On my replying 'Not yet,' he added, 'If you do not learn the rules of Propriety, your character cannot be established.' I then retired, and learned the rules of Propriety.

4. 'I have heard only these two things from him.'

5. Ch'ang K'ang retired, and, quite delighted, said, 'I asked one thing, and I have got three things. I have heard about the Odes. I have heard about the rules of Propriety. I have also heard that the superior man maintains a distant reserve towards his son.'

CHAP. XIV. The wife of the prince of a state is called by him FU-ZAN. She calls herself HSIAO T'UNG. The people of the State call her CHUN FU-ZAN, and, to the people of other States, they call her K'WA HSIAO CHUN. The people of other states also call her CHUN FU-ZAN.

BOOK XVII. YANG HO

CHAP. I. 1. Yang Ho wished to see Confucius, but Confucius would not go to see him. On this, he sent a present of a pig to Confucius, who, having chosen a time when Ho was not at home, went to pay his respects for the gift. He met him, however, on the way.

2. Ho said to Confucius, 'Come, let me speak with you.' He then asked, 'Can he be called benevolent who keeps his jewel in his bosom, and leaves his country to confusion?' Confucius replied, 'No.' 'Can he be called wise, who is anxious to be engaged in public employment, and yet is constantly losing the opportunity of being so?' Confucius again said, 'No.' 'The days and months are passing away; the years do not wait for us.' Confucius said, 'Right; I will go into office.'

CHAP. II. The Master said, 'By nature, men are nearly alike; by practice, they get to be wide apart.'

CHAP. III. The Master said, 'There are only the wise of the highest class, and the stupid of the lowest class, who cannot be changed.'

CHAP. IV. 1. The Master, having come to Wu-ch'ang, heard there the sound of stringed instruments and singing.

2. Well pleased and smiling, he said, 'Why use an ox knife to kill a fowl?'

3. Tsze-yu replied, 'Formerly, Master, I heard you say,—"When the man of high station is well instructed, he loves men; when the man of low station is well instructed, he is easily ruled."'

4. The Master said, 'My disciples, Yen's words are right. What I said was only in sport.'

CHAP. V. 1. Kung-shan Fu-zao, when he was holding Pi, and in an attitude of rebellion, invited the Master to visit him, who was rather inclined to go.

2. Tsze-lu was displeased, and said, 'Indeed, you cannot go! Why must you think of going to see Kung-shan?'

3. The Master said, 'Can it be without some reason that he has invited ME? If any one employ me, may I not make an

eastern Chau?'

CHAP. VI. Tsze-chang asked Confucius about perfect virtue. Confucius said, 'To be able to practise five things everywhere under heaven constitutes perfect virtue.' He begged to ask what they were, and was told, 'Gravity, generosity of soul, sincerity, earnestness, and kindness. If you are grave, you will not be treated with disrespect. If you are generous, you will win all. If you are sincere, people will repose trust in you. If you are earnest, you will accomplish much. If you are kind, this will enable you to employ the services of others.

CHAP. VII. 1. Pi Hsi inviting him to visit him, the Master was inclined to go.

2. Tsze-lu said, 'Master, formerly I have heard you say, "When a man in his own person is guilty of doing evil, a superior man will not associate with him." Pi Hsi is in rebellion, holding possession of Chung-mau; if you go to him, what shall be said?'

3. The Master said, 'Yes, I did use these words. But is it not said, that, if a thing be really hard, it may be ground without being made thin? Is it not said, that, if a thing be really white, it may be steeped in a dark fluid without being made black?

4. 'Am I a bitter gourd! How can I be hung up out of the way of being eaten?'

CHAP. VIII. 1. The Master said, 'Yu, have you heard the six words to which are attached six becloudings?' Yu replied, 'I have not.'

2. 'Sit down, and I will tell them to you.

3. 'There is the love of being benevolent without the love of learning;—the beclouding here leads to a foolish simplicity. There is the love of knowing without the love of learning;— the beclouding here leads to dissipation of mind. There is the love of being sincere without the love of learning;—the beclouding here leads to an injurious disregard of consequences. There is the love of straightforwardness without the love of learning;—the beclouding here leads to rudeness. There is the love of boldness without the love of learning;—the beclouding here leads to insubordination.

There is the love of firmness without the love of learning;—the beclouding here leads to extravagant conduct.'

CHAP. IX. 1. The Master said, 'My children, why do you not study the Book of Poetry?

2. 'The Odes serve to stimulate the mind.

3. 'They may be used for purposes of self-contemplation.

4. 'They teach the art of sociability.

5. 'They show how to regulate feelings of resentment.

6. 'From them you learn the more immediate duty of serving
one's father, and the remoter one of serving one's prince.

7. 'From them we become largely acquainted with the names of birds, beasts, and plants.'

CHAP. X. The Master said to Po-yu, 'Do you give yourself to the Chau-nan and the Shao-nan. The man who has not studied the Chau-nan and the Shao-nan, is like one who stands with his face right against a wall. Is he not so?'

CHAP. XI. The Master said, '"It is according to the rules of propriety," they say.—"It is according to the rules of propriety," they say. Are gems and silk all that is meant by propriety? "It is music," they say.—"It is music," they say. Are bells and drums all that is meant by music?'

CHAP. XII. The Master said, 'He who puts on an appearance of stern firmness, while inwardly he is weak, is like one of the small, mean people;—yea, is he not like the thief who breaks through, or climbs over, a wall?'

CHAP. XIII. The Master said, 'Your good, careful people of the villages are the thieves of virtue.'

CHAP. XIV. The Master said, 'To tell, as we go along, what we have heard on the way, is to cast away our virtue.'

CHAP. XV. 1. The Master said, 'There are those mean creatures! How impossible it is along with them to serve one's prince!

2. 'While they have not got their aims, their anxiety is how to get them. When they have got them, their anxiety is lest they should lose them.

3. 'When they are anxious lest such things should be lost, there is nothing to which they will not proceed.'

CHAP. XVI. 1. The Master said, 'Anciently, men had three failings, which now perhaps are not to be found.

2. 'The high-mindedness of antiquity showed itself in a disregard of small things; the high-mindedness of the present day shows itself in wild license. The stern dignity of antiquity showed itself in grave reserve; the stern dignity of the present day shows itself in quarrelsome perverseness. The stupidity of antiquity showed itself in straightforwardness; the stupidity of the present day shows itself in sheer deceit.'

CHAP. XVII. The Master said, 'Fine words and an insinuating appearance are seldom associated with virtue.'

CHAP. XVIII. The Master said, 'I hate the manner in which purple takes away the luster of vermilion. I hate the way in which the songs of Chang confound the music of the Ya. I hate those who with their sharp mouths overthrow kingdoms and families.'

CHAP. XIX. 1. The Master said, 'I would prefer not speaking.'

2. Tsze-kung said, 'If you, Master, do not speak, what shall we, your disciples, have to record?'

3. The Master said, 'Does Heaven speak? The four seasons pursue their courses, and all things are continually being produced, but does Heaven say anything?'

CHAP. XX. Zu Pei wished to see Confucius, but Confucius declined, on the ground of being sick, to see him. When the bearer of this message went out at the door, (the Master) took his lute and sang to it, in order that Pei might hear him.

CHAP. XXI. 1. Tsai Wo asked about the three years' mourning for parents, saying that one year was long enough.

2. 'If the superior man,' said he, 'abstains for three years from the observances of propriety, those observances will be quite lost. If for three years he abstains from music, music will be ruined.

3. 'Within a year the old grain is exhausted, and the new grain has sprung up, and, in procuring fire by friction, we go through all the changes of wood for that purpose. After a complete year, the mourning may stop.'

4. The Master said, 'If you were, after a year, to eat good

rice, and wear embroidered clothes, would you feel at ease?' 'I should,' replied Wo.

5. The Master said, 'If you can feel at ease, do it. But a superior man, during the whole period of mourning, does not enjoy pleasant food which he may eat, nor derive pleasure from music which he may hear. He also does not feel at ease, if he is comfortably lodged. Therefore he does not do what you propose. But now you feel at ease and may do it.'

6. Tsai Wo then went out, and the Master said, 'This shows Yu's want of virtue. It is not till a child is three years old that it is allowed to leave the arms of its parents. And the three years' mourning is universally observed throughout the empire. Did Yu enjoy the three years' love of his parents?'

CHAP. XXII. The Master said, 'Hard is it to deal with him, who will stuff himself with food the whole day, without applying his mind to anything good! Are there not gamesters and chess players? To be one of these would still be better than doing nothing at all.'

CHAP. XXIII. Tsze-lu said, 'Does the superior man esteem valour?' The Master said, 'The superior man holds righteousness to be of highest importance. A man in a superior situation, having valour without righteousness, will be guilty of insubordination; one of the lower people having valour without righteousness, will commit robbery.'

CHAP. XXIV. 1. Tsze-kung said, 'Has the superior man his hatreds also?' The Master said, 'He has his hatreds. He hates those who proclaim the evil of others. He hates the man who, being in a low station, slanders his superiors. He hates those who have valour merely, and are unobservant of propriety. He hates those who are forward and determined, and, at the same time, of contracted understanding.'

2. The Master then inquired, 'Ts'ze, have you also your hatreds?' Tsze-kung replied, 'I hate those who pry out matters, and ascribe the knowledge to their wisdom. I hate those who are only not modest, and think that they are valourous. I hate those who make known secrets, and think that they are straightforward.'

CHAP. XXV. The Master said, 'Of all people, girls and

116

servants are the most difficult to behave to. If you are familiar with them, they lose their humility. If you maintain a reserve towards them, they are discontented.'

CHAP. XXVI. The Master said, 'When a man at forty is the object of dislike, he will always continue what he is.'

BOOK XVIII. WEI TSZE

CHAP. I. 1. The Viscount of Wei withdrew from the court. The Viscount of Chi became a slave to Chau. Pi-kan remonstrated with him and died. 2. Confucius said, 'The Yin dynasty possessed these three men of virtue.'

CHAP. II. Hui of Liu-hsia being chief criminal judge, was thrice dismissed from his office. Some one said to him, 'Is it not yet time for you, sir, to leave this?' He replied, 'Serving men in an upright way, where shall I go to, and not experience such a thrice-repeated dismissal? If I choose to serve men in a crooked way, what necessity is there for me to leave the country of my parents?'

CHAP. III. The duke Ching of Ch'i, with reference to the manner in which he should treat Confucius, said, 'I cannot treat him as I would the chief of the Chi family. I will treat him in a manner between that accorded to the chief of the Chi, and that given to the chief of the Mang family.' He also said, 'I am old; I cannot use his doctrines.' Confucius took his departure.

CHAP. IV. The people of Ch'i sent to Lu a present of female musicians, which Chi Hwan received, and for three days no court was held. Confucius took his departure.

CHAP. V. 1. The madman of Ch'u, Chieh-yu, passed by Confucius, singing and saying, 'O FANG! O FANG! How is your virtue degenerated! As to the past, reproof is useless; but the future may still be provided against. Give up your vain pursuit. Give up your vain pursuit. Peril awaits those who now engage in affairs of government.'

2. Confucius alighted and wished to converse with him, but Chieh-yu hastened away, so that he could not talk with him.

CHAP. VI. 1. Ch'ang-tsu and Chieh-ni were at work in the field together, when Confucius passed by them, and sent Tsze-lu to inquire for the ford.

2. Ch'ang-tsu said, 'Who is he that holds the reins in the carriage there?' Tsze-lu told him, 'It is K'ung Ch'iu.' 'Is it not K'ung Ch'iu of Lu?' asked he. 'Yes,' was the reply, to which

the other rejoined, 'He knows the ford.'

3. Tsze-lu then inquired of Chieh-ni, who said to him, 'Who are you, sir?' He answered, 'I am Chung Yu.' 'Are you not the disciple of K'ung Ch'iu of Lu?' asked the other. 'I am,' replied he, and then Chieh-ni said to him, 'Disorder, like a swelling flood, spreads over the whole empire, and who is he that will change its state for you? Than follow one who merely withdraws from this one and that one, had you not better follow those who have withdrawn from the world altogether?' With this he fell to covering up the seed, and proceeded with his work, without stopping.

4. Tsze-lu went and reported their remarks, when the Master observed with a sigh, 'It is impossible to associate with birds and beasts, as if they were the same with us. If I associate not with these people,—with mankind,—with whom shall I associate? If right principles prevailed through the empire, there would be no use for me to change its state.'

CHAP. VII. 1. Tsze-lu, following the Master, happened to fall behind, when he met an old man, carrying across his shoulder on a staff a basket for weeds. Tsze-lu said to him, 'Have you seen my master, sir!' The old man replied, 'Your four limbs are unaccustomed to toil; you cannot distinguish the five kinds of grain:—who is your master?' With this, he planted his staff in the ground, and proceeded to weed.

2. Tsze-lu joined his hands across his breast, and stood before him.

3. The old man kept Tsze-lu to pass the night in his house, killed a fowl, prepared millet, and feasted him. He also introduced to him his two sons.

4. Next day, Tsze-lu went on his way, and reported his adventure. The Master said, 'He is a recluse,' and sent Tsze-lu back to see him again, but when he got to the place, the old man was gone.

5. Tsze-lu then said to the family, 'Not to take office is not righteous. If the relations between old and young may not be neglected, how is it that he sets aside the duties that should be observed between sovereign and minister? Wishing to maintain his personal purity, he allows that great relation to

119

come to confusion. A superior man takes office, and performs the righteous duties belonging to it. As to the failure of right principles to make progress, he is aware of that.'

CHAP. VIII. 1. The men who have retired to privacy from the world have been Po-i, Shu-ch'i, Yu-chung, I-yi, Chu-chang, Hui of Liu-hsia, and Shao-lien.

2. The Master said, 'Refusing to surrender their wills, or to submit to any taint in their persons;—such, I think, were Po-i and Shu-ch'i.

3. 'It may be said of Hui of Liu-hsia, and of Shao-lien, that they surrendered their wills, and submitted to taint in their persons, but their words corresponded with reason, and their actions were such as men are anxious to see. This is all that is to be remarked in them.

4. 'It may be said of Yu-chung and I-yi, that, while they hid themselves in their seclusion, they gave a license to their words; but, in their persons, they succeeded in preserving their purity, and, in their retirement, they acted according to the exigency of the times.

5. 'I am different from all these. I have no course for which I am predetermined, and no course against which I am predetermined.'

CHAP. IX. 1. The grand music master, Chih, went to Ch'i.

2. Kan, the master of the band at the second meal, went to Ch'u. Liao, the band master at the third meal, went to Ts'ai. Chueh, the band master at the fourth meal, went to Ch'in.

3. Fang-shu, the drum master, withdrew to the north of the river.

4. Wu, the master of the hand drum, withdrew to the Han.

5. Yang, the assistant music master, and Hsiang, master of the musical stone, withdrew to an island in the sea.

CHAP. X. The duke of Chau addressed his son, the duke of Lu, saying, 'The virtuous prince does not neglect his relations. He does not cause the great ministers to repine at his not employing them. Without some great cause, he does not dismiss from their offices the members of old families. He does not seek in one man talents for every employment.'

CHAP. XI. To Chau belonged the eight officers, Po-ta, Po-kwo, Chung-tu, Chung-hwu, Shu-ya, Shu-hsia, Chi-sui, and Chi-kwa.

BOOK XIX. TSZE-CHANG

CHAP. I. Tsze-chang said, 'The scholar, trained for public duty, seeing threatening danger, is prepared to sacrifice his life. When the opportunity of gain is presented to him, he thinks of righteousness. In sacrificing, his thoughts are reverential. In mourning, his thoughts are about the grief which he should feel. Such a man commands our approbation indeed.'

CHAP. II. Tsze-chang said, 'When a man holds fast to virtue, but without seeking to enlarge it, and believes right principles, but without firm sincerity, what account can be made of his existence or non-existence?'

CHAP. III. The disciples of Tsze-hsia asked Tsze-chang about the principles that should characterize mutual intercourse. Tsze-chang asked, 'What does Tsze-hsia say on the subject?' They replied, 'Tsze-hsia says:—"Associate with those who can advantage you. Put away from you those who cannot do so."' Tsze-chang observed, 'This is different from what I have learned. The superior man honours the talented and virtuous, and bears with all. He praises the good, and pities the incompetent. Am I possessed of great talents and virtue?— who is there among men whom I will not bear with? Am I devoid of talents and virtue?—men will put me away from them. What have we to do with the putting away of others?'

CHAP. IV. Tsze-hsia said, 'Even in inferior studies and employments there is something worth being looked at; but if it be attempted to carry them out to what is remote, there is a danger of their proving inapplicable. Therefore, the superior man does not practise them.'

CHAP. V. Tsze-hsia said, 'He, who from day to day recognises what he has not yet, and from month to month does not forget what he has attained to, may be said indeed to love to learn.'

CHAP. VI. Tsze-hsia said, 'There are learning extensively, and having a firm and sincere aim; inquiring with earnestness, and reflecting with self-application:—virtue is in such a course.'

CHAP. VII. Tsze-hsia said, 'Mechanics have their shops to dwell in, in order to accomplish their works. The superior man learns, in order to reach to the utmost of his principles.'

CHAP. VIII. Tsze-hsia said, 'The mean man is sure to gloss his faults.'

CHAP. IX. Tsze-hsia said, 'The superior man undergoes three changes. Looked at from a distance, he appears stern; when approached, he is mild; when he is heard to speak, his language is firm and decided.'

CHAP. X. Tsze-hsia said, 'The superior man, having obtained their confidence, may then impose labours on his people. If he have not gained their confidence, they will think that he is oppressing them. Having obtained the confidence of his prince, one may then remonstrate with him. If he have not gained his confidence, the prince will think that he is vilifying him.'

CHAP. XI. Tsze-hsia said, 'When a person does not transgress the boundary line in the great virtues, he may pass and repass it in the small virtues.'

CHAP. XII. 1. Tsze-yu said, 'The disciples and followers of Tsze-hsia, in sprinkling and sweeping the ground, in answering and replying, in advancing and receding, are sufficiently accomplished. But these are only the branches of learning, and they are left ignorant of what is essential.—How can they be acknowledged as sufficiently taught?'

2. Tsze-hsia heard of the remark and said, 'Alas! Yen Yu is wrong. According to the way of the superior man in teaching, what departments are there which he considers of prime importance, and delivers? what are there which he considers of secondary importance, and allows himself to be idle about? But as in the case of plants, which are assorted according to their classes, so he deals with his disciples. How can the way of a superior man be such as to make fools of any of them? Is it not the sage alone, who can unite in one the beginning and the consummation of learning?'

CHAP. XIII. Tsze-hsia said, 'The officer, having discharged all his duties, should devote his leisure to learning. The student, having completed his learning, should apply himself to be an officer.'

CHAP. XIV. Tsze-hsia said, 'Mourning, having been carried to the utmost degree of grief, should stop with that.'

CHAP. XV. Tsze-hsia said, 'My friend Chang can do things which are hard to be done, but yet he is not perfectly virtuous.'

CHAP. XVI. The philosopher Tsang said, 'How imposing is the manner of Chang! It is difficult along with him to practise virtue.'

CHAP. XVII. The philosopher Tsang said, 'I heard this from our Master:—"Men may not have shown what is in them to the full extent, and yet they will be found to do so, on occasion of mourning for their parents."'

CHAP. XVIII. The philosopher Tsang said, 'I have heard this from our Master:—"The filial piety of Mang Chwang, in other matters, was what other men are competent to, but, as seen in his not changing the ministers of his father, nor his father's mode of government, it is difficult to be attained to."'

CHAP. XIX. The chief of the Mang family having appointed Yang Fu to be chief criminal judge, the latter consulted the philosopher Tsang. Tsang said, 'The rulers have failed in their duties, and the people consequently have been disorganised, for a long time. When you have found out the truth of any accusation, be grieved for and pity them, and do not feel joy at your own ability.'

CHAP. XX. Tsze-kung said, 'Chau's wickedness was not so great as that name implies. Therefore, the superior man hates to dwell in a low-lying situation, where all the evil of the world will flow in upon him.'

CHAP. XXI. Tsze-kung said, 'The faults of the superior man are like the eclipses of the sun and moon. He has his faults, and all men see them; he changes again, and all men look up to him.'

CHAP. XXII. 1. Kung-sun Ch'ao of Wei asked Tsze-kung, saying, 'From whom did Chung-ni get his learning?'

2. Tsze-kung replied, 'The doctrines of Wan and Wu have not yet fallen to the ground. They are to be found among men. Men of talents and virtue remember the greater principles of them, and others, not possessing such talents and virtue,

remember the smaller. Thus, all possess the doctrines of Wan and Wu. Where could our Master go that he should not have an opportunity of learning them? And yet what necessity was there for his having a regular master?'

CHAP. XXIII. 1. Shu-sun Wu-shu observed to the great officers in the court, saying, 'Tsze-kung is superior to Chung-ni.'

2. Tsze-fu Ching-po reported the observation to Tsze-kung, who said, 'Let me use the comparison of a house and its encompassing wall. My wall only reaches to the shoulders. One may peep over it, and see whatever is valuable in the apartments.

3. 'The wall of my Master is several fathoms high. If one do not find the door and enter by it, he cannot see the ancestral temple with its beauties, nor all the officers in their rich array.

4. 'But I may assume that they are few who find the door. Was not the observation of the chief only what might have been expected?'

CHAP. XXIV. Shu-sun Wu-shu having spoken revilingly of Chung-ni, Tsze-kung said, 'It is of no use doing so. Chung-ni cannot be reviled. The talents and virtue of other men are hillocks and mounds which may be stepped over. Chung-ni is the sun or moon, which it is not possible to step over. Although a man may wish to cut himself off from the sage, what harm can he do to the sun or moon? He only shows that he does not know his own capacity.

CHAP. XXV. 1. Ch'an Tsze-ch'in, addressing Tsze-kung, said, 'You are too modest. How can Chung-ni be said to be superior to you?'

2. Tsze-kung said to him, 'For one word a man is often deemed to be wise, and for one word he is often deemed to be foolish. We ought to be careful indeed in what we say.

3. 'Our Master cannot be attained to, just in the same way as the heavens cannot be gone up to by the steps of a stair.

4. 'Were our Master in the position of the ruler of a State or the chief of a Family, we should find verified the description which has been given of a sage's rule:—he would plant the people, and forthwith they would be established; he would lead

them on, and forthwith they would follow him; he would make them happy, and forthwith multitudes would resort to his dominions; he would stimulate them, and forthwith they would be harmonious. While he lived, he would be glorious. When he died, he would be bitterly lamented. How is it possible for him to be attained to?'

BOOK XX. YAO YUEH

CHAP. I. 1. Yao said, 'Oh! you, Shun, the Heaven-determined order of succession now rests in your person. Sincerely hold fast the due Mean. If there shall be distress and want within the four seas, the Heavenly revenue will come to a perpetual end.'

2. Shun also used the same language in giving charge to Yu.

3. T'ang said, 'I the child Li, presume to use a dark-coloured victim, and presume to announce to Thee, O most great and sovereign God, that the sinner I dare not pardon, and thy ministers, O God, I do not keep in obscurity. The examination of them is by thy mind, O God. If, in my person, I commit offences, they are not to be attributed to you, the people of the myriad regions. If you in the myriad regions commit offences, these offences must rest on my person.'

4. Chau conferred great gifts, and the good were enriched.

5. 'Although he has his near relatives, they are not equal to my virtuous men. The people are throwing blame upon me, the One man.'

6. He carefully attended to the weights and measures, examined the body of the laws, restored the discarded officers, and the good government of the kingdom took its course.

7. He revived States that had been extinguished, restored families whose line of succession had been broken, and called to office those who had retired into obscurity, so that throughout the kingdom the hearts of the people turned towards him.

8. What he attached chief importance to, were the food of the people, the duties of mourning, and sacrifices.

9. By his generosity, he won all. By his sincerity, he made the people repose trust in him. By his earnest activity, his achievements were great. By his justice, all were delighted.

CHAP. II. 1. Tsze-chang asked Confucius, saying, 'In what way should a person in authority act in order that he may conduct government properly?' The Master replied, 'Let him honour the five excellent, and banish away the four bad, things;—then may he conduct government properly.' Tsze-chang said, 'What are meant by the five excellent things?' The Master said, 'When the person in authority is beneficent without great expenditure; when he lays tasks on the people without their repining; when he pursues what he desires without being covetous; when he maintains a dignified ease without being proud; when he is majestic without being fierce.'

2. Tsze-chang said, 'What is meant by being beneficent without great expenditure?' The Master replied, 'When the person in authority makes more beneficial to the people the things from which they naturally derive benefit;—is not this being beneficent without great expenditure? When he chooses the labours which are proper, and makes them labour on them, who will repine? When his desires are set on benevolent government, and he secures it, who will accuse him of covetousness? Whether he has to do with many people or few, or with things great or small, he does not dare to indicate any disrespect;—is not this to maintain a dignified ease without any pride? He adjusts his clothes and cap, and throws a dignity into his looks, so that, thus dignified, he is looked at with awe;—is not this to be majestic without being fierce?'

3. Tsze-chang then asked, 'What are meant by the four bad things?' The Master said, 'To put the people to death without having instructed them;—this is called cruelty. To require from them, suddenly, the full tale of work, without having given them warning;—this is called oppression. To issue orders as if without urgency, at first, and, when the time comes, to insist on them with severity;—this is called injury. And, generally, in the giving pay or rewards to men, to do it in a stingy way;—this is called acting the part of a mere official.'

CHAP III. 1. The Master said, 'Without recognising the ordinances of Heaven, it is impossible to be a superior man.

2. 'Without an acquaintance with the rules of Propriety, it is impossible for the character to be established.

3. 'Without knowing the force of words, it is impossible to know men.'

THE WORKS OF MENCIUS

THE WORKS OF MENCIUS

BOOK I. KING HUI OF LIANG, PART I

CHAP. I. 1. Mencius went to see king Hui of Liang.

2. The king said, 'Venerable sir, since you have not counted it far to come here, a distance of a thousand li, may I presume that you are provided with counsels to profit my kingdom?'

3. Mencius replied, 'Why must your Majesty use that word "profit?" What I am provided with, are counsels to benevolence and righteousness, and these are my only topics.

4. 'If your Majesty say, "What is to be done to profit my kingdom?" the great officers will say, "What is to be done to profit our families?" and the inferior officers and the common people will say, "What is to be done to profit our persons?" Superiors and inferiors will try to snatch this profit the one from the other, and the kingdom will be endangered. In the kingdom of ten thousand chariots, the murderer of his sovereign shall be the chief of a family of a thousand chariots. In the kingdom of a thousand chariots, the murderer of his prince shall be the chief of a family of a hundred chariots. To have a thousand in ten thousand, and a hundred in a thousand, cannot be said not to be a large allotment, but if righteousness be put last, and profit be put first, they will not be satisfied without snatching all.

5. 'There never has been a benevolent man who neglected his parents. There never has been a righteous man who made his sovereign an after consideration.

6. 'Let your Majesty also say, "Benevolence and righteousness, and let these be your only themes." Why must you use that word—"profit?".

CHAP. II. 1. Mencius, another day, saw King Hui of Liang. The king went and stood with him by a pond, and, looking round at the large geese and deer, said, 'Do wise and good princes also find pleasure in these things?'

2. Mencius replied, 'Being wise and good, they have

pleasure in these things. If they are not wise and good, though they have these things, they do not find pleasure.

3. 'It is said in the Book of Poetry,
"He measured out and commenced his marvellous tower;
He measured it out and planned it.
The people addressed themselves to it,
And in less than a day completed it.
When he measured and began it, he said to them—
Be not so earnest:
But the multitudes came as if they had been his children.
The king was in his marvellous park;
The does reposed about,
The does so sleek and fat:
And the white birds came glistening.
The king was by his marvellous pond;
How full was it of fishes leaping about!"'

'King Wan used the strength of the people to make his tower and his pond, and yet the people rejoiced to do the work, calling the tower "the marvellous tower," calling the pond "the marvellous pond," and rejoicing that he had his large deer, his fishes, and turtles. The ancients caused the people to have pleasure as well as themselves, and therefore they could enjoy it.

4. 'In the Declaration of T'ang it is said, "O sun, when wilt thou expire? We will die together with thee." The people wished for Chieh's death, though they should die with him. Although he had towers, ponds, birds, and animals, how could he have pleasure alone?'

CHAP. III. 1. King Hui of Liang said, 'Small as my virtue is, in the government of my kingdom, I do indeed exert my mind to the utmost. If the year be bad on the inside of the river, I remove as many of the people as I can to the east of the river, and convey grain to the country in the inside. When the year is bad on the east of the river, I act on the same plan. On examining the government of the neighbouring kingdoms, I do not find that there is any prince who exerts his mind as I do. And yet the people of the neighbouring kingdoms do not decrease, nor do my people increase. How is this?'

2. Mencius replied, 'Your majesty is fond of war;—let me take an illustration from war.—The soldiers move forward to the sound of the drums; and after their weapons have been crossed, on one side they throw away their coats of mail, trail their arms behind them, and run. Some run a hundred paces and stop; some run fifty paces and stop. What would you think if those who run fifty paces were to laugh at those who run a hundred paces?' The kind said, 'They should not do so. Though they did not run a hundred paces, yet they also ran away.' 'Since your Majesty knows this,' replied Mencius, 'you need not hope that your people will become more numerous than those of the neighbouring kingdoms.

3. 'If the seasons of husbandry be not interfered with, the grain will be more than can be eaten. If close nets are not allowed to enter the pools and ponds, the fishes and turtles will be more than can be consumed. If the axes and bills enter the hills and forests only at the proper time, the wood will be more than can be used. When the grain and fish and turtles are more than can be eaten, and there is more wood than can be used, this enables the people to nourish their living and mourn for their dead, without any feeling against any. This condition, in which the people nourish their living and bury their dead without any feeling against any, is the first step of royal government.

4. 'Let mulberry trees be planted about the homesteads with their five mau, and persons of fifty years may be clothed with silk. In keeping fowls, pigs, dogs, and swine, let not their times of breeding be neglected, and persons of seventy years may eat flesh. Let there not be taken away the time that is proper for the cultivation of the farm with its hundred ma, and the family of several mouths that is supported by it shall not suffer from hunger. Let careful attention be paid to education in schools, inculcating in it especially the filial and fraternal duties, and grey-haired men will not be seen upon the roads, carrying burdens on their backs or on their heads. It never has been that the ruler of a State, where such results were seen,—persons of seventy wearing silk and eating flesh, and the black-haired people suffering neither from hunger nor cold,—did

not attain to the royal dignity.

5. 'Your dogs and swine eat the food of men, and you do not make any restrictive arrangements. There are people dying from famine on the roads, and you do not issue the stores of your granaries for them. When people die, you say, "It is not owing to me; it is owing to the year." In what does this differ from stabbing a man and killing him, and then saying—"It was not I; it was the weapon?" Let your Majesty cease to lay the blame on the year, and instantly from all the nation the people will come to you.'

CHAP. IV. 1. King Hui of Liang said, 'I wish quietly to receive your instructions.'

2. Mencius replied, 'Is there any difference between killing a man with a stick and with a sword?' The king said, 'There is no difference!

3. 'Is there any difference between doing it with a sword and with the style of government? 'There is no difference,' was the reply.

4. Mencius then said, 'In your kitchen there is fat meat; in your stables there are fat horses. But your people have the look of hunger, and on the wilds there are those who have died of famine. This is leading on beasts to devour men.

5. 'Beasts devour one another, and men hate them for doing so. When a prince, being the parent of his people, administers his government so as to be chargeable with leading on beasts to devour men, where is his parental relation to the people?'

6. Chung-ni said, 'Was he not without posterity who first made wooden images to bury with the dead? So he said, because that man made the semblances of men, and used them for that purpose:—what shall be thought of him who causes his people to die of hunger?'

CHAP. V. 1. King Hui of Liang said, 'There was not in the nation a stronger State than Tsin, as you, venerable Sir, know. But since it descended to me, on the east we have been defeated by Ch'i, and then my eldest son perished; on the west we have lost seven hundred li of territory to Ch'in; and on the south we have sustained disgrace at the hands of Ch'u. I have brought shame on my departed predecessors, and wish on their account to wipe it away, once for all. What course is to be pursued to accomplish this?'

2. Mencius replied, 'With a territory which is only a hundred li square, it is possible to attain to the royal dignity.

3. 'If Your Majesty will indeed dispense a benevolent government to the people, being sparing in the use of punishments and fines, and making the taxes and levies light, so causing that the fields shall be ploughed deep, and the weeding of them be carefully attended to, and that the strong-bodied, during their days of leisure, shall cultivate their filial piety, fraternal respectfulness, sincerity, and truthfulness, serving thereby, at home, their fathers and elder brothers, and, abroad, their elders and superiors,—you will then have a people who can be employed, with sticks which they have prepared, to oppose the strong mail and sharp weapons of the troops of Ch'in and Ch'u.

4. 'The rulers of those States rob their people of their time, so that they cannot plough and weed their fields, in order to support their parents. Their parents suffer from cold and hunger. Brothers, wives, and children are separated and scattered abroad.

5. 'Those rulers, as it were, drive their people into pit-falls, or drown them. Your Majesty will go to punish them. In such a case, who will oppose your Majesty?

6. 'In accordance with this is the saying,—"The benevolent has no enemy." I beg your Majesty not to doubt what I say.'

CHAP. VI. 1. Mencius went to see the king Hsiang of Liang.

2. On coming out from the interview, he said to some persons, 'When I looked at him from a distance, he did not appear like a sovereign; when I drew near to him, I saw nothing venerable about him. Abruptly he asked me, "How can the kingdom be settled?" I replied, "It will be settled by being united under one sway."

3. '"Who can so unite it?"

4. 'I replied, "He who has no pleasure in killing men can so unite it."

5. '"Who can give it to him?"

6. 'I replied, "All the people of the nation will unanimously

135

give it to him. Does your Majesty understand the way of the growing grain? During the seventh and eighth months, when drought prevails, the plants become dry. Then the clouds collect densely in the heavens, they send down torrents of rain, and the grain erects itself, as if by a shoot. When it does so, who can keep it back? Now among the shepherds of men throughout the nation, there is not one who does not find pleasure in killing men. If there were one who did not find pleasure in killing men, all the people in the nation would look towards him with outstretched necks. Such being indeed the case, the people would flock to him, as water flows downwards with a rush, which no one can repress.'"

CHAP. VII. 1. The king Hsuan of Ch'i asked, saying, 'May I be informed by you of the transactions of Hwan of Ch'i, and Wan of Tsin?'

2. Mencius replied, 'There were none of the disciples of Chung-ni who spoke about the affairs of Hwan and Wan, and therefore they have not been transmitted to these after-ages ;—your servant has not heard them. If you will have me speak, let it be about royal government.'

3. The king said, 'What virtue must there be in order to attain to royal sway?' Mencius answered, 'The love and protection of the people; with this there is no power which can prevent a ruler from attaining to it.'

4. The king asked again, 'Is such an one as I competent to love and protect the people?' Mencius said, 'Yes.' 'How do you know that I am competent for that?' 'I heard the following incident from Hu Ho:—"The king," said he, "was sitting aloft in the hall, when a man appeared, leading an ox past the lower part of it. The king saw him, and asked, Where is the ox going? The man replied, We are going to consecrate a bell with its blood. The king said, Let it go. I cannot bear its frightened appearance, as if it were an innocent person going to the place of death. The man answered, Shall we then omit the consecration of the bell? The king said, How can that be omitted? Change it for a sheep." I do not know whether this incident really occurred.'

5. The king replied, 'It did,' and then Mencius said, 'The

heart seen in this is sufficient to carry you to the royal sway. The people all supposed that your Majesty grudged the animal, but your servant knows surely, that it was your Majesty's not being able to bear the sight, which made you do as you did.'

6. The king said, 'You are right. And yet there really was an appearance of what the people condemned. But though Chi be a small and narrow State, how should I grudge one ox? Indeed it was because I could not bear its frightened appearance, as if it were an innocent person going to the place of death, that therefore I changed it for a sheep.'

7. Mencius pursued, 'Let not your Majesty deem it strange that the people should think you were grudging the animal. When you changed a large one for a small, how should they know the true reason? If you felt pained by its being led without guilt to the place of death, what was there to choose between an ox and a sheep? The king laughed and said, 'What really was my mind in the matter? I did not grudge the expense of it, and changed it for a sheep!—There was reason in the people's saying that I grudged it.'

8. 'There is no harm in their saying so,' said Mencius. 'Your conduct was an artifice of benevolence. You saw the ox, and had not seen the sheep. So is the superior man affected towards animals, that, having seen them alive, he cannot bear to see them die; having heard their dying cries, he cannot bear to eat their flesh. Therefore he keeps away from his slaughter-house and cook-room.'

9. The king was pleased, and said, 'It is said in the Book of Poetry, "The minds of others, I am able by reflection to measure;"—this is verified, my Master, in your discovery of my motive. I indeed did the thing, but when I turned my thoughts inward, and examined into it, I could not discover my own mind. When you, Master, spoke those words, the movements of compassion began to work in my mind. How is it that this heart has in it what is equal to the royal sway?'

10. Mencius replied, 'Suppose a man were to make this statement to your Majesty:—"My strength is sufficient to lift three thousand catties, but it is not sufficient to lift one feather;—my eyesight is sharp enough to examine the point of

an autumn hair, but I do not see a waggon-load of faggots;"—
would your Majesty allow what he said?' 'No,' was the answer,
on which Mencius proceeded, 'Now here is kindness sufficient
to reach to animals, and no benefits are extended from it to
the people.—How is this? Is an exception to be made here?
The truth is, the feather is not lifted, because strength is not
used; the waggon-load of firewood is not seen, because the
eyesight is not used; and the people are not loved and
protected, because kindness is not employed. Therefore your
Majesty's not exercising the royal sway, is because you do not
do it, not because you are not able to do it.'

11. The king asked, 'How may the difference between the
not doing a thing, and the not being able to do it, be
represented? Mencius replied, 'In such a thing as taking the
T'ai mountain under your arm, and leaping over the north sea
with it, if you say to people—"I am not able to do it," that is a
real case of not being able. In such a matter as breaking off a
branch from a tree at the order of a superior, if you say to
people—"I am not able to do it," that is a case of not doing it,
it is not a case of not being able to do it. Therefore your
Majesty's not exercising the royal sway, is not such a case as
that of taking the T'ai mountain under your arm, and leaping
over the north sea with it. Your Majesty's not exercising the
royal sway is a case like that of breaking off a branch from a
tree.

12. 'Treat with the reverence due to age the elders in your
own family, so that the elders in the families of others shall be
similarly treated; treat with the kindness due to youth the
young in your own family, so that the young in the families of
others shall be similarly treated:—do this, and the kingdom
may be made to go round in your palm. It is said in the Book
of Poetry, "His example affected his wife. It reached to his
brothers, and his family of the State was governed by it."—
The language shows how king Wan simply took his kindly
heart, and exercised it towards those parties. Therefore the
carrying out his kindness of heart by a prince will suffice for
the love and protection of all within the four seas, and if he do
not carry it out, he will not be able to protect his wife and

children. The way in which the ancients came greatly to surpass other men, was no other but this:—simply that they knew well how to carry out, so as to affect others, what they themselves did. Now your kindness is sufficient to reach to animals, and no benefits are extended from it to reach the people.—How is this? Is an exception to be made here?

13. 'By weighing, we know what things are light, and what heavy. By measuring, we know what things are long, and what short. The relations of all things may be thus determined, and it is of the greatest importance to estimate the motions of the mind. I beg your Majesty to measure it.

14. 'You collect your equipments of war, endanger your soldiers and officers, and excite the resentment of the other princes;—do these things cause you pleasure in your mind?'

15. The king replied, 'No. How should I derive pleasure from these things? My object in them is to seek for what I greatly desire.'

16. Mencius said, 'May I hear from you what it is that you greatly desire?' The king laughed and did not speak. Mencius resumed, 'Are you led to desire it, because you have not enough of rich and sweet food for your mouth? Or because you have not enough of light and warm clothing for your body? Or because you have not enough of beautifully coloured objects to delight your eyes? Or because you have not voices and tones enough to please your ears? Or because you have not enough of attendants and favourites to stand before you and receive your orders? Your Majesty's various officers are sufficient to supply you with those things. How can your Majesty be led to entertain such a desire on account of them?' 'No,' said the king; 'my desire is not on account of them.' Mencius added, 'Then, what your Majesty greatly desires may be known. You wish to enlarge your territories, to have Ch'in and Ch'u wait at your court, to rule the Middle Kingdom, and to attract to you the barbarous tribes that surround it. But doing what you do to seek for what you desire is like climbing a tree to seek for fish.'

17. The king said, 'Is it so bad as that?' 'It is even worse,' was the reply. 'If you climb a tree to seek for fish, although you

do not get the fish, you will not suffer any subsequent calamity. But doing what you do to seek for what you desire, doing it moreover with all your heart, you will assuredly afterwards meet with calamities.' The king asked, 'May I hear from you the proof of that?' Mencius said, 'If the people of Tsau should fight with the people of Ch'u, which of them does your Majesty think would conquer?' 'The people of Ch'u would conquer.' 'Yes;—and so it is certain that a small country cannot contend with a great, that few cannot contend with many, that the weak cannot contend with the strong. The territory within the four seas embraces nine divisions, each of a thousand li square. All Ch'i together is but one of them. If with one part you try to subdue the other eight, what is the difference between that and Tsau's contending with Ch'u? For, with such a desire, you must turn back to the proper course for its attainment.

18. 'Now if your Majesty will institute a government whose action shall be benevolent, this will cause all the officers in the kingdom to wish to stand in your Majesty's court, and all the farmers to wish to plough in your Majesty's fields, and all the merchants, both travelling and stationary, to wish to store their goods in your Majesty's market-places, and all travelling strangers to wish to make their tours on your Majesty's roads, and all throughout the kingdom who feel aggrieved by their rulers to wish to come and complain to your Majesty. And when they are so bent, who will be able to keep them back?'

19. The king said, 'I am stupid, and not able to advance to this. I wish you, my Master, to assist my intentions. Teach me clearly; although I am deficient in intelligence and vigour, I will essay and try to carry your instructions into effect.'

20. Mencius replied, 'They are only men of education, who, without a certain livelihood, are able to maintain a fixed heart. As to the people, if they have not a certain livelihood, it follows that they will not have a fixed heart. And if they have not a fixed heart, there is nothing which they will not do, in the way of self-abandonment, of moral deflection, of depravity, and of wild license. When they thus have been involved in crime, to follow them up and punish them;—this is to entrap the people.

140

How can such a thing as entrapping the people be done under the rule of a benevolent man?

21. 'Therefore an intelligent ruler will regulate the livelihood of the people, so as to make sure that, for those above them, they shall have sufficient wherewith to serve their parents, and, for those below them, sufficient wherewith to support their wives and children; that in good years they shall always be abundantly satisfied, and that in bad years they shall escape the danger of perishing. After this he may urge them, and they will proceed to what is good, for in this case the people will follow after it with ease.

22. 'Now, the livelihood of the people is so regulated, that, above, they have not sufficient wherewith to serve their parents, and, below, they have not sufficient wherewith to support their wives and children. Notwithstanding good years, their lives are continually embittered, and, in bad years, they do not escape perishing. In such circumstances they only try to save themselves from death, and are afraid they will not succeed. What leisure have they to cultivate propriety and righteousness?'

23. 'If your Majesty wishes to effect this regulation of the livelihood of the people, why not turn to that which is the essential step to it?

24. 'Let mulberry-trees be planted about the homesteads with their five mau, and persons of fifty years may be clothed with silk. In keeping fowls, pigs, dogs, and swine, let not their times of breeding be neglected, and persons of seventy years may eat flesh. Let there not be taken away the time that is proper for the cultivation of the farm with its hundred mau, and the family of eight mouths that is supported by it shall not suffer from hunger. Let careful attention be paid to education in schools,—the inculcation in it especially of the filial and fraternal duties, and grey-haired men will not be seen upon the roads, carrying burdens on their backs or on their heads. It never has been that the ruler of a State where such results were seen,—the old wearing silk and eating flesh, and the black-haired people suffering neither from hunger nor cold,—did not attain to the royal dignity.'

141

BOOK I. KING HUI OF LIANG, PART II

CHAP. I. 1. Chwang Pa'o, seeing Mencius, said to him, 'I had an interview with the king. His Majesty told me that he loved music, and I was not prepared with anything to reply to him. What do you pronounce about that love of music?' Mencius replied, 'If the king's love of music were very great, the kingdom of Ch'i would be near to a state of good government!'

2. Another day, Mencius, having an interview with the king, said, 'Your Majesty, I have heard, told the officer Chwang, that you love music;—was it so?' The king changed colour, and said, 'I am unable to love the music of the ancient sovereigns; I only love the music that suits the manners of the present age.'

3. Mencius said, 'If your Majesty's love of music were very great, Ch'i would be near to a state of good government! The music of the present day is just like the music of antiquity, as regards effecting that.'

4. The king said, 'May I hear from you the proof of that?' Mencius asked, 'Which is the more pleasant,—to enjoy music by yourself alone, or to enjoy it with others?' 'To enjoy it with others,' was the reply. 'And which is the more pleasant,—to enjoy music with a few, or to enjoy it with many?' 'To enjoy it with many.'

5. Mencius proceeded, 'Your servant begs to explain what I have said about music to your Majesty.

6. 'Now, your Majesty is having music here.—The people hear the noise of your bells and drums, and the notes of your fifes and pipes, and they all, with aching heads, knit their brows, and say to one another, "That's how our king likes his music! But why does he reduce us to this extremity of distress?—Fathers and sons cannot see one another. Elder brothers and younger brothers, wives and children, are separated and scattered abroad." Now, your Majesty is hunting here.—The people hear the noise of your carriages and horses, and see the beauty of your plumes and streamers, and they all, with aching heads, knit their brows, and say to one another,

143

"That's how our king likes his hunting! But why does he reduce us to this extremity of distress?—Fathers and sons cannot see one another. Elder brothers and younger brothers, wives and children, are separated and scattered abroad." Their feeling thus is from no other reason but that you do not allow the people to have pleasure as well as yourself.

7. 'Now, your Majesty is having music here. The people hear the noise of your bells and drums, and the notes of your fifes and pipes, and they all, delighted, and with joyful looks, say to one another, "That sounds as if our king were free from all sickness! If he were not, how could he enjoy this music?" Now, your Majesty is hunting here.—The people hear the noise of your carriages and horses, and see the beauty of your plumes and streamers, and they all, delighted, and with joyful looks, say to one another, "That looks as if our king were free from all sickness! If he were not, how could he enjoy this hunting?" Their feeling thus is from no other reason but that you cause them to have their pleasure as you have yours.

8. 'If your Majesty now will make pleasure a thing common to the people and yourself, the royal sway awaits you.'

CHAP. II. 1. The king Hsuan of Ch'i asked, 'Was it so, that the park of king Wan contained seventy square li?' Mencius replied, 'It is so in the records.'

2. 'Was it so large as that?' exclaimed the king. 'The people,' said Mencius, 'still looked on it as small.' The king added, 'My park contains only forty square li, and the people still look on it as large. How is this?' 'The park of king Wan,' was the reply, 'contained seventy square li, but the grass-cutters and fuel-gatherers had the privilege of entrance into it; so also had the catchers of pheasants and hares. He shared it with the people, and was it not with reason that they looked on it as small?

3. 'When I first arrived at the borders of your kingdom, I inquired about the great prohibitory regulations, before I would venture to enter it; and I heard, that inside the barrier-gates there was a park of forty square li, and that he who killed a deer in it, was held guilty of the same crime as if he had killed a man.—Thus those forty square li are a pitfall in the middle of the kingdom. Is it not with reason that the people look upon

them as large?'

CHAP. III. 1. The king Hsuan of Ch'i asked, saying, 'Is there any way to regulate one's maintenance of intercourse with neighbouring kingdoms?' Mencius replied, 'There is. But it requires a perfectly virtuous prince to be able, with a great country, to serve a small one,—as, for instance, T'ang served Ko, and king Wan served the Kwan barbarians. And it requires a wise prince to be able, with a small country, to serve a large one,—as the king T'ai served the Hsun-yu, and Kau-ch'ien served Wu.

2. 'He who with a areat State serves a small one, delights in Heaven. He who with a small State serves a large one, stands in awe of Heaven. He who delights in Heaven, will affect with his love and protection the whole kingdom. He who stands in awe of Heaven, will affect with his love and protection his own kingdom.

3. 'It is said in the Book of Poetry, "I fear the Majesty of Heaven, and will thus preserve its favouring decree."'

4. The king said, 'A great saying! But I have an infirmity;— I love valour.'

5. I beg your Majesty,' was the reply, 'not to love small valour. If a man brandishes his sword, looks fiercely, and says, "How dare he withstand me?"—this is the valour of a common man, who can be the opponent only of a single individual. I beg your Majesty to greaten it.

6. 'It is said in the Book of Poetry,
"The king blazed with anger,
And he marshalled his hosts,
To stop the march to Chu,
To consolidate the prosperity of Chau,
To meet the expectations of the nation."
This was the valour of king Wan. King Wan, in one burst of his anger, gave repose to all the people of the kingdom.

7. 'In the Book of History it is said, "Heaven having produced the inferior people, made for them rulers and teachers, with the purpose that they should be assisting to God, and therefore distinguished them throughout the four quarters of the land. Whoever are offenders, and whoever are

innocent, here am I to deal with them. How dare any under heaven give indulgence to their refractory wills?" There was one man pursuing a violent and disorderly course in the kingdom, and king Wu was ashamed of it. This was the valour of king Wu. He also, by one display of his anger, gave repose to all the people of the kingdom.

8. 'Let now your Majesty also, in one burst of anger, give repose to all the people of the kingdom. The people are only afraid that your Majesty does not love valour.'

CHAP. IV. 1. The king Hsuan of Ch'i had an interview with Mencius in the Snow palace, and said to him, 'Do men of talents and worth likewise find pleasure in these things?' Mencius replied, 'They do; and if people generally are not able to enjoy themselves, they condemn their superiors.

2. 'For them, when they cannot enjoy themselves, to condemn their superiors is wrong, but when the superiors of the people do not make enjoyment a thing common to the people and themselves, they also do wrong.

3. 'When a ruler rejoices in the joy of his people, they also rejoice in his joy; when he grieves at the sorrow of his people, they also grieve at his sorrow. A sympathy of joy will pervade the kingdom ; a sympathy of sorrow will do the same:—in such a state of things, it cannot be but that the ruler attain to the royal dignity.

4. 'Formerly, the duke Ching of Ch'i asked the minister Yen, saying, "I wish to pay a visit of inspection to Chwan-fu, and Chao-wu, and then to bend my course southward along the shore, till I come to Lang-ye. What shall I do that my tour may be fit to be compared with the visits of inspection made by the ancient sovereigns?"

5. 'The minister Yen replied, "An excellent inquiry! When the Son of Heaven visited the princes, it was called a tour of inspection, that is, be surveyed the States under their care. When the princes attended at the court of the Son of Heaven, it was called a report of office, that is, they reported their administration of their offices. Thus, neither of the proceedings was without a purpose. And moreover, in the spring they examined the ploughing, and supplied any

deficiency of seed; in the autumn they examined the reaping, and supplied any deficiency of yield. There is the saying of the Hsia dynasty,—If our king do not take his ramble, what will become of our happiness? If our king do not make his excursion, what will become of our help? That ramble, and that excursion, were a pattern to the princes.

6. "'Now, the state of things is different.—A host marches in attendance on the ruler, and stores of provisions are consumed. The hungry are deprived of their food, and there is no rest for those who are called to toil. Maledictions are uttered by one to another with eyes askance, and the people proceed to the commission of wickedness. Thus the royal ordinances are violated, and the people are oppressed, and the supplies of food and drink flow away like water. The rulers yield themselves to the current, or they urge their way against it; they are wild; they are utterly lost:—these things proceed to the grief of the inferior princes.

7. "'Descending along with the current, and forgetting to return, is what I call yielding to it. Pressing up against it, and forgetting to return, is what I call urging their way against it. Pursuing the chase without satiety is what I call being wild. Delighting in wine without satiety is what I call being lost.

8. "'The ancient sovereigns had no pleasures to which they gave themselves as on the flowing stream; no doings which might be so characterized as wild and lost.

9. "'It is for you, my prince, to pursue your course.'"

10. 'The duke Ching was pleased. He issued a proclamation throughout his State, and went out and occupied a shed in the borders. From that time he began to open his granaries to supply the wants of the people, and calling the Grand music-master, he said to him—"Make for me music to suit a prince and his minister pleased with each other." And it was then that the Chi-shao and Chio-shao were made, in the words to which it was said, "Is it a fault to restrain one's prince?" He who restrains his prince loves his prince.'

CHAP. V. 1. The king Hsuan of Ch'i said, 'People all tell me to pull down and remove the Hall of Distinction. Shall I pull it down, or stop the movement for that object?'

147

2. Mencius replied, 'The Hall of Distinction is a Hall appropriate to the sovereigns. If your Majesty wishes to practise the true royal government, then do not pull it down.'

3. The king said, 'May I hear from you what the true royal government is?' 'Formerly,' was the reply, 'king Wan's government of Ch'i was as follows:—The husbandmen cultivated for the government one-ninth of the land; the descendants of officers were salaried; at the passes and in the markets, strangers were inspected, but goods were not taxed: there were no prohibitions respecting the ponds and weirs; the wives and children of criminals were not involved in their guilt. There were the old and wifeless, or widowers; the old and husbandless, or widows; the old and childless, or solitaries ; the young and fatherless, or orphans:—these four classes are the most destitute of the people, and have none to whom they can tell their wants, and king Wan, in the institution of his government with its benevolent action, made them the first objects of his regard, as it is said in the Book of Poetry,

"The rich may get through life well;
But alas! for the miserable and solitary!"'

4. The king said, 'O excellent words!' Mencius said, 'Since your Majesty deems them excellent, why do you not practise them?' 'I have an infirmity,' said the king; 'I am fond of wealth.' The reply was, 'Formerly, Kung-liu was fond of wealth. It is said in the Book of Poetry,

"He reared his ricks, and filled his granaries,
He tied up dried provisions and grain,
In bottomless bags, and sacks,
That he might gather his people together, and glorify his
    State.
With bows and arrows all-displayed,
With shields, and spears, and battle-axes, large and small,
He commenced his march."

In this way those who remained in their old seat had their ricks and granaries, and those who marched had their bags of provisions. It was not till after this that he thought he could begin his march. If your Majesty loves wealth, give the people power to gratify the same feeling, and what difficulty will there be in your attaining the royal sway?'

5. The king said, 'I have an infirmity; I am fond of beauty.' The reply was, 'Formerly, king T'ai was fond of beauty, and loved his wife. It is said in the Book of Poetry,

"Ku-kung T'an-fu
Came in the morning, galloping his horse,
By the banks of the western waters,
As far as the foot of Ch'i hill,
Along with the lady of Chiang;
They came and together chose the site for their settlement."

At that time, in the seclusion of the house, there were no dissatisfied women, and abroad, there were no unmarried men. If your Majesty loves beauty, let the people be able to gratify the same feeling, and what difficulty will there be in your attaining the royal sway?'

CHAP. VI. 1. Mencius said to the king Hsuan of Ch'i, 'Suppose that one of your Majesty's ministers were to entrust his wife and children to the care of his friend, while he himself went into Ch'u to travel, and that, on his return, he should find that the friend had let his wife and children suffer from cold and hunger;—how ought he to deal with him?' The king said, 'He should cast him off.'

2. Mencius proceeded, 'Suppose that the chief criminal judge could not regulate the officers under him, how would you deal with him?' The king said, 'Dismiss him.'

3. Mencius again said, 'If within the four borders of your kingdom there is not good government, what is to be done?' The king looked to the right and left, and spoke of other matters.

CHAP. VII. 1. Mencius, having an interview with the king Hsuan of Ch'i, said to him, 'When men speak of "an ancient kingdom," it is not meant thereby that it has lofty trees in it, but that it has ministers sprung from families which have been noted in it for generations. Your Majesty has no intimate ministers even. Those whom you advanced yesterday are gone to-day, and you do not know it.'

2. The king said, 'How shall I know that they have not ability, and so avoid employing them at all?'

3. The reply was, 'The ruler of a State advances to office men of talents and virtue only as a matter of necessity. Since he will thereby cause the low to overstep the honourable, and distant to overstep his near relatives, ought he to do so but with caution?

4. 'When all those about you say,—"This is a man of talents and worth," you may not therefore believe it. When your great officers all say,—"This is a man of talents and virtue," neither may you for that believe it. When all the people say,—"This is a man of talents and virtue," then examine into the case, and when you find that the man is such, employ him. When all those about you say,—"This man won't do," don't listen to them. When all your great officers say,—"This man won't do," don't listen to them. When the people all say,—"This man won't do," then examine into the case, and when you find that the man won't do, send him away.

5. 'When all those about you say,—"This man deserves death," don't listen to them. When all your great officers say,—"This man deserves death," don't listen to them. When the people all say, "This man deserves death," then inquire into the case, and when you see that the man deserves death, put him to death. In accordance with this we have the saying, "The people killed him."

6. 'You must act in this way in order to be the parent of the people.'

CHAP. VIII. 1. The king Hsuan of Ch'i asked, saying, 'Was it so, that T'ang banished Chieh, and that king Wu smote Chau?' Mencius replied, 'It is so in the records.'

2. The king said, 'May a minister then put his sovereign to death?'

3. Mencius said, 'He who outrages the benevolence proper to his nature, is called a robber; he who outrages righteousness, is called a ruffian. The robber and ruffian we call a mere fellow. I have heard of the cutting off of the fellow Chau, but I have not heard of the putting a sovereign to death, in his case.'

CHAP. IX. 1. Mencius, having an interview with the king Hsuan of Ch'i, said to him, 'If you are going to build a large mansion, you will surely cause the Master of the workmen to look out for large trees, and when he has found such large trees, you will be glad, thinking that they will answer for the intended object. Should the workmen hew them so as to make them too small, then your Majesty will be angry, thinking that they will not answer for the purpose. Now, a man spends his youth in learning the principles of right government, and, being grown up to vigour, he wishes to put them in practice;— if your Majesty says to him, "For the present put aside what you have learned, and follow me," what shall we say?

2. 'Here now you have a gem unwrought, in the stone. Although it may be worth 240,000 taels, you will surely employ a lapidary to cut and polish it. But when you come to the government of the State, then you say,—"For the present put aside what you have learned, and follow me." How is it that you herein act so differently from your conduct in calling in the lapidary to cut the gem?'

CHAP. X. 1. The people of Ch'i attacked Yen, and conquered it.

2. The king Hsuan asked, saying, 'Some tell me not to take possession of it for myself, and some tell me to take possession of it. For a kingdom of ten thousand chariots, attacking another of ten thousand chariots, to complete the conquest of it in fifty days, is an achievement beyond mere human strength. If I do not take possession of it, calamities from Heaven will surely come upon me. What do you say to my taking possession of it?'

3. Mencius replied, 'If the people of Yen will be pleased with your taking possession of it, then do so.—Among the ancients there was one who acted on this principle, namely king Wu. If the people of Yen will not be pleased with your taking possession of it, then do not do so.—Among the ancients there was one who acted on this principle, namely king Wan.

4. 'When, with all the strength of your country of ten thousand chariots, you attacked another country of ten thousand chariots, and the people brought baskets of rice and vessels of congee, to meet your Majesty's host, was there any other reason for this but that they hoped to escape out of fire

and water? If you make the water more deep and the fire more fierce, they will in like manner make another revolution.'

CHAP. XI. 1. The people of Ch'i, having smitten Yen, took possession of it, and upon this, the princes of the various States deliberated together, and resolved to deliver Yen from their power. The king Hsuan said to Mencius, 'The princes have formed many plans to attack me:—how shall I prepare myself for them?' Mencius replied, 'I have heard of one who with seventy li exercised all the functions of government throughout the kingdom. That was T'ang. I have never heard of a prince with a thousand li standing in fear of others.'

2. 'It is said in the Book of History, As soon as T'ang began his work of executing justice, he commenced with Ko. The whole kingdom had confidence in him. When he pursued his work in the east, the rude tribes on the west murmured. So did those on the north, when he was engaged in the south. Their cry was—"Why does he put us last?" Thus, the people looked to him, as we look in a time of great drought to the clouds and rainbows. The frequenters of the markets stopped not. The husbandmen made no change in their operations. While he punished their rulers, he consoled the people. His progress was like the falling of opportune rain, and the people were delighted. It is said again in the Book of History, "We have waited for our prince long; the prince's coming will be our reviving!"

3. 'Now the ruler of Yen was tyrannizing over his people, and your Majesty went and punished him. The people supposed that you were going to deliver them out of the water and the fire, and brought baskets of rice and vessels of congee, to meet your Majesty's host. But you have slain their fathers and elder brothers, and put their sons and younger brothers in confinement. You have pulled down the ancestral temple of the State, and are removing to Ch'i its precious vessels. How can such a course be deemed proper? The rest of the kingdom is indeed jealously afraid of the strength of Ch'i; and now, when with a doubled territory you do not put in practice a benevolent government;—it is this which sets the arms of the kingdom in in motion.

4. 'If your Majesty will make haste to issue an ordinance, restoring your captives, old and young, stopping the removal of the precious vessels, and saying that, after consulting with the people of Yen, you will appoint them a ruler, and withdraw from the country;—in this way you may still be able to stop the threatened attack.'

CHAP. XII. 1. There had been a brush between Tsau and Lu, when the duke Mu asked Mencius, saying, 'Of my officers there were killed thirty-three men, and none of the people would die in their defence. Though I sentenced them to death for their conduct, it is impossible to put such a multitude to death. If I do not put them to death, then there is the crime unpunished of their looking angrily on at the death of their officers, and not saving them. How is the exigency of the case to be met?'

2. Mencius replied, 'In calamitous years and years of famine, the old and weak of your people, who have been found lying in the ditches and water-channels, and the able-bodied who have been scattered about to the four quarters, have amounted to several thousands. All the while, your granaries, O prince, have been stored with grain, and your treasuries and arsenals have been full, and not one of your officers has told you of the distress. Thus negligent have the superiors in your State been, and cruel to their inferiors. The philosopher Tsang said, "Beware, beware. What proceeds from you, will return to you again." Now at length the people have paid back the conduct of their officers to them. Do not you, O prince, blame them.

3. 'If you will put in practice a benevolent government, this people will love you and all above them, and will die for their officers.'

CHAP. XIII. 1. The duke Wan of T'ang asked Mencius, saying, 'T'ang is a small kingdom, and lies between Ch'i and Ch'u. Shall I serve Ch'i? Or shall I serve Chu?'

2. Mencius replied, 'This plan which you propose is beyond me. If you will have me counsel you, there is one thing I can suggest. Dig deeper your moats; build higher your walls; guard them as well as your people. In case of attack, be prepared to die in your defence, and have the people so that they will not

leave you;—this is a proper course.

CHAP. XIV. 1. The duke Wan of T'ang asked Mencius, saying, 'The people of Ch'i are going to fortify Hsieh. The movement occasions me great alarm. What is the proper course for me to take in the case?'

2. Mencius replied, 'Formerly, when king T'ai dwelt in Pin, the barbarians of the north were continually making incursions upon it. He therefore left it, went to the foot of mount Ch'i, and there took up his residence. He did not take that situation, as having selected it. It was a matter of necessity with him.

3. 'If you do good, among your descendants, in after generations, there shall be one who will attain to the royal dignity. A prince lays the foundation of the inheritance, and hands down the beginning which he has made, doing what may be continued by his successors. As to the accomplishment of the great result, that is with Heaven. What is that Ch'i to you, O prince? Be strong to do good. That is all your business.'

CHAP. XV. 1. The duke Wan of T'ang asked Mencius, saying, 'T'ang is a small State. Though I do my utmost to serve those large kingdoms on either side of it, we cannot escape suffering from them. What course shall I take that we may do so?' Mencius replied, 'Formerly, when king T'ai dwelt in Pin, the barbarians of the north were constantly making incursions upon it. He served them with skins and silks, and still he suffered from them. He served them with dogs and horses, and still he suffered from them. He served them with pearls and gems, and still he suffered from them. Seeing this, he assembled the old men, and announced to them, saying, "What the barbarians want is my territory. I have heard this,—that a ruler does not injure his people with that wherewith he nourishes them. My children, why should you be troubled about having no prince? I will leave this." Accordingly, he left Pin, crossed the mountain Liang, built a town at the foot of mount Ch'i, and dwelt there. The people of Pin said, "He is a benevolent man. We must not lose him." Those who followed him looked like crowds hastening to market.

2. 'On the other hand, some say, "The kingdom is a thing to be kept from generation to generation. One individual

cannot undertake to dispose of it in his own person. Let him be prepared to die for it. Let him not quit it."

3. 'I ask you, prince, to make your election between these two courses.'

CHAP. XVI. 1. The duke P'ing of Lu was about to leave his palace, when his favourite, one Tsang Ts'ang, made a request to him, saying, 'On other days, when you have gone out, you have given instructions to the officers as to where you were going. But now, the horses have been put to the carriage, and the officers do not yet know where you are going. I venture to ask.' The duke said, 'I am going to see the scholar Mang.' 'How is this?' said the other. 'That you demean yourself, prince, in paying the honour of the first visit to a common man, is, I suppose, because you think that he is a man of talents and virtue. By such men the rules of ceremonial proprieties and right are observed. But on the occasion of this Mang's second mourning, his observances exceeded those of the former. Do not go to see him, my prince.' The duke said, 'I will not.'

2. The officer Yo-chang entered the court, and had an audience. He said, 'Prince, why have you not gone to see Mang K'o?' the duke said, 'One told me that, on the occasion of the scholar Mang's second mourning, his observances exceeded those of the former. It is on that account that I have not gone to see him.' 'How is this!' answered Yo-chang. 'By what you call "exceeding," you mean, I suppose, that, on the first occasion, he used the rites appropriate to a scholar, and, on the second, those appropriate to a great officer; that he first used three tripods, and afterwards five tripods.' The duke said, 'No; I refer to the greater excellence of the coffin, the shell, the grave-clothes, and the shroud.' Yo-chang said, 'That cannot be called "exceeding." That was the difference between being poor and being rich.'

3. After this, Yo-chang saw Mencius, and said to him, 'I told the prince about you, and he was consequently coming to see you, when one of his favourites, named Tsang Ts'ang, stopped him, and therefore he did not come according to his purpose.' Mencius said, 'A man's advancement is effected, it may be, by others, and the stopping him is, it may be, from the efforts of

others. But to advance a man or to stop his advance is really beyond the power of other men. My not finding in the prince of Lu a ruler who would confide in me, and put my counsels into practice, is from Heaven. How could that scion of the Tsang family cause me not to find the ruler that would suit me?'

BOOK II. KUNG-SUN CH'AU, PART I

CHAP. I. 1. Kung-sun Ch'au asked Mencius, saying, 'Master, if you were to obtain the ordering of the government in Ch'i, could you promise yourself to accomplish anew such results as those realized by Kwan Chung and Yen?'

2. Mencius said, 'You are indeed a true man of Ch'i. You know about Kwan Chung and Yen, and nothing more,

3. 'Some one asked Tsang Hsi, saying, "Sir, to which do you give the superiority,—to yourself or to Tsze-lu?" Tsang Hsi looked uneasy, and said, "He was an object of veneration to my grandfather." "Then," pursued the other, "Do you give the superiority to yourself or to Kwan Chung?" Tsang Hsi, flushed with anger and displeased, said, "How dare you compare me with Kwan Chung? Considering how entirely Kwan Chung possessed the confidence of his prince, how long he enjoyed the direction of the government of the State, and how low, after all, was what he accomplished,—how is it that you liken me to him?"

4. 'Thus,' concluded Mencius, 'Tsang Hsi would not play Kwan Chung, and is it what you desire for me that I should do so?'

5. Kung-sun Ch'au said, 'Kwan Chung raised his prince to be the leader of all the other princes, and Yen made his prince illustrious, and do you still think it would not be enough for you to do what they did?'

6. Mencius answered, 'To raise Ch'i to the royal dignity would be as easy as it is to turn round the hand.'

7. 'So!' returned the other. 'The perplexity of your disciple is hereby very much increased. There was king Wan, moreover, with all the virtue which belonged to him; and who did not die till he had reached a hundred years:—and still his influence had not penetrated throughout the kingdom. It required king Wu and the duke of Chau to continue his course, before that influence greatly prevailed. Now you say that the royal dignity might be so easily obtained:—is king Wan then not a sufficient object for imitation?'

157

8. Mencius said, 'How can king Wan be matched? From T'ang to Wu-ting there had appeared six or seven worthy and sage sovereigns. The kingdom had been attached to Yin for a long time, and this length of time made a change difficult. Wu-ting had all the princes coming to his court, and possessed the kingdom as if it had been a thing which he moved round in his palm. Then, Chau was removed from Wu-ting by no great interval of time. There were still remaining some of the ancient families and of the old manners, of the influence also which had emanated from the earlier sovereigns, and of their good government. Moreover, there were the viscount of Wei and his second son, their Royal Highnesses Pi-kan and the viscount of Ch'i, and Kao-ko, all men of ability and virtue, who gave their joint assistance to Chau in his government. In consequence of these things, it took a long time for him to lose the throne. There was not a foot of ground which he did not possess. There was not one of all the people who was not his subject. So it was on his side, and king Wan at his beginning had only a territory of one hundred square li. On all these accounts, it was difficult for him immediately to attain to the royal dignity.

9. 'The people of Ch'i have a saying—"A man may have wisdom and discernment, but that is not like embracing the favourable opportunity. A man may have instruments of husbandry, but that is not like waiting for the farming seasons." The present time is one in which the royal dignity may be easily attained.

10. 'In the flourishing periods of the Hsia, Yin, and Chau dynasties, the royal domain did not exceed a thousand li, and Ch'i embraces so much territory. Cocks crow and dogs bark to one another, all the way to the four borders of the State:—so Ch'i possesses the people. No change is needed for the enlarging of its territory: no change is needed for the collecting of a population. If its ruler will put in practice a benevolent government, no power will be able to prevent his becoming sovereign.

11. 'Moreover, never was there a time farther removed than the present from the rise of a true sovereign: never was there

a time when the sufferings of the people from tyrannical government were more intense than the present. The hungry readily partake of any food, and the thirsty of any drink.'

12. 'Confucius said, "The flowing progress of virtue is more rapid than the transmission of royal orders by stages and couriers."

13. 'At the present time, in a country of ten thousand chariots, let benevolent government be put in practice, and the people will be delighted with it, as if they were relieved from hanging by the heels. With half the merit of the ancients, double their achievements is sure to be realized. It is only at this time that such could be the case.'

CHAP. II. 1. Kung-sun Ch'au asked Mencius, saying, 'Master, if you were to be appointed a high noble and the prime minister of Ch'i, so as to be able to carry your principles into practice, though you should thereupon raise the ruler to the headship of all the other princes, or even to the royal dignity, it would not be to be wondered at.—In such a position would your mind be perturbed or not?' Mencius replied, 'No. At forty, I attained to an unperturbed mind.'

2. Ch'au said, 'Since it is so with you, my Master, you are far beyond Mang Pan.' 'The mere attainment,' said Mencius, 'is not difficult. The scholar Kao had attained to an unperturbed mind at an earlier period of life than I did.'

3. Ch'au asked, 'Is there any way to an unperturbed mind?' The answer was, 'Yes.

4. 'Pi-kung Yu had this way of nourishing his valour:—He did not flinch from any strokes at his body. He did not turn his eyes aside from any thrusts at them. He considered that the slightest push from any one was the same as if he were beaten before the crowds in the market-place, and that what he would not receive from a common man in his loose large garments of hair, neither should he receive from a prince of ten thousand chariots. He viewed stabbing a prince of ten thousand chariots just as stabbing a fellow dressed in cloth of hair. He feared not any of all the princes. A bad word addressed to him be always returned.

5. 'Mang Shih-she had this way of nourishing his valour:—

He said, "I look upon not conquering and conquering in the same way. To measure the enemy and then advance; to calculate the chances of victory and then engage:—this is to stand in awe of the opposing force. How can I make certain of conquering? I can only rise superior to all fear."

6. 'Mang Shih-she resembled the philosopher Tsang. Pi-kung Yu resembled Tsze-hsia. I do not know to the valour of which of the two the superiority should be ascribed, but yet Mang Shih-she attended to what was of the greater importance.

7. 'Formerly, the philosopher Tsang said to Tsze-hsiang, "Do you love valour? I heard an account of great valour from the Master. It speaks thus:—'If, on self-examination, I find that I am not upright, shall I not be in fear even of a poor man in his loose garments of hair-cloth? If, on self-examination, I find that I am upright, I will go forward against thousands and tens of thousands.'"

8. Yet, what Mang Shih-she maintained, being merely his physical energy, was after all inferior to what the philosopher Tsang maintained, which was indeed of the most importance.'

9. Kung-sun Ch'au said, 'May I venture to ask an explanation from you, Master, of how you maintain an unperturbed mind, and how the philosopher Kao does the same?' Mencius answered, 'Kao says,—"What is not attained in words is not to be sought for in the mind; what produces dissatisfaction in the mind, is not to be helped by passion-effort." This last,—when there is unrest in the mind, not to seek for relief from passion-effort, may be conceded. But not to seek in the mind for what is not attained in words cannot be conceded. The will is the leader of the passion-nature. The passion-nature pervades and animates the body. The will is first and chief, and the passion-nature is subordinate to it. Therefore I say,—Maintain firm the will, and do no violence to the passion-nature.'

10. Ch'au observed, 'Since you say—"The will is chief, and the passion-nature is subordinate," how do you also say, "Maintain firm the will, and do no violence to the passion-nature?"' Mencius replied, 'When it is the will alone which is

active, it moves the passion-nature. When it is the passion-nature alone which is active, it moves the will. For instance now, in the case of a man falling or running, that is from the passion-nature, and yet it moves the mind.'

11. 'I venture to ask,' said Ch'au again, 'wherein you, Master, surpass Kao.' Mencius told him, 'I understand words. I am skilful in nourishing my vast, flowing passion-nature.'

12. Ch'au pursued, 'I venture to ask what you mean by your vast, flowing passion-nature!' The reply was, 'It is difficult to describe it.

13. 'This is the passion-nature:—It is exceedingly great, and exceedingly strong. Being nourished by rectitude, and sustaining no injury, it fills up all between heaven and earth.

14. 'This is the passion-nature:—It is the mate and assistant of righteousness and reason. Without it, man is in a state of starvation.

15. 'It is produced by the accumulation of righteous deeds; it is not to be obtained by incidental acts of righteousness. If the mind does not feel complacency in the conduct, the nature becomes starved. I therefore said, "Kao has never understood righteousness, because he makes it something external."

16. 'There must be the constant practice of this righteousness, but without the object of thereby nourishing the passion-nature. Let not the mind forget its work, but let there be no assisting the growth of that nature. Let us not be like the man of Sung. There was a man of Sung, who was grieved that his growing corn was not longer, and so he pulled it up. Having done this, he returned home, looking very stupid, and said to his people, "I am tired to-day. I have been helping the corn to grow long." His son ran to look at it, and found the corn all withered. There are few in the world, who do not deal with their passion-nature, as if they were assisting the corn to grow long. Some indeed consider it of no benefit to them, and let it alone:—they do not weed their corn. They who assist it to grow long, pull out their corn. What they do is not only of no benefit to the nature, but it also injures it.'

17. Kung-sun Ch'au further asked, 'What do you mean by saying that you understand whatever words you hear?'

Mencius replied, 'When words are one-sided, I know how the mind of the speaker is clouded over. When words are extravagant, I know how the mind is fallen and sunk. When words are all-depraved, I know how the mind has departed from principle. When words are evasive, I know how the mind is at its wit's end. These evils growing in the mind, do injury to government, and, displayed in the government, are hurtful to the conduct of affairs. When a Sage shall again arise, he will certainly follow my words.'

18. On this Ch'au observed, 'Tsai Wo and Tsze-kung were skilful in speaking. Zan Niu, the disciple Min, and Yen Yuan, while their words were good, were distinguished for their virtuous conduct. Confucius united the qualities of the disciples in himself, but still he said, "In the matter of speeches, I am not competent."—Then, Master, have you attained to be a Sage?'

19. Mencius said, 'Oh! what words are these? Formerly Tsze-kung asked Confucius, saying, "Master, are you a Sage?" Confucius answered him, "A Sage is what I cannot rise to. I learn without satiety, and teach without being tired." Tsze-kung said, "You learn without satiety:—that shows your wisdom. You teach without being tired:—that shows your benevolence. Benevolent and wise:—Master, you ARE a Sage." Now, since Confucius would not allow himself to be regarded as a Sage, what words were those?'

20. Ch'au said, 'Formerly, I once heard this:—Tsze-hsia, Tsze-yu, and Tsze-chang had each one member of the Sage. Zan Niu, the disciple Min, and Yen Yuan had all the members, but in small proportions. I venture to ask,—With which of these are you pleased to rank yourself?'

21. Mencius replied, 'Let us drop speaking about these, if you please.'

22. Ch'au then asked, 'What do you say of Po-i and I Yin?' 'Their ways were different from mine,' said Mencius. 'Not to serve a prince whom he did not esteem, nor command a people whom he did not approve; in a time of good government to take office, and on the occurrence of confusion to retire:—this was the way of Po-i. To say—"Whom may I

not serve? My serving him makes him my ruler. What people may I not command? My commanding them makes them my people." In a time of good government to take office, and when disorder prevailed, also to take office:—that was the way of I Yin. When it was proper to go into office, then to go into it; when it was proper to keep retired from office, then to keep retired from it; when it was proper to continue in it long, then to continue in it long - when it was proper to withdraw from it quickly, then to withdraw quickly:—that was the way of Confucius. These were all sages of antiquity, and I have not attained to do what they did. But what I wish to do is to learn to be like Confucius.'

23. Ch'au said, 'Comparing Po-i and I Yin with Confucius, are they to be placed in the same rank?' Mencius replied, 'No. Since there were living men until now, there never was another Confucius.'

24. Ch'au said, 'Then, did they have any points of agreement with him?' The reply was,—'Yes. If they had been sovereigns over a hundred li of territory, they would, all of them, have brought all the princes to attend in their court, and have obtained the throne. And none of them, in order to obtain the throne, would have committed one act of unrighteousness, or put to death one innocent person. In those things they agreed with him.'

25. Ch'au said, 'I venture to ask wherein he differed from them.' Mencius replied, 'Tsai Wo, Tsze-kung, and Yu Zo had wisdom sufficient to know the sage. Even had they been ranking themselves low, they would not have demeaned themselves to flatter their favourite.

26. 'Now, Tsai Wo said, "According to my view of our Master, he was far superior to Yao and Shun."

27. 'Tsze-kung said, "By viewing the ceremonial ordinances of a prince, we know the character of his government. By hearing his music, we know the character of his virtue. After the lapse of a hundred ages I can arrange, according to their merits, the kings of a hundred ages;—not one of them can escape me. From the birth of mankind till now, there has never been another like our Master."

28. 'Yu Zo said, "Is it only among men that it is so? There is the Ch'i-lin among quadrupeds, the Fang-hwang among birds, the T'ai mountain among mounds and ant-hills, and rivers and seas among rain-pools. Though different in degree, they are the same in kind. So the sages among mankind are also the same in kind. But they stand out from their fellows, and rise above the level, and from the birth of mankind till now, there never has been one so complete as Confucius."'

CHAP. III. 1. Mencius said, 'He who, using force, makes a pretence to benevolence is the leader of the princes. A leader of the princes requires a large kingdom. He who, using virtue, practises benevolence is the sovereign of the kingdom. To become the sovereign of the kingdom, a prince need not wait for a large kingdom. T'ang did it with only seventy li, and king Wan with only a hundred.

2. 'When one by force subdues men, they do not submit to him in heart. They submit, because their strength is not adequate to resist. When one subdues men by virtue, in their hearts' core they are pleased, and sincerely submit, as was the case with the seventy disciples in their submission to Confucius. What is said in the Book of Poetry,

"From the west, from the east,
From the south, from the north,
There was not one who thought of refusing submission,"
is an illustration of this.'

CHAP. IV. 1. Mencius said, 'Benevolence brings glory to a prince, and the opposite of it brings disgrace. For the princes of the present day to hate disgrace and yet to live complacently doing what is not benevolent, is like hating moisture and yet living in a low situation.

2. 'If a prince hates disgrace, the best course for him to pursue, is to esteem virtue and honour virtuous scholars, giving the worthiest among them places of dignity, and the able offices of trust. When throughout his kingdom there is leisure and rest from external troubles, let him, taking advantage of such a season, clearly digest the principles of his government with its legal sanctions, and then even great kingdoms will be constrained to stand in awe of him.

3. 'It is said in the Book of Poetry,
"Before the heavens were dark with rain,
I gathered the bark from the roots of the mulberry trees,
And wove it closely to form the window and door of my
    nest;
Now, I thought, ye people below,
Perhaps ye will not dare to insult me."
Confucius said, "Did not he who made this ode understand
the way of governing?" If a prince is able rightly to govern his
kingdom, who will dare to insult him?

4. 'But now the princes take advantage of the time when
throughout their kingdoms there is leisure and rest from
external troubles, to abandon themselves to pleasure and
indolent indifference;—they in fact seek for calamities for
themselves.

5. 'Calamity and happiness in all cases are men's own
seeking.

6. 'This is illustrated by what is said in the Book of
Poetry,—
Be always studious to be in harmony with the ordinances
    of God,
So you will certainly get for yourself much happiness;"
and by the passage of the Tai Chiah,—"When Heaven sends
down calamities, it is still possible to escape from them; when
we occasion the calamities ourselves, it is not possible any
longer to live."'

CHAP. V. 1. Mencius said, 'If a ruler give honour to men of
talents and virtue and employ the able, so that offices shall all
be filled by individuals of distinction and mark;—then all the
scholars of the kingdom will be pleased, and wish to stand in
his court.

2. 'If, in the market-place of his capital, he levy a ground-
rent on the shops but do not tax the goods, or enforce the
proper regulations without levying a ground-rent;—then all
the traders of the kingdom will be pleased, and wish to store
their goods in his market-place.

3. 'If, at his frontier-passes, there be an inspection of
persons, but no taxes charged on goods or other articles, then

all the travellers of the kingdom will be pleased, and wish to make their tours on his roads.

4. 'If he require that the husbandmen give their mutual aid to cultivate the public field, and exact no other taxes from them;—then all the husbandmen of the kingdom will be pleased, and wish to plough in his fields.

5. 'If from the occupiers of the shops in his market-place he do not exact the fine of the individual idler, or of the hamlet's quota of cloth, then all the people of the kingdom will be pleased, and wish to come and be his people.

6. 'If a ruler can truly practise these five things, then the people in the neighbouring kingdoms will look up to him as a parent. From the first birth of mankind till now, never has any one led children to attack their parent, and succeeded in his design. Thus, such a ruler will not have an enemy in all the kingdom, and he who has no enemy in the kingdom is the minister of Heaven. Never has there been a ruler in such a case who did not attain to the royal dignity.'

CHAP. VI. 1. Mencius said, 'All men have a mind which cannot bear to see the sufferings of others.

2. 'The ancient kings had this commiserating mind, and they, as a matter of course, had likewise a commiserating government. When with a commiserating mind was practised a commiserating government, to rule the kingdom was as easy a matter as to make anything go round in the palm.

3. 'When I say that all men have a mind which cannot bear to see the sufferings of others, my meaning may be illustrated thus:—even now-a-days, if men suddenly see a child about to fall into a well, they will without exception experience a feeling of alarm and distress. They will feel so, not as a ground on which they may gain the favour of the child's parents, nor as a ground on which they may seek the praise of their neighbours and friends, nor from a dislike to the reputation of having been unmoved by such a thing.

4. 'From this case we may perceive that the feeling of commiseration is essential to man, that the feeling of shame and dislike is essential to man, that the feeling of modesty and complaisance is essential to man, and that the feeling of

approving and disapproving is essential to man.

5. 'The feeling of commiseration is the principle of benevolence. The feeling of shame and dislike is the principle of righteousness. The feeling of modesty and complaisance is the principle of propriety. The feeling of approving and disapproving is the principle of knowledge.

6. 'Men have these four principles just as they have their four limbs. When men, having these four principles, yet say of themselves that they cannot develop them, they play the thief with themselves, and he who says of his prince that he cannot develop them plays the thief with his prince.

7. 'Since all men have these four principles in themselves, let them know to give them all their development and completion, and the issue will be like that of fire which has begun to burn, or that of a spring which has begun to find vent. Let them have their complete development, and they will suffice to love and protect all within the four seas. Let them be denied that development, and they will not suffice for a man to serve his parents with.'

CHAP. VII. 1. Mencius said, 'Is the arrow-maker less benevolent than the maker of armour of defence? And yet, the arrow-maker's only fear is lest men should not be hurt, and the armour-maker's only fear is lest men should be hurt. So it is with the priest and the coffin-maker. The choice of a profession, therefore, is a thing in which great caution is required.

2. 'Confucius said, "It is virtuous manners which constitute the excellence of a neighbourhood. If a man, in selecting a residence, do not fix on one where such prevail, how can he be wise?" Now, benevolence is the most honourable dignity conferred by Heaven, and the quiet home in which man should dwell. Since no one can hinder us from being so, if yet we are not benevolent;—this is being not wise.

3. 'From the want of benevolence and the want of wisdom will ensue the entire absence of propriety and righteousness;— he who is in such a case must be the servant of other men. To be the servant of men and yet ashamed of such servitude, is like a bowmaker's being ashamed to make bows, or an arrow-

maker's being ashamed to make arrows.

4. 'If he be ashamed of his case, his best course is to practise benevolence.

5. 'The man who would be benevolent is like the archer. The archer adjusts himself and then shoots. If he misses, he does not murmur against those who surpass himself. He simply turns round and seeks the cause of his failure in himself.'

CHAP. VIII. 1. Mencius said, 'When any one told Tsze-lu that he had a fault, he rejoiced.

2. 'When Yu heard good words, he bowed to the speaker.

3. 'The great Shun had a still greater delight in what was good. He regarded virtue as the common property of himself and others, giving up his own way to follow that of others, and delighting to learn from others to practise what was good.

4. 'From the time when he ploughed and sowed, exercised the potter's art, and was a fisherman, to the time when he became emperor, he was continually learning from others.

5. 'To take example from others to practise virtue, is to help them in the same practice. Therefore, there is no attribute of the superior man greater than his helping men to practise virtue.'

CHAP. IX. 1. Mencius said, 'Po-i would not serve a prince whom he did not approve, nor associate with a friend whom he did not esteem. He would not stand in a bad prince's court, nor speak with a bad man. To stand in a bad prince's court, or to speak with a bad man, would have been to him the same as to sit with his court robes and court cap amid mire and ashes. Pursuing the examination of his dislike to what was evil, we find that he thought it necessary, if he happened to be standing with a villager whose cap was not rightly adjusted, to leave him with a high air, as if he were going to be defiled. Therefore, although some of the princes made application to him with very proper messages, he would not receive their gifts.—He would not receive their gifts, counting it inconsistent with his purity to go to them.

2. 'Hui of Liu-hsia was not ashamed to serve an impure prince, nor did he think it low to be an inferior officer. When

advanced to employment, he did not conceal his virtue, but made it a point to carry out his principles. When neglected and left without office, he did not murmur. When straitened by poverty, he did not grieve. Accordingly, he had a saying, "You are you, and I am I. Although you stand by my side with breast and aims bare, or with your body naked, how can you defile me?" Therefore, self-possessed, he companied with men indifferently, at the same time not losing himself. When he wished to leave, if pressed to remain in office, he would remain.—He would remain in office, when pressed to do so, not counting it required by his purity to go away.'

3. Mencius said, 'Po-i was narrow-minded, and Hui of Liu-hsia was wanting in self-respect. The superior man will not manifest either narrow-mindedness, or the want of self-respect.'

BOOK II. KUNG-SUN CH'AU, PART II

CHAP. I. 1. Mencius said, 'Opportunities of time vouchsafed by Heaven are not equal to advantages of situation afforded by the Earth, and advantages of situation afforded by the Earth are not equal to the union arising from the accord of Men.

2. 'There is a city, with an inner wall of three li in circumference, and an outer wall of seven.—The enemy surround and attack it, but they are not able to take it. Now, to surround and attack it, there must have been vouchsafed to them by Heaven the opportunity of time, and in such case their not taking it is because opportunities of time vouchsafed by Heaven are not equal to advantages of situation afforded by the Earth.

3. 'There is a city, whose walls are distinguished for their height, and whose moats are distinguished for their depth, where the arms of its defenders, offensive and defensive, are distinguished for their strength and sharpness, and the stores of rice and other grain are very large. Yet it is obliged to be given up and abandoned. This is because advantages of situation afforded by the Earth are not equal to the union arising from the accord of Men.

4. 'In accordance with these principles it is said, "A people is bounded in, not by the limits of dykes and borders; a State is secured, not by the strengths of mountains and rivers; the kingdom is overawed, not by the sharpness and strength of arms." He who finds the proper course has many to assist him. He who loses the proper course has few to assist him. When this,—the being assisted by few,—reaches its extreme point, his own relations revolt from the prince. When the being assisted by many reaches its highest point, the whole kingdom becomes obedient to the prince.

5. 'When one to whom the whole kingdom is prepared to be obedient, attacks those from whom their own relations revolt, what must be the result? Therefore, the true ruler will prefer not to fight; but if he do fight, he must overcome.'

CHAP. II. 1. As Mencius was about to go to court to see the king, the king sent a person to him with this message,—'I was wishing to come and see you. But I have got a cold, and may not expose myself to the wind. In the morning I will hold my court. I do not know whether you will give me the opportunity of seeing you then.' Mencius replied, 'Unfortunately, I am unwell, and not able to go to the court.'

2. Next day, he went out to pay a visit of condolence to some one of the Tung-kwoh family, when Kung-sun Ch'au said to him, 'Yesterday, you declined going to the court on the ground of being unwell, and to-day you are going to pay a visit of condolence. May this not be regarded as improper?' 'Yesterday,' said Mencius, 'I was unwell; to-day, I am better:— why should I not pay this visit?'

3. In the mean time, the king sent a messenger to inquire about his sickness, and also a physician. Mang Chung replied to them, 'Yesterday, when the king's order came, he was feeling a little unwell, and could not go to the court. To-day he was a little better, and hastened to go to court. I do not know whether he can have reached it by this time or not.' Having said this, he sent several men to look for Mencius on the way, and say to him, 'I beg that, before you return home, you will go to the court.'

4. On this, Mencius felt himself compelled to go to Ching Ch'au's, and there stop the night. Mr. Ching said to him, 'In the family, there is the relation of father and son; abroad, there is the relation of prince and minister. These are the two great relations among men. Between father and son the ruling principle is kindness. Between prince and minister the ruling principle is respect. I have seen the respect of the king to you, Sir, but I have not seen in what way you show respect to him.' Mencius replied, 'Oh! what words are these? Among the people of Ch'i there is no one who speaks to the king about benevolence and righteousness. Are they thus silent because they do not think that benevolence and righteousness are admirable? No, but in their hearts they say, "This man is not fit to be spoken with about benevolence and righteousness." Thus they manifest a disrespect than which there can be none

greater. I do not dare to set forth before the king any but the ways of Yao and Shun. There is therefore no man of Ch'i who respects the king so much as I do.'

5. Mr. Ching said, 'Not so. That was not what I meant. In the Book of Rites it is said, "When a father calls, the answer must be without a moment's hesitation. When the prince's order calls, the carriage must not be waited for." You were certainly going to the court, but when you heard the king's order, then you did not carry your purpose out. This does seem as if it were not in accordance with that rule of propriety.'

6. Mencius answered him, 'How can you give that meaning to my conduct? The philosopher Tsang said, "The wealth of Tsin and Ch'u cannot be equalled. Let their rulers have their wealth:—I have my benevolence. Let them have their nobility:—I have my righteousness. Wherein should I be dissatisfied as inferior to them?" Now shall we say that these sentiments are not right? Seeing that the philosopher Tsang spoke them, there is in them, I apprehend, a real principle.— In the kingdom there are three things universally acknowledged to be honourable. Nobility is one of them; age is one of them; virtue is one of them. In courts, nobility holds the first place of the three; in villages, age holds the first place; and for helping one's generation and presiding over the people, the other two are not equal to virtue. How can the possession of only one of these be presumed on to despise one who possesses the other two?

7. 'Therefore a prince who is to accomplish great deeds will certainly have ministers whom he does not call to go to him. When he wishes to consult with them, he goes to them. The prince who does not honour the virtuous, and delight in their ways of doing, to this extent, is not worth having to do with.

8. 'Accordingly, there was the behaviour of T'ang to I Yin:—he first learned of him, and then employed him as his minister; and so without difficulty he became sovereign. There was the behaviour of the duke Hwan to Kwan Chung:—he first learned of him, and then employed him as his minister; and so without difficulty he became chief of all the princes.

9. 'Now throughout the kingdom, the territories of the

princes are of equal extent, and in their achievements they are on a level. Not one of them is able to exceed the others. This is from no other reason, but that they love to make ministers of those whom they teach, and do not love to make ministers of those by whom they might be taught.

10. 'So did T'ang behave to I Yin, and the duke Hwan to Kwan Chung, that they would not venture to call them to go to them. If Kwan Chung might not be called to him by his prince, how much less may he be called, who would not play the part of Kwan Chung!'

CHAP. III. 1. Ch'an Tsin asked Mencius, saying, 'Formerly, when you were in Ch'i, the king sent you a present Of 2,400 taels of fine silver, and you refused to accept it. When you were in Sung, 1,680 taels were sent to you, which you accepted; and when you were in Hsieh, 1,200 taels were sent, which you likewise accepted. If your declining to accept the gift in the first case was right, your accepting it in the latter cases was wrong. If your accepting it in the latter cases was right, your declining to do so in the first case was wrong. You must accept, Master, one of these alternatives.'

2. Mencius said, 'I did right in all the cases.

3. 'When I was in Sung, I was about to take a long journey. Travellers must be provided with what is necessary for their expenses. The prince's message was, "A present against travelling-expenses." Why should I have declined the gift?

4. 'When I was in Hsieh, I was apprehensive for my safety, and taking measures for my protection. The message was, "I have heard that you are taking measures to protect yourself, and send this to help you in procuring arms." Why should I have declined the gift?

5. 'But when I was in Ch'i, I had no occasion for money. To send a man a gift when he has no occasion for it, is to bribe him. How is it possible that a superior man should be taken with a bribe?'

CHAP. IV. 1. Mencius having gone to P'ing-lu, addressed the governor of it, saying, 'If one of your spearmen should lose his place in the ranks three times in one day, would you, Sir, put him to death or not?' 'I would not wait for three times to do so,' was the reply.

2. Mencius said, 'Well then, you, Sir, have likewise lost your place in the ranks many times. In bad calamitous years, and years of famine, the old and feeble of your people, who have been found lying in the ditches and water-channels, and the able-bodied, who have been scattered about to the four quarters, have amounted to several thousand.' The governor replied, 'That is a state of things in which it does not belong to me Chu-hsin to act.'

3. 'Here,' said Mencius, 'is a man who receives charge of the cattle and sheep of another, and undertakes to feed them for him;—of course he must search for pasture-ground and grass for them. If, after searching for those, he cannot find them, will he return his charge to the owner? or will he stand by and see them die?' 'Herein,' said the officer, 'I am guilty.'

4. Another day, Mencius had an audience of the king, and said to him, 'Of the governors of your Majesty's cities I am acquainted with five, but the only one of them who knows his faults is K'ung Chu-hsin.' He then repeated the conversation to the king, who said, 'In this matter, I am the guilty one.'

CHAP. V. 1. Mencius said to Ch'i Wa, 'There seemed to be reason in your declining the governorship of Ling-ch'iu, and requesting to be appointed chief criminal judge, because the latter office would afford you the opportunity of speaking your views. Now several months have elapsed, and have you yet found nothing of which you might speak?'

2. On this, Ch'i Wa remonstrated on some matter with the king, and, his counsel not being taken, resigned his office and went away.

3. The people of Ch'i said, 'In the course which he marked out for Ch'i Wa he did well, but we do not know as to the course which he pursues for himself.'

4. His disciple Kung-tu told him these remarks.

5. Mencius said, 'I have heard that he who is in charge of an office, when he is prevented from fulfilling its duties, ought to take his departure, and that he on whom is the responsibility of giving his opinion, when he finds his words unattended to, ought to do the same. But I am in charge of no office; on me

devolves no duty of speaking out my opinion:—may not I therefore act freely and without any constraint, either in going forward or in retiring?'

CHAP. VI. 1. Mencius, occupying the position of a high dignitary in Ch'i, went on a mission of condolence to T'ang. The king also sent Wang Hwan, the governor of Ka, as assistant-commissioner. Wang Hwan, morning and evening, waited upon Mencius, who, during all the way to T'ang and back, never spoke to him about the business of their mission.

2. Kung-sun Ch'au. said to Mencius, 'The position of a high dignitary of Ch'i is not a small one; the road from Ch'i to T'ang is not short. How was it that during all the way there and back, you never spoke to Hwan about the matters of your mission?' Mencius replied, 'There were the proper officers who attended to them. What occasion had I to speak to him about them?'

CHAP. VII. 1. Mencius went from Ch'i to Lu to bury his mother. On his return to Ch'i, he stopped at Ying, where Ch'ung Yu begged to put a question to him, and said, 'Formerly, in ignorance of my incompetency, you employed me to superintend the making of the coffin. As you were then pressed by the urgency of the business, I did not venture to put any question to you. Now, however, I wish to take the liberty to submit the matter. The wood of the coffin, it appeared to me, was too good.'

2. Mencius replied, 'Anciently, there was no rule for the size of either the inner or the outer coffin. In middle antiquity, the inner coffin was made seven inches thick, and the outer one the same. This was done by all, from the sovereign to the common people, and not simply for the beauty of the appearance, but because they thus satisfied the natural feelings of their hearts.

3. 'If prevented by statutory regulations from making their coffins in this way, men cannot have the feeling of pleasure. If they have not the money to make them in this way, they cannot have the feeling of pleasure. When they were not prevented, and had the money, the ancients all used this style. Why should I alone not do so?

4. 'And moreover, is there no satisfaction to the natural

feelings of a man, in preventing the earth from getting near to the bodies of his dead?

5. 'I have heard that the superior man will not for all the world be niggardly to his parents.'

CHAP. VIII. 1. Shan T'ung, on his own impulse, asked Mencius, saying, 'May Yen be smitten?' Mencius replied, 'It may. Tsze-k'wai had no right to give Yen to another man, and Tsze-chih had no right to receive Yen from Tsze-k'wai. Suppose there were an officer here, with whom you, Sir, were pleased, and that, without informing the king, you were privately to give to him your salary and rank; and suppose that this officer, also without the king's orders, were privately to receive them from you—would such a transaction be allowable? And where is the difference between the case of Yen and this?'

2. The people of Ch'i smote Yen. Some one asked Mencius, saying, 'Is it really the case that you advised Ch'i to smite Yen?' He replied, 'No. Shan T'ung asked me whether Yen might be smitten, and I answered him, "It may." They accordingly went and smote it. If he had asked me—"Who may smite it?" I would have answered him, "He who is the minister of Heaven may smite it." Suppose the case of a murderer, and that one asks me—"May this man be put to death?" I will answer him—"He may." If he ask me—"Who may put him to death?" I will answer him, "The chief criminal judge may put him to death." But now with one Yen to smite another Yen:—how should I have advised this?'

CHAP. IX. 1. The people of Yen having rebelled, the king of Ch'i said, 'I feel very much ashamed when I think of Mencius.'

2. Ch'an Chia said to him, 'Let not your Majesty be grieved. Whether does your Majesty consider yourself or Chau-kung the more benevolent and wise?' The king replied, 'Oh! what words are those?' 'The duke of Chau,' said Chia, 'appointed Kwan-shu to oversee the heir of Yin, but Kwan-shu with the power of the Yin State rebelled. If knowing that this would happen he appointed Kwan-shu, he was deficient in benevolence. If he appointed him, not knowing that it would

happen, he was deficient in knowledge. If the duke of Chau was not completely benevolent and wise, how much less can your Majesty be expected to be so! I beg to go and see Mencius, and relieve your Majesty from that feeling.'

3. Ch'an Chia accordingly saw Mencius, and asked him, saying, 'What kind of man was the duke of Chau?' 'An ancient sage,' was the reply. 'Is it the fact, that he appointed Kwan-shu to oversee the heir of Yin, and that Kwan-shu with the State of Yin rebelled?' 'It is.' 'Did the duke of Chau. know that he would rebel, and purposely appoint him to that office?' Mencius said, 'He did not know.' 'Then, though a sage, he still fell into error?' 'The duke of Chau,' answered Mencius, 'was the younger brother. Kwan-shu was his elder brother. Was not the error of Chau-kung in accordance with what is right?

4. 'Moreover, when the superior men of old had errors, they reformed them. The superior men of the present time, when they have errors, persist in them. The errors of the superior men of old were like eclipses of the sun and moon. All the people witnessed them, and when they had reformed them, all the people looked up to them with their former admiration. But do the superior men of the present day only persist in their errors? They go on to apologize for them likewise.'

CHAP. X. 1. Mencius gave up his office, and made arrangements for returning to his native State.

2. The king came to visit him, and said, 'Formerly, I wished to see you, but in vain. Then, I got the opportunity of being by your side, and all my court joyed exceedingly along with me. Now again you abandon me, and are returning home. I do not know if hereafter I may expect to have another opportunity of seeing you.' Mencius replied, 'I dare not request permission to visit you at any particular time, but, indeed, it is what I desire.'

3. Another day, the king said to the officer Shih, 'I wish to give Mencius a house, somewhere in the middle of the kingdom, and to support his disciples with an allowance of 10,000 chung, that all the officers and the people may have such an example to reverence and imitate. Had you not better tell him this for me?'

4. Shih took advantage to convey this message by means of

the disciple Ch'an, who reported his words to Mencius.

5. Mencius said, 'Yes; but how should the officer Shih know that the thing could not be? Suppose that I wanted to be rich, having formerly declined 100,000 chung, would my now accepting 10,000 be the conduct of one desiring riches?

6. 'Chi-sun said, "A strange man was Tsze-shu I. He pushed himself into the service of government. His prince declining to employ him, he had to retire indeed, but he again schemed that his son or younger brother should be made a high officer. Who indeed is there of men but wishes for riches and honour? But he only, among the seekers of these, tried to monopolize the conspicuous mound.

7. "'Of old time, the market-dealers exchanged the articles which they had for others which they had not, and simply had certain officers to keep order among them. It happened that there was a mean fellow, who made it a point to look out for a conspicuous mound, and get up upon it. Thence he looked right and left, to catch in his net the whole gain of the market. The people all thought his conduct mean, and therefore they proceeded to lay a tax upon his wares. The taxing of traders took its rise from this mean fellow.'"

CHAP. XI. 1. Mencius, having taken his leave of Ch'i, was passing the night in Chau.

2. A person who wished to detain him on behalf of the king, came and sat down, and began to speak to him. Mencius gave him no answer, but leant upon his stool and slept.

3. The visitor was displeased, and said, 'I passed the night in careful vigil, before I would venture to speak to you, and you, Master, sleep and do not listen to me. Allow me to request that I may not again presume to see you.' Mencius replied, 'Sit down, and I will explain the case clearly to you. Formerly, if the duke Mu had not kept a person by the side of Tsze-sze, he could not have induced Tsze-sze to remain with him. If Hsieh Liu and Shan Hsiang had not had a remembrancer by the side of the duke Mu, he would not have been able to make them feel at home and remain with him.

4. 'You anxiously form plans with reference to me, but you do not treat me as Tsze-sze was treated. Is it you, Sir, who cut

me? Or is it I who cut you?

CHAP. XII. 1. When Mencius had left Ch'i, Yin Shih spoke about him to others, saying, 'If he did not know that the king could not be made a T'ang or a Wu, that showed his want of intelligence. If he knew that he could not be made such, and came notwithstanding, that shows he was seeking his own benefit. He came a thousand li to wait on the king; because he did not find in him a ruler to suit him, he took his leave, but how dilatory and lingering was his departure, stopping three nights before he quitted Chau! I am dissatisfied on account of this.'

2. The disciple Kao informed Mencius of these remarks.

3. Mencius said, 'How should Yin Shih know me! When I came a thousand li to wait on the king, it was what I desired to do. When I went away because I did not find in him a ruler to suit me, was that what I desired to do? I felt myself constrained to do it.

4. 'When I stopped three nights before I quitted Chau, in my own mind I still considered my departure speedy. I was hoping that the king might change. If the king had changed, he would certainly have recalled me.

5. 'When I quitted Chau, and the king had not sent after me, then, and not till then, was my mind resolutely bent on returning to Tsau. But, notwithstanding that, how can it be said that I give up the king? The king, after all, is one who may be made to do what is good. If he were to use me, would it be for the happiness of the people of Ch'i only? It would be for the happiness of the people of the whole kingdom. I am hoping that the king will change. I am daily hoping for this.

6. 'Am I like one of your little-minded people? They will remonstrate with their prince, and on their remonstrance not being accepted, they get angry; and, with their passion displayed in their countenance, they take their leave, and travel with all their strength for a whole day, before they will stop for the night.'

7. When Yin Shih heard this explanation, he said, 'I am indeed a small man.'

CHAP. XIII. 1. When Mencius left Ch'i, Ch'ung Yu

questioned him upon the way, saying, 'Master, you look like one who carries an air of dissatisfaction in his countenance. But formerly I heard you say—"The superior man does not murmur against Heaven, nor grudge against men."'

2. Mencius said, 'That was one time, and this is another.

3. 'It is a rule that a true royal sovereign should arise in the course of five hundred years, and that during that time there should be men illustrious in their generation.

4. 'From the commencement of the Chau dynasty till now, more than seven hundred years have elapsed. Judging numerically, the date is past. Examining the character of the present time, we might expect the rise of such individuals in it.

5. 'But Heaven does not yet wish that the kingdom should enjoy tranquillity and good order. If it wished this, who is there besides me to bring it about? How should I be otherwise than dissatisfied?'

CHAP. XIV. 1. When Mencius left Ch'i, he dwelt in Hsiu. There Kung-sun Ch'au asked him, saying, 'Was it the way of the ancients to hold office without receiving salary?'

2. Mencius replied, 'No; when I first saw the king in Ch'ung, it was my intention, on retiring from the interview, to go away. Because I did not wish to change this intention, I declined to receive any salary.

3. 'Immediately after, there came orders for the collection of troops, when it would have been improper for me to beg permission to leave. But to remain so long in Ch'i was not my purpose.'

BOOK III. T'ANG WAN KUNG, PART I

CHAP. I. 1. When the prince, afterwards duke Wan of T'ang, had to go to Ch'u, he went by way of Sung, and visited Mencius.

2. Mencius discoursed to him how the nature of man is good, and when speaking, always made laudatory reference to Yao and Shun.

3. When the prince was returning from Ch'u, he again visited Mencius. Mencius said to him, 'Prince, do you doubt my words? The path is one, and only one.

4. 'Ch'ang Chi'en said to duke King of Ch'i, "They were men. I am a man. Why should I stand in awe of them?" Yen Yuan said, "What kind of man was Shun? What kind of man am I? He who exerts himself will also become such as he was." Kung-Ming I said, "King Wan is my teacher. How should the duke of Chau deceive me by those words?"

5. 'Now, T'ang, taking its length with its breadth, will amount, I suppose, to fifty li. It is small, but still sufficient to make a good State. It is said in the Book of History, "If medicine do not raise a commotion in the patient, his disease will not be cured by it."'

CHAP. II. 1. When the duke Ting of T'ang died, the prince said to Yen Yu, 'Formerly, Mencius spoke with me in Sung, and in my mind I have never forgotten his words. Now, alas! this great duty to my father devolves upon me; I wish to send you to ask the advice of Mencius, and then to proceed to its various services'

2. Zan Yu accordingly proceeded to Tsau, and consulted Mencius. Mencius said, 'Is this not good? In discharging the funeral duties to parents, men indeed feel constrained to do their utmost. The philosopher Tsang said, "When parents are alive, they should be served according to propriety; when they are dead, they should be buried according to propriety; and they should be sacrificed to according to propriety:—this may be called filial piety." The ceremonies to be observed by the princes I have not learned, but I have heard these points:—

that the three years' mourning, the garment of coarse cloth with its lower edge even, and the eating of congee, were equally prescribed by the three dynasties, and binding on all, from the sovereign to the mass of the people.'

3. Zan Yu reported the execution of his commission, and the prince determined that the three years' mourning should be observed. His aged relatives, and the body of the officers, did not wish that it should be so, and said, 'The former princes of Lu, that kingdom which we honour, have, none of them, observed this practice, neither have any of our own former princes observed it. For you to act contrary to their example is not proper. Moreover, the History says,—"In the observances of mourning and sacrifice, ancestors are to be followed," meaning that they received those things from a proper source to hand them down.'

4. The prince said again to Zan Yu, 'Hitherto, I have not given myself to the pursuit of learning, but have found my pleasure in horsemanship and sword-exercise, and now I don't come up to the wishes of my aged relatives and the officers. I am afraid I may not be able to discharge my duty in the great business that I have entered on; do you again consult Mencius for me.' On this, Zan Yu went again to Tsau, and consulted Mencius. Mencius said, 'It is so, but he may not seek a remedy in others, but only in himself. Confucius said, "When a prince dies, his successor entrusts the administration to the prime minister. He sips the congee. His face is of a deep black. He approaches the place of mourning, and weeps. Of all the officers and inferior ministers there is not one who will presume not to join in the lamentation, he setting them this example. What the superior loves, his inferiors will be found to love exceedingly. The relation between superiors and inferiors is like that between the wind and grass. The grass must bend when the wind blows upon it." The business depends on the prince.'

5. Zan Yu returned with this answer to his commission, and the prince said, 'It is so. The matter does indeed depend on me.' So for five months he dwelt in the shed, without issuing an order or a caution. All the officers and his relatives said, 'He

may be said to understand the ceremonies.' When the time of interment arrived, they came from all quarters of the State to witness it. Those who had come from other States to condole with him, were greatly pleased with the deep dejection of his countenance and the mournfulness of his wailing and weeping.

CHAP. III. 1. The duke Wan of T'ang asked Mencius about the proper way of governing a kingdom.

2. Mencius said, 'The business of the people may not be remissly attended to. It is said in the Book of Poetry,

"In the day-light go and gather the grass,
And at night twist your ropes;
Then get up quickly on the roofs;—
Soon must we begin sowing again the grain."

3. 'The way of the people is this:—If they have a certain livelihood, they will have a fixed heart; if they have not a certain livelihood, they have not a fixed heart. If they have not a fixed heart, there is nothing which they will not do in the way of self-abandonment, of moral deflection, of depravity, and of wild license. When they have thus been involved in crime, to follow them up and punish them:—this is to entrap the people. How can such a thing as entrapping the people be done under the rule of a benevolent man?

4. 'Therefore, a ruler who is endowed with talents and virtue will be gravely complaisant and economical, showing a respectful politeness to his ministers, and taking from the people only in accordance with regulated limits.

5. 'Yang Hu said, "He who seeks to be rich will not be benevolent. He who wishes to be benevolent will not be rich."

6. 'The sovereign of the Hsia dynasty enacted the fifty mau allotment, and the payment of a tax. The founder of the Yin enacted the seventy mau allotment, and the system of mutual aid. The founder of the Chau enacted the hundred mau allotment, and the share system. In reality, what was paid in all these was a tithe. The share system means mutual division. The aid system means mutual dependence.

7. 'Lung said, "For regulating the lands, there is no better system than that of mutual aid, and none which is not better than that of taxing. By the tax system, the regular amount was

fixed by taking the average of several years. In good years, when the grain lies about in abundance, much might be taken without its being oppressive, and the actual exaction would be small. But in bad years, the produce being not sufficient to repay the manuring of the fields, this system still requires the taking of the full amount. When the parent of the people causes the people to wear looks of distress, and, after the whole year's toil, yet not to be able to nourish their parents, so that they proceed to borrowing to increase their means, till the old people and children are found lying in the ditches and water-channels:—where, in such a case, is his parental relation to the people?"

8. 'As to the system of hereditary salaries, that is already observed in T'ang.

9. 'It is said in the Book of Poetry,
"May the rain come down on our public field,
And then upon our private fields!"
It is only in the system of mutual aid that there is a public field, and from this passage we perceive that even in the Chau dynasty this system has been recognised.

10. 'Establish hsiang, hsu, hsio, and hsiao,—all those educational institutions,—for the instruction of the people. The name hsiang indicates nourishing as its object; hsiao, indicates teaching; and hsu indicates archery. By the Hsia dynasty the name hsiao was used; by the Yin, that of hsu; and by the Chau, that of hsiang. As to the hsio, they belonged to the three dynasties, and by that name. The object of them all is to illustrate the human relations. When those are thus illustrated by superiors, kindly feeling will prevail among the inferior people below.

11. 'Should a real sovereign arise, he will certainly come and take an example from you; and thus you will be the teacher of the true sovereign.

12. 'It is said in the Book of Poetry,
"Although Chau was an old country,
It received a new destiny."
That is said with reference to king Wan. Do you practise those things with vigour, and you also will by them make new your

184

kingdom.'

13. The duke afterwards sent Pi Chan to consult Mencius about the nine-squares system of dividing the land. Mencius said to him, 'Since your prince, wishing to put in practice a benevolent government, has made choice of you and put you into this employment, you must exert yourself to the utmost. Now, the first thing towards a benevolent government must be to lay down the boundaries. If the boundaries be not defined correctly, the division of the land into squares will not be equal, and the produce available for salaries will not be evenly distributed. On this account, oppressive rulers and impure ministers are sure to neglect this defining of the boundaries. When the boundaries have been defined correctly, the division of the fields and the regulation of allowances may be determined by you, sitting at your ease.

14. 'Although the territory of T'ang is narrow and small, yet there must be in it men of a superior grade, and there must be in it country-men. If there were not men of a superior grade, there would be none to rule the country-men. If there were not country-men, there would be none to support the men of superior grade.

15. 'I would ask you, in the remoter districts, observing the nine-squares division, to reserve one division to be cultivated on the system of mutual aid, and in the more central parts of the kingdom, to make the people pay for themselves a tenth part of their produce.

16. 'From the highest officers down to the lowest, each one must have his holy field, consisting of fifty mau.

17. 'Let the supernumerary males have their twenty-five mau.

18. 'On occasions of death, or removal from one dwelling to another, there will be no quitting the district. In the fields of a district, those who belong to the same nine squares render all friendly offices to one another in their going out and coming in, aid one another in keeping watch and ward, and sustain one another in sickness. Thus the people are brought to live in affection and harmony.

19. 'A square li covers nine squares of land, which nine

185

squares contain nine hundred mau. The central square is the public field, and eight families, each having its private hundred mau, cultivate in common the public field. And not till the public work is finished, may they presume to attend to their private affairs. This is the way by which the country-men are distinguished from those of a superior grade.

20. 'Those are the great outlines of the system. Happily to modify and adapt it depends on the prince and you.'

CHAP. IV. 1. There came from Ch'u to T'ang one Hsu Hsing, who gave out that he acted according to the words of Shan-nang. Coming right to his gate, he addressed the duke Wan, saying, 'A man of a distant region, I have heard that you, Prince, are practising a benevolent government, and I wish to receive a site for a house, and to become one of your people.' The duke Wan gave him a dwelling-place. His disciples, amounting to several tens, all wore clothes of haircloth, and made sandals of hemp and wove mats for a living.

2. At the same time, Ch'an Hsiang, a disciple of Ch'an Liang, and his younger brother, Hsin, with their plough-handles and shares on their backs, came from Sung to T'ang, saying, 'We have heard that you, Prince, are putting into practice the government of the ancient sages, showing that you are likewise a sage. We wish to become the subjects of a sage.'

3. When Ch'an Hsiang saw Hsu Hsing, he was greatly pleased with him, and, abandoning entirely whatever he had learned, became his disciple. Having an interview with Mencius, he related to him with approbation the words of Hsu Hsing to the following effect:—'The prince of T'ang is indeed a worthy prince. He has not yet heard, however, the real doctrines of antiquity. Now, wise and able princes should cultivate the ground equally and along with their people, and eat the fruit of their labour. They should prepare their own meals, morning and evening, while at the same time they carry on their government. But now, the prince of T'ang has his granaries, treasuries, and arsenals, which is an oppressing of the people to nourish himself. How can he be deemed a real worthy prince?'

4. Mencius said, 'I suppose that Hsu Hsing sows grain and

eats the produce. Is it not so?' 'It is so,' was the answer. 'I suppose also he weaves cloth, and wears his own manufacture. Is it not so?' 'No. Hsu wears clothes of haircloth.' 'Does he wear a cap?' 'He wears a cap.' 'What kind of cap?' 'A plain cap.' 'Is it woven by himself?' 'No. He gets it in exchange for grain.' 'Why does Hsu not weave it himself?' 'That would injure his husbandry.' 'Does Hsu cook his food in boilers and earthenware pans, and does he plough with an iron share?' 'Yes.' 'Does he make those articles himself?' 'No. He gets them in exchange for grain.'

5. Mencius then said, 'The getting those various articles in exchange for grain, is not oppressive to the potter and the founder, and the potter and the founder in their turn, in exchanging their various articles for grain, are not oppressive to the husbandman. How should such a thing be supposed? And moreover, why does not Hsu act the potter and founder, supplying himself with the articles which he uses solely from his own establishment? Why does he go confusedly dealing and exchanging with the handicraftsmen? Why does he not spare himself so much trouble?' Ch'an Hsiang replied, 'The business of the handicraftsman can by no means be carried on along with the business of husbandry.'

6. Mencius resumed, 'Then, is it the government of the kingdom which alone can be carried on along with the practice of husbandry? Great men have their proper business, and little men have their proper business. Moreover, in the case of any single individual, whatever articles he can require are ready to his hand, being produced by the various handicraftsmen:—if he must first make them for his own use, this way of doing would keep all the people running about upon the roads. Hence, there is the saying, "Some labour with their minds, and some labour with their strength. Those who labour with their minds govern others; those who labour with their strength are governed by others. Those who are governed by others support them; those who govern others are supported by them." This is a principle universally recognised.

7. 'In the time of Yao, when the world had not yet been perfectly reduced to order, the vast waters, flowing out of their

channels, made a universal inundation. Vegetation was luxuriant, and birds and beasts swarmed. The various kinds of grain could not be grown. The birds and beasts pressed upon men. The paths marked by the feet of beasts and prints of birds crossed one another throughout the Middle Kingdom. To Yao alone this caused anxious sorrow. He raised Shun to office, and measures to regulate the disorder were set forth. Shun committed to Yi the direction of the fire to be employed, and Yi set fire to, and consumed, the forests and vegetation on the mountains and in the marshes, so that the birds and beasts fled away to hide themselves. Yu separated the nine streams, cleared the courses of the Tsi and T'a, and led them all to the sea. He opened a vent also for the Zu and Han, and regulated the course of the Hwa'i and Sze, so that they all flowed into the Chiang. When this was done, it became possible for the people of the Middle Kingdom to cultivate the ground and get food for themselves. During that time, Yu was eight years away from his home, and though he thrice passed the door of it, he did not enter. Although he had wished to cultivate the ground, could he have done so?'

8. 'The Minister of Agriculture taught the people to sow and reap, cultivating the five kinds of grain. When the five kinds of grain were brought to maturity, the people all obtained a subsistence. But men possess a moral nature; and if they are well fed, warmly clad, and comfortably lodged, without being taught at the same time, they become almost like the beasts. This was a subject of anxious solicitude to the sage Shun, and he appointed Hsieh to be the Minister of Instruction, to teach the relations of humanity:—how, between father and son, there should be affection; between sovereign and minister, righteousness; between husband and wife, attention to their separate functions; between old and young, a proper order; and between friends, fidelity. The high meritorious sovereign said to him, "Encourage them; lead them on; rectify them; straighten them; help them; give them wings:—thus causing them to become possessors of themselves. Then follow this up by stimulating them, and conferring benefits on them." When the sages were exercising

their solicitude for the people in this way, had they leisure to cultivate the ground?

9. 'What Yao felt giving him anxiety was the not getting Shun. What Shun felt giving him anxiety was the not getting Yu and Kao Yao. But he whose anxiety is about his hundred mau not being properly cultivated, is a mere husbandman.

10. 'The imparting by a man to others of his wealth, is called "kindness." The teaching others what is good, is called "the exercise of fidelity." The finding a man who shall benefit the kingdom, is called "benevolence." Hence to give the throne to another man would be easy; to find a man who shall benefit the kingdom is difficult.

11. 'Confucius said, "Great indeed was Yao as a sovereign. It is only Heaven that is great, and only Yao corresponded to it. How vast was his virtue! The people could find no name for it. Princely indeed was Shun! How majestic was he, having possession of the kingdom, and yet seeming as if it were nothing to him!" In their governing the kingdom, were there no subjects on which Yao and Shun employed their minds? There were subjects, only they did not employ their minds on the cultivation of the ground.

12. 'I have heard of men using the doctrines of our great land to change barbarians, but I have never yet heard of any being changed by barbarians. Ch'an Liang was a native of Ch'u. Pleased with the doctrines of Chau-kung and Chung-ni, he came northwards to the Middle Kingdom and studied them. Among the scholars of the northern regions, there was perhaps no one who excelled him. He was what you call a scholar of high and distinguished qualities. You and your brother followed him some tens of years, and when your master died, you forthwith turned away from him.

13. 'Formerly, when Confucius died, after three years had elapsed, his disciples collected their baggage, and prepared to return to their several homes. But on entering to take their leave of Tsze-kung, as they looked towards one another, they wailed, till they all lost their voices. After this they returned to their homes, but Tsze-kung went back, and built a house for himself on the altar-ground, where he lived alone other three

189

years, before he returned home. On another occasion, Tsze-hsia, Tsze-chang, and Tsze-yu, thinking that Yu Zo resembled the sage, wished to render to him the same observances which they had rendered to Confucius. They tried to force the disciple Tsang to join with them, but he said, "This may not be done. What has been washed in the waters of the Chiang and Han, and bleached in the autumn sun:—how glistening is it! Nothing can be added to it."

14. 'Now here is this shrike-tongued barbarian of the south, whose doctrines are not those of the ancient kings. You turn away from your master and become his disciple. Your conduct is different indeed from that of the philosopher Tsang.

15. 'I have heard of birds leaving dark valleys to remove to lofty trees, but I have not heard of their descending from lofty trees to enter into dark valleys.

16. 'In the Praise-songs of Lu it is said,
"He smote the barbarians of the west and the north,
He punished Ching and Shu."
Thus Chau-kung would be sure to smite them, and you become their disciple again; it appears that your change is not good.'

17. Ch'an Hsiang said, 'If Hsu's doctrines were followed, then there would not be two prices in the market, nor any deceit in the kingdom. If a boy of five cubits were sent to the market, no one would impose on him; linen and silk of the same length would be of the same price. So it would be with bundles of hemp and silk, being of the same weight; with the different kinds of grain, being the same in quantity; and with shoes which were of the same size.'

18. Mencius replied, 'It is the nature of things to be of unequal quality. Some are twice, some five times, some ten times, some a hundred times, some a thousand times, some ten thousand times as valuable as others. If you reduce them all to the same standard, that must throw the kingdom into confusion. If large shoes and small shoes were of the same price, who would make them? For people to follow the doctrines of Hsu, would be for them to lead one another on to practise deceit. How can they avail for the government of a

State?'

CHAP. V. 1. The Mohist, I Chih, sought, through Hsu Pi, to see Mencius. Mencius said, 'I indeed wish to see him, but at present I am still unwell. When I am better, I will myself go and see him. He need not come here again.'

2. Next day, I Chih again sought to see Mencius. Mencius said, 'To-day I am able to see him. But if I do not correct his errors, the true principles will not be fully evident. Let me first correct him. I have heard that this I is a Mohist. Now Mo considers that in the regulation of funeral matters a spare simplicity should be the rule. I thinks with Mo's doctrines to change the customs of the kingdom;—how does he regard them as if they were wrong, and not honour them? Notwithstanding his views, I buried his parents in a sumptuous manner, and so he served them in the way which his doctrines discountenance.'

3. The disciple Hsu informed I of these remarks. I said, 'Even according to the principles of the learned, we find that the ancients acted towards the people "as if they were watching over an infant." What does this expression mean? To me it sounds that we are to love all without difference of degree; but the manifestation of love must begin with our parents.' Hsu reported this reply to Mencius, who said, 'Now, does I really think that a man's affection for the child of his brother is merely like his affection for the infant of a neighbour? What is to be approved in that expression is simply this:—that if an infant crawling about is likely to fall into a well, it is no crime in the infant. Moreover, Heaven gives birth to creatures in such a way that they have one root, and I makes them to have two roots. This is the cause of his error.

4. 'And, in the most ancient times, there were some who did not inter their parents. When their parents died, they took them up and threw them into some water-channel. Afterwards, when passing by them, they saw foxes and wild-cats devouring them, and flies and gnats biting at them. The perspiration started out upon their foreheads, and they looked away, unable to bear the sight. It was not on account of other people that this perspiration flowed. The emotions of their

hearts affected their faces and eyes, and instantly they went home, and came back with baskets and spades and covered the bodies. If the covering them thus was indeed right, you may see that the filial son and virtuous man, in interring in a handsome manner their parents, act according to a proper rule.'

5. The disciple Hsu informed I of what Mencius had said. I was thoughtful for a short time, and then said, 'He has instructed me.'

BOOK III. T'ANG WAN KUNG, PART II

CHAP. I. 1. Ch'an Tai said to Mencius, 'In not going to wait upon any of the princes, you seem to me to be standing on a small point. If now you were once to wait upon them, the result might be so great that you would make one of them sovereign, or, if smaller, that you would make one of them chief of all the other princes. Moreover, the History says, "By bending only one cubit, you make eight cubits straight." It appears to me like a thing which might be done.'

2. Mencius said, 'Formerly, the duke Ching of Ch'i, once when he was hunting, called his forester to him by a flag. The forester would not come, and the duke was going to kill him. With reference to this incident, Confucius said, "The determined officer never forgets that his end may be in a ditch or a stream; the brave officer never forgets that he may lose his head." What was it in the forester that Confucius thus approved? He approved his not going to the duke, when summoned by the article which was not appropriate to him. If one go to see the princes without waiting to be invited, what can be thought of him?

3. 'Moreover, that sentence, "By bending only one cubit, you make eight cubits straight," is spoken with reference to the gain that may be got. If gain be the object, then, if it can be got by bending eight cubits to make one cubit straight, may we likewise do that?

4. 'Formerly, the officer Chao Chien made Wang Liang act as charioteer for his favourite Hsi, when, in the course of a whole day, they did not get a single bird. The favourite Hsi reported this result, saying, "He is the poorest charioteer in the world." Some one told this to Wang Liang, who said, "I beg leave to try again." By dint of pressing, this was accorded to him, when in one morning they got ten birds. The favourite, reporting this result, said, "He is the best charioteer in the world." Chien said, "I will make him always drive your chariot for you." When he told Wang Liang so, however, Liang refused, saying, "I drove for him, strictly observing the proper

193

rules for driving, and in the whole day he did not get one bird. I drove for him so as deceitfully to intercept the birds, and in one morning he got ten. It is said in the Book of Poetry,

'There is no failure in the management of their horses;
The arrows are discharged surely, like the blows of an axe.'

I am not accustomed to drive for a mean man. I beg leave to decline the office."

5. 'Thus this charioteer even was ashamed to bend improperly to the will of such an archer. Though, by bending to it, they would have caught birds and animals sufficient to form a hill, he would not do so. If I were to bend my principles and follow those princes, of what kind would my conduct be? And you are wrong. Never has a man who has bent himself been able to make others straight.'

CHAP. II. 1. Ching Ch'un said to Mencius, 'Are not Kung-sun Yen and Chang I really great men? Let them once be angry, and all the princes are afraid. Let them live quietly, and the flames of trouble are extinguished throughout the kingdom.'

2. Mencius said, 'How can such men be great men? Have you not read the Ritual Usages?—"At the capping of a young man, his father admonishes him. At the marrying away of a young woman, her mother admonishes her, accompanying her to the door on her leaving, and cautioning her with these words, 'You are going to your home. You must be respectful; you must be careful. Do not disobey your husband.'" Thus, to look upon compliance as their correct course is the rule for women.

3. 'To dwell in the wide house of the world, to stand in the correct seat of the world, and to walk in the great path of the world; when he obtains his desire for office, to practise his principles for the good of the people; and when that desire is disappointed, to practise them alone; to be above the power of riches and honours to make dissipated, of poverty and mean condition to make swerve from principle, and of power and force to make bend:—these characteristics constitute the great man.'

CHAP. III. 1. Chau Hsiao asked Mencius, saying, 'Did superior men of old time take office?' Mencius replied, 'They did. The Record says, "If Confucius was three months without being employed by some ruler, he looked anxious and unhappy. When he passed from the boundary of a State, he was sure to carry with him his proper gift of introduction." Kung-ming I said, "Among the ancients, if an officer was three months unemployed by a ruler, he was condoled with.'"

2. Hsiao said, 'Did not this condoling, on being three months unemployed by a ruler, show a too great urgency?'

3. Mencius answered, 'The loss of his place to an officer is like the loss of his State to a prince. It is said in the Book of Rites, "A prince ploughs himself, and is assisted by the people, to supply the millet for sacrifice. His wife keeps silkworms, and unwinds their cocoons, to make the garments for sacrifice." If the victims be not perfect, the millet not pure, and the dress not complete, he does not presume to sacrifice. "And the scholar who, out of office, has no holy field, in the same way, does not sacrifice. The victims for slaughter, the vessels, and the garments, not being all complete, he does not presume to sacrifice, and then neither may he dare to feel happy." Is there not here sufficient ground also for condolence?'

4. Hsiao again asked, 'What was the meaning of Confucius's always carrying his proper gift of introduction with him, when he passed over the boundaries of the State where he had been?'

5. 'An officer's being in office,' was the reply, 'is like the ploughing of a husbandman. Does a husbandman part with his plough, because he goes from one State to another?'

6. Hsiao pursued, 'The kingdom of Tsin is one, as well as others, of official employments, but I have not heard of anyone being thus earnest about being in office. If there should be this urge why does a superior man make any difficulty about taking it?' Mencius answered, 'When a son is born, what is desired for him is that he may have a wife; when a daughter is born, what is desired for her is that she may have a husband. This feeling of the parents is possessed by all men. If the young people, without waiting for the orders of their parents, and the arrangements of the go-betweens, shall bore holes to steal a sight of each other, or get over the wall to be with each other, then their parents and all other people will

195

despise them. The ancients did indeed always desire to be in office, but they also hated being so by any improper way. To seek office by an improper way is of a class with young people's boring holes.'

CHAP. IV. 1. P'ang Kang asked Mencius, saying, 'Is it not an extravagant procedure to go from one prince to another and live upon them, followed by several tens of carriages, and attended by several hundred men?' Mencius replied, 'If there be not a proper ground for taking it, a single bamboo-cup of rice may not be received from a man. If there be such a proper ground, then Shun's receiving the kingdom from Yao is not to be considered excessive. Do you think it was excessive?'

2. Kang said, 'No. But for a scholar performing no service to receive his support notwithstanding is improper.'

3. Mencius answered, 'If you do not have an intercommunication of the productions of labour, and an interchange of men's services, so that one from his overplus may supply the deficiency of another, then husbandmen will have a superfluity of grain, and women will have a superfluity of cloth. If you have such an interchange, carpenters and carriage-wrights may all get their food from you. Here now is a man, who, at home, is filial, and abroad, respectful to his elders; who watches over the principles of the ancient kings, awaiting the rise of future learners:—and yet you will refuse to support him. How is it that you give honour to the carpenter and carriage-wright, and slight him who practises benevolence and righteousness?'

4. P'ang Kang said, 'The aim of the carpenter and carriage-wright is by their trades to seek for a living. Is it also the aim of the superior man in his practice of principles thereby to seek for a living?' 'What have you to do,' returned Mencius, 'with his purpose? He is of service to you. He deserves to be supported, and should be supported. And let me ask,—Do you remunerate a man's intention, or do you remunerate his service.' To this Kang replied, 'I remunerate his intention.'

5. Mencius said, 'There is a man here, who breaks your tiles, and draws unsightly figures on your walls;—his purpose may be thereby to seek for his living, but will you indeed

remunerate him?' 'No,' said Kang; and Mencius then concluded, 'That being the case, it is not the purpose which you remunerate, but the work done.'

CHAP. V. 1. Wan Chang asked Mencius, saying, 'Sung is a small State. Its ruler is now setting about to practise the true royal government, and Ch'i and Ch'u hate and attack him. What in this case is to be done?'

2. Mencius replied, 'When T'ang dwelt in Po, he adjoined to the State of Ko, the chief of which was living in a dissolute state and neglecting his proper sacrifices. T'ang sent messengers to inquire why he did not sacrifice. He replied, "I have no means of supplying the necessary victims." On this, T'ang caused oxen and sheep to be sent to him, but he ate them, and still continued not to sacrifice. T'ang again sent messengers to ask him the same question as before, when he replied, "I have no means of obtaining the necessary millet." On this, T'ang sent the mass of the people of Po to go and till the ground for him, while the old and feeble carried their food to them. The chief of Ko led his people to intercept those who were thus charged with wine, cooked rice, millet, and paddy, and took their stores from them, while they killed those who refused to give them up. There was a boy who had some millet and flesh for the labourers, who was thus slain and robbed. What is said in the Book of History, "The chief of Ko behaved as an enemy to the provision-carriers," has reference to this.

3. 'Because of his murder of this boy, T'ang proceeded to punish him. All within the four seas said, "It is not because he desires the riches of the kingdom, but to avenge a common man and woman."

4. 'When T'ang began his work of executing justice, he commenced with Ko, and though he made eleven punitive expeditions, he had not an enemy in the kingdom. When he pursued his work in the east, the rude tribes in the west murmured. So did those on the north, when he was engaged in the south. Their cry was—"Why does he make us last." Thus, the people's longing for him was like their longing for rain in a time of great drought. The frequenters of the markets stopped not. Those engaged in weeding in the fields made no

change in their operations. While he punished their rulers, he consoled the people. His progress was like the falling of opportune rain, and the people were delighted. It is said in the Book of History, "We have waited for our prince. When our prince comes, we may escape from the punishments under which we suffer."

5. 'There being some who would not become the subjects of Chau, king Wu proceeded to punish them on the east. He gave tranquillity to their people, who welcomed him with baskets full of their black and yellow silks, saying—"From henceforth we shall serve the sovereign of our dynasty of Chau, that we may be made happy by him." So they joined themselves, as subjects, to the great city of Chau. Thus, the men of station of Shang took baskets full of black and yellow silks to meet the men of station of Chau, and the lower classes of the one met those of the other with baskets of rice and vessels of congee. Wu saved the people from the midst of fire and water, seizing only their oppressors, and destroying them.'

6. 'In the Great Declaration it is said, "My power shall be put forth, and, invading the territories of Shang, I will seize the oppressor. I will put him to death to punish him:—so shall the greatness of my work appear, more glorious than that of T'ang."

7. 'Sung is not, as you say, practising true royal government, and so forth. If it were practising royal government, all within the four seas would be lifting up their heads, and looking for its prince, wishing to have him for their sovereign. Great as Ch'i and Ch'u are, what would there be to fear from them?'

CHAP. VI. 1. Mencius said to Tai Pu-shang, 'I see that you are desiring your king to be virtuous, and will plainly tell you how he may be made so. Suppose that there is a great officer of Ch'u here, who wishes his son to learn the speech of Ch'i. Will he in that case employ a man of Ch'i as his tutor, or a man of Ch'u?' 'He will employ a man of Ch'i to teach him,' said Pu-shang. Mencius went on, 'If but one man of Ch'i be teaching him, and there be a multitude of men of Ch'u continually shouting out about him, although his father beat him every day, wishing him to learn the speech of Ch'i, it will be impossible for him to do so. But in the same way, if he were to be taken and placed for several years in Chwang or Yo, though his father should beat him, wishing him to speak the language of Ch'u, it would be impossible for him to do so.

2. 'You supposed that Hsieh Chu-chau was a scholar of virtue, and you have got him placed in attendance on the king. Suppose that all in attendance on the king, old and young, high and low, were Hsieh Chu-chaus, whom would the king have to do evil with? And suppose that all in attendance on the king, old and young, high and low, are not Hsieh Chu-chaus, whom will the king gave to do good with? What can one Hsieh Chu-chau do alone for the king of Sung?'

CHAP. VII. 1. Kung-sun Chau asked Mencius, saying, 'What is the point of righteousness involved in your not going to see the princes?' Mencius replied, 'Among the ancients, if one had not been a minister in a State, he did not go to see the sovereign.

2. 'Twan Kan-mu leaped over his wall to avoid the prince. Hsieh Liu shut his door, and would not admit the prince. These two, however, carried their scrupulosity to excess. When a prince is urgent, it is not improper to see him.

3. 'Yang Ho wished to get Confucius to go to see him, but disliked doing so by any want of propriety. As it is the rule, therefore, that when a great officer sends a gift to a scholar, if the latter be not at home to receive it, he must go to the officer's to pay his respects, Yang Ho watched when Confucius was out, and sent him a roasted pig. Confucius, in his turn, watched when Ho was out, and went to pay his respects to him. At that time, Yang Ho had taken the initiative;—how could Confucius decline going to see him?

4. 'Tsang-tsze said, "They who shrug up their shoulders, and laugh in a flattering way, toil harder than the summer labourer in the fields." Tsze-lu said, "There are those who talk with people with whom they have no great community of feeling. If you look at their countenances, they are full of blushes. I do not desire to know such persons." By considering these remarks, the spirit which the superior man nourishes may be known.'

CHAP. VIII. 1. Tai Ying-chih said to Mencius, 'I am not able at present and immediately to do with the levying of a tithe only, and abolishing the duties charged at the passes and in the markets. With your leave I will lighten, however, both the tax and the duties, until next year, and will then make an end of them. What do you think of such a course?'

2. Mencius said, 'Here is a man, who every day appropriates some of his neighbour's strayed fowls. Some one says to him, "Such is not the way of a good man;" and he replies, "With your leave I will diminish my appropriations, and will take only one fowl a month, until next year, when I will make an end of the practice."

3. 'If you know that the thing is unrighteous, then use all despatch in putting an end to it:—why wait till next year?'

CHAP. IX. 1. The disciple Kung-tu said to Mencius, 'Master, the people beyond our school all speak of you as being fond of disputing. I venture to ask whether it be so.' Mencius replied, 'Indeed, I am not fond of disputing, but I am compelled to do it.

2. 'A long time has elapsed since this world of men received its being, and there has been along its history now a period of good order, and now a period of confusion.

3. 'In the time of Yao, the waters, flowing out of their channels, inundated the Middle Kingdom. Snakes and dragons occupied it, and the people had no place where they could settle themselves. In the low grounds they made nests for themselves on the trees or raised platforms, and in the high grounds they made caves. It is said in the Book of History, "The waters in their wild course warned me." Those "waters in their wild course" were the waters of the great inundation.

4. 'Shun employed Yu to reduce the waters to order. Yu dug open their obstructed channels, and conducted them to the sea. He drove away the snakes and dragons, and forced them into the grassy marshes. On this, the waters pursued their course through the country, even the waters of the Chiang, the Hwai, the Ho, and the Han, and the dangers and obstructions which they had occasioned were removed. The birds and beasts which had injured the people also disappeared, and after

this men found the plains available for them, and occupied them.

5. 'After the death of Yao and Shun, the principles that mark sages fell into decay. Oppressive sovereigns arose one after another, who pulled down houses to make ponds and lakes, so that the people knew not where they could rest in quiet; they threw fields out of cultivation to form gardens and parks, so that the people could not get clothes and food. Afterwards, corrupt speakings and oppressive deeds became more rife; gardens and parks, ponds and lakes, thickets and marshes became more numerous, and birds and beasts swarmed. By the time of the tyrant Chau, the kingdom was again in a state of great confusion.

6. 'Chau-kung assisted king Wu, and destroyed Chau. He smote Yen, and after three years put its sovereign to death. He drove Fei-lien to a corner by the sea, and slew him. The States which he extinguished amounted to fifty. He drove far away also the tigers, leopards, rhinoceroses, and elephants;—and all the people was greatly delighted. It is said in the Book of History, "Great and splendid were the plans of king Wan! Greatly were they carried out by the energy of king Wu! They are for the assistance and instruction of us who are of an after day. They are all in principle correct, and deficient in nothing."

7. 'Again the world fell into decay, and principles faded away. Perverse speakings and oppressive deeds waxed rife again. There were instances of ministers who murdered their sovereigns, and of sons who murdered their fathers.

8. 'Confucius was afraid, and made the "Spring and Autumn." What the "Spring and Autumn" contains are matters proper to the sovereign. On this account Confucius said, "Yes! It is the Spring and Autumn which will make men know me, and it is the Spring and Autumn which will make men condemn me."

9. 'Once more, sage sovereigns cease to arise, and the princes of the States give the reins to their lusts. Unemployed scholars indulge in unreasonable discussions. The words of Yang Chu and Mo Ti fill the country. If you listen to people's discourses throughout it, you will find that they have adopted

the views either of Yang or of Mo. Now, Yang's principle is—"each one for himself," which does not acknowledge the claims of the sovereign. Mo's principle is—"to love all equally," which does not acknowledge the peculiar affection due to a father. But to acknowledge neither king nor father is to be in the state of a beast. Kung-ming I said, "In their kitchens, there is fat meat. In their stables, there are fat horses. But their people have the look of hunger, and on the wilds there are those who have died of famine. This is leading on beasts to devour men." If the principles of Yang and Mo be not stopped, and the principles of Confucius not set forth, then those perverse speakings will delude the people, and stop up the path of benevolence and righteousness. When benevolence and righteousness are stopped up, beasts will be led on to devour men, and men will devour one another.

10. 'I am alarmed by these things, and address myself to the defence of the doctrines of the former sages, and to oppose Yang and Mo. I drive away their licentious expressions, so that such perverse speakers may not be able to show themselves. Their delusions spring up in men's minds, and do injury to their practice of affairs. Shown in their practice of affairs, they are pernicious to their government. When sages shall rise up again, they will not change my words.

11. 'In former times, Yu repressed the vast waters of the inundation, and the country was reduced to order. Chau-kung's achievements extended even to the barbarous tribes of the east and north, and he drove away all ferocious animals, and the people enjoyed repose. Confucius completed the "Spring and Autumn," and rebellious ministers and villainous sons were struck with terror.

12. 'It is said in the Book of Poetry,
"He smote the barbarians of the west and the north;
He punished Ching and Shu
And no one dared to resist us."
These father-deniers and king-deniers would have been smitten by Chau-kung.

13. 'I also wish to rectify men's hearts, and to put an end to those perverse doctrines, to oppose their one-sided actions

and banish away their licentious expressions;—and thus to carry on the work of the three sages. Do I do so because I am fond of disputing? I am compelled to do it.

14. 'Whoever is able to oppose Yang and Mo is a disciple of the sages.'

CHAP. X. 1. K'wang Chang said to Mencius, 'Is not Ch'an Chung a man of true self-denying purity? He was living in Wu-ling, and for three days was without food, till he could neither hear nor see. Over a well there grew a plum-tree, the fruit of which had been more than half eaten by worms. He crawled to it, and tried to eat some of the fruit, when, after swallowing three mouthfuls, he recovered his sight and hearing.'

2. Mencius replied, 'Among the scholars of Ch'i, I must regard Chung as the thumb among the fingers. But still, where is the self-denying purity he pretends to? To carry out the principles which he holds, one must become an earthworm, for so only can it be done.

3. 'Now, an earthworm eats the dry mould above, and drinks the yellow spring below. Was the house in which Chung dwells built by a Po-i? or was it built by a robber like Chih? Was the millet which he eats planted by a Po-i? or was it planted by a robber like Chih? These are things which cannot be known.'

4. 'But,' said Chang, 'what does that matter? He himself weaves sandals of hemp, and his wife twists and dresses threads of hemp to sell or exchange them.'

5. Mencius rejoined, 'Chung belongs to an ancient and noble family of Ch'i. His elder brother Tai received from Ka a revenue of 10,000 chung, but he considered his brother's emolument to be unrighteous, and would not eat of it, and in the same way he considered his brother's house to be unrighteous, and would not dwell in it. Avoiding his brother and leaving his mother, he went and dwelt in Wu-ling. One day afterwards, he returned to their house, when it happened that some one sent his brother a present of a live goose. He, knitting his eyebrows, said, "What are you going to use that cackling thing for?" By-and-by his mother killed the goose, and gave him some of it to eat. Just then his brother came into

the house, and said, "It is the flesh of that cackling thing," upon which he went out and vomited it.

6. 'Thus, what his mother gave him he would not eat, but what his wife gives him he eats. He will not dwell in his brother's house, but he dwells in Wu-ling. How can he in such circumstances complete the style of life which he professes? With such principles as Chung holds, a man must be an earthworm, and then he can carry them out.'

BOOK IV. LI LAU, PART I

CHAP. I. 1. Mencius said, 'The power of vision of Li Lau, and skill of hand of Kung-shu, without the compass and square, could not form squares and circles. The acute ear of the music-master K'wang, without the pitch-tubes, could not determine correctly the five notes. The principles of Yao and Shun, without a benevolent government, could not secure the tranquil order of the kingdom.

2. 'There are now princes who have benevolent hearts and a reputation for benevolence, while yet the people do not receive any benefits from them, nor will they leave any example to future ages;—all because they do not put into practice the ways of the ancient kings.

3. 'Hence we have the saying:—"Virtue alone is not sufficient for the exercise of government; laws alone cannot carry themselves into practice."

4. It is said in the Book of Poetry,
"Without transgression, without forgetfulness,
Following the ancient statutes."
Never has any one fallen into error, who followed the laws of the ancient kings.

5. 'When the sages had used the vigour of their eyes, they called in to their aid the compass, the square, the level, and the line, to make things square, round, level, and straight:—the use of the instruments is inexhaustible. When they had used their power of hearing to the utmost, they called in the pitch-tubes to their aid to determine the five notes:—the use of those tubes is inexhaustible. When they had exerted to the utmost the thoughts of their hearts, they called in to their aid a government that could not endure to witness the sufferings of men:—and their benevolence overspread the kingdom.

6. 'Hence we have the saying:—"To raise a thing high, we must begin from the top of a mound or a hill; to dig to a great depth, we must commence in the low ground of a stream or a marsh." Can he be pronounced wise, who, in the exercise of government, does not proceed according to the ways of the

former kings?

7. 'Therefore only the benevolent ought to be in high stations. When a man destitute of benevolence is in a high station, he thereby disseminates his wickedness among all below him.

8. 'When the prince has no principles by which he examines his administration, and his ministers have no laws by which they keep themselves in the discharge of their duties, then in the court obedience is not paid to principle, and in the office obedience is not paid to rule. Superiors violate the laws of righteousness, and inferiors violate the penal laws. It is only by a fortunate chance that a State in such a case is preserved.

9. 'Therefore it is said, "It is not the exterior and interior walls being incomplete, and the supply of weapons offensive and defensive not being large, which constitutes the calamity of a kingdom. It is not the cultivable area not being extended, and stores and wealth not being accumulated, which occasions the ruin of a State." When superiors do not observe the rules of propriety, and inferiors do not learn, then seditious people spring up, and that State will perish in no time.

10. 'It is said in the Book of Poetry,
"When such an overthrow of Chau is being produced by
    Heaven,
Be not ye so much at your ease!"

11. '"At your ease;"—that is, dilatory.

12. 'And so dilatory may those officers be deemed, who serve their prince without righteousness, who take office and retire from it without regard to propriety, and who in their words disown the ways of the ancient kings.

13. 'Therefore it is said, "To urge one's sovereign to difficult achievements may be called showing respect for him. To set before him what is good and repress his perversities may be called showing reverence for him. He who does not do these things, saying to himself,—My sovereign is incompetent to this, may be said to play the thief with him."'

CHAP. II. 1. Mencius said, 'The compass and square produce perfect circles and squares. By the sages, the human relations are perfectly exhibited.

2. 'He who as a sovereign would perfectly discharge the duties of a sovereign, and he who as a minister would perfectly discharge the duties of a minister, have only to imitate—the one Yao, and the other Shun. He who does not serve his sovereign as Shun served Yao, does not respect his sovereign; and he who does not rule his people as Yao ruled his, injures his people.

3. 'Confucius said, "There are but two courses, which can be pursued, that of virtue and its opposite."

4. 'A ruler who carries the oppression of his people to the highest pitch, will himself be slain, and his kingdom will perish. If one stop short of the highest pitch, his life will notwithstanding be in danger, and his kingdom will be weakened. He will be styled "The Dark," or "The Cruel," and though he may have filial sons and affectionate grandsons, they will not be able in a hundred generations to change the designation.

5. 'This is what is intended in the words of the Book of Poetry,

"The beacon of Yin is not remote,
It is in the time of the (last) sovereign of Hsia."'

CHAP. III. 1. Mencius said, 'It was by benevolence that the three dynasties gained the throne, and by not being benevolent that they lost it.

2. 'It is by the same means that the decaying and flourishing, the preservation and perishing, of States are determined.

3. 'If the sovereign be not benevolent, be cannot preserve the throne from passing from him. If the Head of a State be not benevolent, he cannot preserve his rule. If a high noble or great officer be not benevolent, he cannot preserve his ancestral temple. If a scholar or common man be not benevolent, be cannot preserve his four limbs.

4. 'Now they hate death and ruin, and yet delight in being not benevolent;—this is like hating to be drunk, and yet being strong to drink wine!

CHAP. IV. 1. Mencius said, 'If a man love others, and no responsive attachment is shown to him, let him turn inwards and examine his own benevolence. If he is trying to rule others, and his government is unsuccessful, let him turn inwards and examine his wisdom. If he treats others politely, and they do not return his politeness, let him turn inwards and examine his own feeling of respect.

2. 'When we do not, by what we do, realise what we desire, we must turn inwards, and examine ourselves in every point. When a man's person is correct, the whole kingdom will turn to him with recognition and submission.

3. 'It is said in the Book of Poetry,

"Be always studious to be in harmony with the ordinances
  of God,
And you will obtain much happiness.""

CHAP. V. Mencius said, 'People have this common saying,—"The kingdom, the State, the family." The root of the kingdom is in the State. The root of the State is in the family. The root of the family is in the person of its Head.'

CHAP. VI. Mencius said, 'The administration of government is not difficult;—it lies in not offending the great families. He whom the great families affect, will be affected by the whole State; and he whom any one State affects, will be affected by the whole kingdom. When this is the case, such an one's virtue and teachings will spread over all within the four seas like the rush of water.'

CHAP. VII. 1. Mencius said, 'When right government prevails in the kingdom, princes of little virtue are submissive to those of great, and those of little worth to those of great. When bad government prevails in the kingdom, princes of small power are submissive to those of great, and the weak to the strong. Both these cases are the rule of Heaven. They who accord with Heaven are preserved, and they who rebel against Heaven perish.

2. 'The duke Ching of Ch'i said, "Not to be able to command others, and at the same time to refuse to receive their commands, is to cut one's self off from all intercourse with others." His tears flowed forth while he gave his daughter to be married to the prince of Wu.

3. 'Now the small States imitate the large, and yet are ashamed to receive their commands. This is like a scholar's

being ashamed to receive the commands of his master.

4. 'For a prince who is ashamed of this, the best plan is to imitate king Wan. Let one imitate king Wan, and in five years, if his State be large, or in seven years, if it be small, he will be sure to give laws to the kingdom.

5. 'It is said in the Book of Poetry,

"The descendants of the sovereigns of the Shang dynasty,
Are in number more than hundreds of thousands,
But, God having passed His decree,
They are all submissive to Chau.
They are submissive to Chau,
Because the decree of Heaven is not unchanging.
The officers of Yin, admirable and alert,
Pour out the libations, and assist in the capital of Chau."

Confucius said, "As against so benevolent a sovereign, they could not be deemed a multitude." Thus, if the prince of a state love benevolence, he will have no opponent in all the kingdom.

6. 'Now they wish to have no opponent in all the kingdom, but they do not seek to attain this by being benevolent. This is like a man laying hold of a heated substance, and not having first dipped it in water. It is said in the Book of Poetry,

"Who can take up a heated substance,
Without first dipping it (in water)?"'

CHAP. VIII. 1. Mencius said, 'How is it possible to speak with those princes who are not benevolent? Their perils they count safety, their calamities they count profitable, and they have pleasure in the things by which they perish. If it were possible to talk with them who so violate benevolence, how could we have such destruction of States and ruin of Families?

2. 'There was a boy singing,

"When the water of the Ts'ang-lang is clear,
It does to wash the strings of my cap;
When the water of the Ts'ang-lang is muddy,
It does to wash my feet."

3. 'Confucius said, "Hear what he sings, my children. When clear, then he will wash his cap-strings; and when muddy, he will wash his feet with it. This different application is brought

by the water on itself."

4. 'A man must first despise himself, and then others will despise him. A family must first destroy itself, and then others will destroy it. A State must first smite itself, and then others will smite it.

5. 'This is illustrated in the passage of the T'ai Chia, "When Heaven sends down calamities, it is still possible to escape them. When we occasion the calamities ourselves, it is not possible any longer to live."'

CHAP. IX. 1. Mencius said, 'Chieh and Chau's losing the throne, arose from their losing the people, and to lose the people means to lose their hearts. There is a way to get the kingdom:—get the people, and the kingdom is got. There is a way to get the people:—get their hearts, and the people are got. There is a way to get their hearts:—it is simply to collect for them what they like, and not to lay on them what they dislike.

2. 'The people turn to a benevolent rule as water flows downwards, and as wild beasts fly to the wilderness.

3. 'Accordingly, as the otter aids the deep waters, driving the fish into them, and the hawk aids the thickets, driving the little birds to them, so Chieh and Chau aided T'ang and Wu, driving the people to them.

4. 'If among the present rulers of the kingdom, there were one who loved benevolence, all the other princes would aid him, by driving the people to him. Although he wished not to become sovereign, he could not avoid becoming so.

5. 'The case of one of the present princes wishing to become sovereign is like the having to seek for mugwort three years old, to cure a seven years' sickness. If it have not been kept in store, the patient may all his life not get it. If the princes do not set their wills on benevolence, all their days will be in sorrow and disgrace, and they will be involved in death and ruin.

6. 'This is illustrated by what is said in the Book of Poetry, "How otherwise can you improve the kingdom?
You will only with it go to ruin."'

CHAP. X. 1. Mencius said, 'With those who do violence to

themselves, it is impossible to speak. With those who throw themselves away, it is impossible to do anything. To disown in his conversation propriety and righteousness, is what we mean by doing violence to one's self. To say—"I am not able to dwell in benevolence or pursue the path of righteousness," is what we mean by throwing one's self away.

2. 'Benevolence is the tranquil habitation of man, and righteousness is his straight path.

3. 'Alas for them, who leave the tranquil dwelling empty and do not reside in it, and who abandon the right path and do not pursue it?'

CHAP. XI. Mencius said, 'The path of duty lies in what is near, and men seek for it in what is remote. The work of duty lies in what is easy, and men seek for it in what is difficult. If each man would love his parents and show the due respect to his elders, the whole land would enjoy tranquillity.'

CHAP. XII. 1. Mencius said, 'When those occupying inferior situations do not obtain the confidence of the sovereign, they cannot succeed in governing the people. There is a way to obtain the confidence of the sovereign:—if one is not trusted by his friends, he will not obtain the confidence of his sovereign. There is a way of being trusted by one's friends:— if one do not serve his parents so as to make them pleased, he will not be trusted by his friends. There is a way to make one's parents pleased:—if one, on turning his thoughts inwards, finds a want of sincerity, he will not give pleasure to his parents. There is a way to the attainment of sincerity in one's self:—if a man do not understand what is good, he will not attain sincerity in himself.

2. 'Therefore, sincerity is the way of Heaven. To think how to be sincere is the way of man.

3. Never has there been one possessed of complete sincerity, who did not move others. Never has there been one who had not sincerity who was able to move others.'

CHAP. XIII. 1. Mencius said, 'Po-I, that he might avoid Cha'u, was dwelling on the coast of the northern sea. When he heard of the rise of king Wan, he roused himself, and said, "Why should I not go and follow him? I have heard that the chief of the West knows well how to nourish the old." T'ai-kung, that he might avoid Chau, was dwelling on the coast of the eastern sea. When he heard of the rise of king Wan, he roused himself, and said, "Why should I not go and follow him? I have heard that the chief of the West knows well how to nourish the old."

2. 'Those two old men were the greatest old men of the kingdom. When they came to follow king Wan, it was the fathers of the kingdom coming to follow him. When the fathers of the kingdom joined him, how could the sons go to any other?

3. 'Were any of the princes to practise the government of king Wan, within seven years he would be sure to be giving laws to the kingdom.'

CHAP. XIV. 1. Mencius said, 'Ch'iu acted as chief officer to the head of the Chi family, whose evil ways he was unable to change, while he exacted from the people double the grain formerly paid. Confucius said, "He is no disciple of mine. Little children, beat the drum and assail him."

2. 'Looking at the subject from this case, we perceive that when a prince was not practising benevolent government, all his ministers who enriched him were rejected by Confucius:— how much more would he have rejected those who are vehement to fight for their prince! When contentions about territory are the ground on which they fight, they slaughter men till the fields are filled with them. When some struggle for a city is the ground on which they fight, they slaughter men till the city is filled with them. This is what is called "leading on the land to devour human flesh." Death is not enough for such a crime.

3. 'Therefore, those who are skilful to fight should suffer the highest punishment. Next to them should be punished those who unite some princes in leagues against others; and next to them, those who take in grassy commons, imposing the cultivation of the ground on the people.'

CHAP. XV. 1. Mencius said, 'Of all the parts of a man's body there is none more excellent than the pupil of the eye. The pupil cannot be used to hide a man's wickedness. If within the breast all be correct, the pupil is bright. If within the breast all be not correct, the pupil is dull.

2. 'Listen to a man's words and look at the pupil of his eye. How can a man conceal his character?'

CHAP. XVI. Mencius said, 'The respectful do not despise others. The economical do not plunder others. The prince who treats men with despite and plunders them, is only afraid that they may not prove obedient to him:—how can he be regarded as respectful or economical? How can respectfulness and economy be made out of tones of the voice, and a smiling manner?'

CHAP. XVII. 1. Shun-yu K'wan said, 'Is it the rule that males and females shall not allow their hands to touch in giving or receiving anything?' Mencius replied, 'It is the rule.' K'wan asked, 'If a man's sister-in-law be drowning, shall he rescue her with his hand?' Mencius said, 'He who would not so rescue the drowning woman is a wolf. For males and females not to allow their hands to touch in giving and receiving is the general rule; when a sister-in-law is drowning, to rescue her with the hand is a peculiar exigency.'

2. K'wan said, 'The whole kingdom is drowning. How strange it is that you will not rescue it!'

3. Mencius answered, 'A drowning kingdom must be rescued with right principles, as a drowning sister-in-law has to be rescued with the hand. Do you wish me to rescue the kingdom with my hand?'

CHAP. XVIII. 1. Kung-sun Ch'au said, 'Why is it that the superior man does not himself teach his son?'

2. Mencius replied, 'The circumstances of the case forbid its being done. The teacher must inculcate what is correct. When he inculcates what is correct, and his lessons are not practised, he follows them up with being angry. When he follows them up with being angry, then, contrary to what should be, he is offended with his son. At the same time, the pupil says, "My master inculcates on me what is correct, and he himself does not proceed in a correct path." The result of this is, that father and son are offended with each other. When father and son come to be offended with each other, the case

is evil.

3. 'The ancients exchanged sons, and one taught the son of another.

4. 'Between father and son, there should be no reproving admonitions to what is good. Such reproofs lead to alienation, and than alienation there is nothing more inauspicious.'

CHAP. XIX. 1. Mencius said, 'Of services, which is the greatest? The service of parents is the greatest. Of charges, which is the greatest? The charge of one's self is the greatest. That those who do not fail to keep themselves are able to serve their parents is what I have heard. But I have never heard of any, who, having failed to keep themselves, were able notwithstanding to serve their parents.

2. 'There are many services, but the service of parents is the root of all others. There are many charges, but the charge of one's self is the root of all others.

3. 'The philosopher Tsang, in nourishing Tsang Hsi, was always sure to have wine and flesh provided. And when they were being removed, he would ask respectfully to whom he should give what was left. If his father asked whether there was anything left, he was sure to say, "There is." After the death of Tsing Hsi, when Tsang Yuan came to nourish Tsing-tsze, he was always sure to have wine and flesh provided. But when the things were being removed, he did not ask to whom he should give what was left, and if his father asked whether there was anything left, he would answer "No;"—intending to bring them in again. This was what is called—"nourishing the mouth and body." We may call Tsang-tsze's practice—"nourishing the will."

4. 'To serve one's parents as Tsang-tsze served his, may be accepted as filial piety.'

CHAP. XX. Mencius said, 'It is not enough to remonstrate with a sovereign on account of the mal-employment of ministers, nor to blame errors of government. It is only the great man who can rectify what is wrong in the sovereign's mind. Let the prince be benevolent, and all his acts will be benevolent. Let the prince be righteous, and all his acts will be righteous. Let the prince be correct, and everything will be correct. Once rectify the ruler, and the kingdom will be firmly settled.'

CHAP. XXI. Mencius said, 'There are cases of praise which could not be expected, and of reproach when the parties have been seeking to be perfect.'

CHAP. XXII. Mencius said, 'Men's being ready with their tongues arises simply from their not having been reproved.'

CHAP. XXIII. Mencius said, 'The evil of men is that they like to be teachers of others.'

CHAP. XXIV. 1. The disciple Yo-chang went in the train of Tsze-ao to Ch'i.

2. He came to see Mencius, who said to him, 'Are you also come to see me?' Yo-chang replied, 'Master, why do you speak such words?' 'How many days have you been here?' asked Mencius. 'I came yesterday.' 'Yesterday! Is it not with reason then that I thus speak?' 'My lodging-house was not arranged.' 'Have you heard that a scholar's lodging-house must be arranged before he visit his elder?'

3. Yo-chang said, 'I have done wrong.'

CHAP. XXV. Mencius, addressing the disciple Yo-chang, said to him, 'Your coming here in the train of Tsze-ao was only because of the food and the drink. I could not have thought that you, having learned the doctrine of the ancients, would have acted with a view to eating and drinking.'

CHAP. XXVI. 1. Mencius said, 'There are three things which are unfilial, and to have no posterity is the greatest of them.

2. 'Shun married without informing his parents because of this,—lest he should have no posterity. Superior men consider that his doing so was the same as if he had informed them.'

CHAP. XXVII. 1. Mencius said, 'The richest fruit of benevolence is this,—the service of one's parents. The richest fruit of righteousness is this,—the obeying one's elder brothers.

2. 'The richest fruit of wisdom is this,—the knowing those two things, and not departing from them. The richest fruit of propriety is this,—the ordering and adorning those two things. The richest fruit of music is this,—the rejoicing in those two

things. When they are rejoiced in, they grow. Growing, how can they be repressed? When they come to this state that they cannot be repressed, then unconsciously the feet begin to dance and the hands to move.'

CHAP. XXVIII. 1. Mencius said, 'Suppose the case of the whole kingdom turning in great delight to an individual to submit to him.—To regard the whole kingdom thus turning to him in great delight but as a bundle of grass;—only Shun was capable of this. He considered that if one could not get the hearts of his parents he could not be considered a man, and that if he could not get to an entire accord with his parents, he could not be considered a son.

2. 'By Shun's completely fulfilling everything by which a parent could be served, Ku-sau was brought to find delight in what was good. When Ku-sau was brought to find that delight, the whole kingdom was transformed. When Ku-sau was brought to find that delight, all fathers and sons in the kingdom were established in their respective duties. This is called great filial piety.'

BOOK IV. LI LAU, PART II

CHAP. I. 1. Mencius said, 'Shun was born in Chu-fang, removed to Fu-hsia, and died in Ming-t'iao;—a man near the wild tribes on the east.

2. 'King Wan was born in Chau by mount Ch'i, and died in Pi-ying;—a man near the wild tribes on the west.

3. 'Those regions were distant from one another more than a thousand li, and the age of the one sage was posterior to that of the other more than a thousand years. But when they got their wish, and carried their principles into practice throughout the Middle Kingdom, it was like uniting the two halves of a seal.

4. 'When we examine those sages, both the earlier and the later, their principles are found to be the same.'

CHAP. II. 1. When Tsze-ch'an was chief minister of the State of Chang, he would convey people across the Chan and Wei in his own carriage.

2. Mencius said, 'It was kind, but showed that he did not understand the practice of government.

3. 'When in the eleventh month of the year the foot-bridges are completed, and the carriage-bridges in the twelfth month, the people have not the trouble of wading.

4. 'Let a governor conduct his rule on principles of equal justice, and, when he goes abroad, he may cause people to be removed out of his path. But how can he convey everybody across the rivers?

5. 'It follows that if a governor will try to please everybody, he will find the days not sufficient for his work.'

CHAP. III. 1. Mencius said to the king Hsuan of Ch'i, 'When the prince regards his ministers as his hands and feet, his ministers regard their prince as their belly and heart; when he regards them as his dogs and horses, they regard him as another man; when he regards them as the ground or as grass, they regard him as a robber and an enemy.'

2. The king said, 'According to the rules of propriety, a minister wears mourning when he has left the service of a

217

prince. How must a prince behave that his old ministers may thus go into mourning?'

3. Mencius replied, 'The admonitions of a minister having been followed, and his advice listened to, so that blessings have descended on the people, if for some cause he leaves the country, the prince sends an escort to conduct him beyond the boundaries. He also anticipates with recommendatory intimations his arrival in the country to which he is proceeding. When he has been gone three years and does not return, only then at length does he take back his fields and residence. This treatment is what is called a "thrice-repeated display of consideration." When a prince acts thus, mourning will be worn on leaving his service.

4. 'Now-a-days, the remonstrances of a minister are not followed, and his advice is not listened to, so that no blessings descend on the people. When for any cause he leaves the country, the prince tries to seize him and hold him a prisoner. He also pushes him to extremity in the country to which he has gone, and on the very day of his departure, takes back his fields and residence. This treatment shows him to be what we call "a robber and an enemy." What mourning can be worn for a robber and an enemy?'

CHAP. IV. Mencius said, 'When scholars are put to death without any crime, the great officers may leave the country. When the people are slaughtered without any crime, the scholars may remove.'

CHAP. V. Mencius said, 'If the sovereign be benevolent, all will be benevolent. If the sovereign be righteous, all will be righteous.'

CHAP. VI. Mencius said, 'Acts of propriety which are not really proper, and acts of righteousness which are not really righteous, the great man does not do.'

CHAP. VII. Mencius said, 'Those who keep the Mean, train up those who do not, and those who have abilities, train up those who have not, and hence men rejoice in having fathers and elder brothers who are possessed of virtue and talent. If they who keep the Mean spurn those who do not, and they who have abilities spurn those who have not, then the space between them—those so gifted and the ungifted—will not admit an inch.'

CHAP. VIII. Mencius said, 'Men must be decided on what they will NOT do, and then they are able to act with vigour in what they ought to do.'

CHAP. IX. Mencius said, 'What future misery have they and ought they to endure, who talk of what is not good in others!'

CHAP. X. Mencius said, 'Chung-ni did not do extraordinary things.'

CHAP. XI. Mencius said, 'The great man does not think beforehand of his words that they may be sincere, nor of his actions that they may be resolute;—he simply speaks and does what is right.'

CHAP. XII. Mencius said, 'The great man is he who does not lose his child's-heart.'

CHAP. XIII. Mencius said, 'The nourishment of parents when living is not sufficient to be accounted the great thing. It is only in the performing their obsequies when dead that we have what can be considered the great thing.'

CHAP. XIV. Mencius said, 'The superior man makes his advances in what he is learning with deep earnestness and by the proper course, wishing to get hold of it as in himself. Having got hold of it in himself, he abides in it calmly and firmly. Abiding in it calmly and firmly, he reposes a deep reliance on it. Reposing a deep reliance on it, he seizes it on the left and right, meeting everywhere with it as a fountain from which things flow. It is on this account that the superior man wishes to get hold of what he is learning as in himself.'

CHAP. XV. Mencius said, 'In learning extensively and discussing minutely what is learned, the object of the superior man is that he may be able to go back and set forth in brief what is essential.'

CHAP. XVI. Mencius said, 'Never has he who would by his excellence subdue men been able to subdue them. Let a prince seek by his excellence to nourish men, and he will be able to subdue the whole kingdom. It is impossible that any one should become ruler of the people to whom they have not yielded the subjection of the heart.'

CHAP. XVII. Mencius said, 'Words which are not true are inauspicious, and the words which are most truly obnoxious to the name of inauspicious, are those which throw into the shade men of talents and virtue.'

CHAP. XVIII. 1. The disciple Hsu said, 'Chung-ni often praised water, saying, "O water! O water!" What did he find in water to praise?'

2. Mencius replied, 'There is a spring of water; how it gushes out! It rests not day nor night. It fills up every hole, and then advances, flowing onto the four seas. Such is water having a spring! It was this which he found in it to praise.

3. 'But suppose that the water has no spring.—In the seventh and eighth when the rain falls abundantly, the channels in the fields are all filled, but their being dried up again may be expected in a short time. So a superior man is ashamed of a reputation beyond his merits.'

CHAP. XIX. 1. Mencius said, 'That whereby man differs from the lower animals is but small. The mass of people cast it away, while superior men preserve it.

2. 'Shun clearly understood the multitude of things, and closely observed the relations of humanity. He walked along the path of benevolence and righteousness; he did not need to pursue benevolence and righteousness.'

CHAP. XX. 1. Mencius said, 'Yu hated the pleasant wine, and loved good words.

2. 'T'ang held fast the Mean, and employed men of talents and virtue without regard to where they came from.

3. 'King Wan looked on the people as he would on a man who was wounded, and he looked towards the right path as if he could not see it.

4. King Wu did not slight the near, and did not forget the distant.

5. 'The duke of Chau desired to unite in himself the virtues of those kings, those founders of the three dynasties, that he might display in his practice the four things which they did. If he saw any thing in them not suited to his time, he looked up and thought about it, from daytime into the night, and when he was fortunate enough to master the difficulty, he sat waiting

for the morning.'

CHAP. XXI. 1. Mencius said, 'The traces of sovereign rule were extinguished, and the royal odes ceased to be made. When those odes ceased to be made, then the Ch'un Ch'iu was produced. 2. 'The Shang of Tsin, the Tao-wu of Ch'u, and the Ch'un Ch'iu of Lu were books of the same character. 3. 'The subject of the Ch'un Ch'iu was the affairs of Hwan of Chi and Wan of Tsin, and its style was the historical. Confucius said, "Its righteous decisions I ventured to make."'

CHAP. XXII. 1. Mencius said, 'The influence of a sovereign sage terminates in the fifth generation. The influence of a mere sage does the same. 2. 'Although I could not be a disciple of Confucius himself, I have endeavoured to cultivate my virtue by means of others who were.'

CHAP. XXIII. Mencius said, 'When it appears proper to take a thing, and afterwards not proper, to take it is contrary to moderation. When it appears proper to give a thing and afterwards not proper, to give it is contrary to kindness. When it appears proper to sacrifice one's life, and afterwards not proper, to sacrifice it is contrary to bravery.'

CHAP. XXIV. 1. P'ang Mang learned archery of I. When he had acquired completely all the science of I, he thought that in all the kingdom only I was superior to himself, and so he slew him. Mencius said, 'In this case I also was to blame. Kung-ming I indeed said, "It would appear as if he were not to be blamed," but he thereby only meant that his blame was slight. How can he be held without any blame?'

2. 'The people of Chang sent Tsze-cho Yu to make a stealthy attack on Wei, which sent Yu-kung Sze to pursue him. Tsze-cho Yu said, "To-day I feel unwell, so that I cannot hold my bow. I am a dead man!" At the same time he asked his driver, "Who is it that is pursuing me?" The driver said, "It is Yu-kung Sze," on which, he exclaimed, "I shall live." The driver said, "Yu-kung Sze is the best archer of Wei, what do you mean by saying 'I shall live?'" Yu replied, "Yu-kung Sze learned archery from Yin-kung T'o, who again learned it from

me. Now, Yin-kung T'o is an upright man, and the friends of his selection must be upright also." When Yu-kung Sze came up, he said, "Master, why are you not holding your bow?" Yu answered him, "To-day I am feeling unwell, and cannot hold my bow." On this Sze said, "I learned archery from Yin-kung T'o, who again learned it from you. I cannot bear to injure you with your own science. The business of to-day, however, is the prince's business, which I dare not neglect." He then took his arrows, knocked off their steel points against the carriage-wheel, discharged four of them, and returned.

CHAP. XXV. 1. Mencius said, 'If the lady Hsi had been covered with a filthy head-dress, all people would have stopped their noses in passing her.

2. 'Though a man may be wicked, yet if he adjust his thoughts, fast, and bathe, he may sacrifice to God.'

CHAP. XXVI. 1. Mencius said, 'All who speak about the natures of things, have in fact only their phenomena to reason from, and the value of a phenomenon is in its being natural.

2. 'What I dislike in your wise men is their boring out their conclusions. If those wise men would only act as Yu did when he conveyed away the waters, there would be nothing to dislike in their wisdom. The manner in which Yu conveyed away the waters was by doing what gave him no trouble. If your wise men would also do that which gave them no trouble, their knowledge would also be great.

3. 'There is heaven so high; there are the stars so distant. If we have investigated their phenomena, we may, while sitting in our places, go back to the solstice of a thousand years ago.'

CHAP. XXVII. 1. The officer Kung-hang having on hand the funeral of one of his sons, the Master of the Right went to condole with him. When this noble entered the door, some called him to them and spoke with him, and some went to his place and spoke with him.

2. Mencius did not speak with him, so that he was displeased, and said, 'All the gentlemen have spoken with me. There is only Mencius who does not speak to me, thereby slighting me.'

3. Mencius having heard of this remark, said, 'According to

the prescribed rules, in the court, individuals may not change their places to speak with one another, nor may they pass from their ranks to bow to one another. I was wishing to observe this rule, and Tsze-ao understands it that I was slighting him:—is not this strange?'

CHAP. XXVIII. 1. Mencius said, 'That whereby the superior man is distinguished from other men is what he preserves in his heart;—namely, benevolence and propriety.

2. 'The benevolent man loves others. The man of propriety shows respect to others.

3. 'He who loves others is constantly loved by them. He who respects others is constantly respected by them.

4. 'Here is a man, who treats me in a perverse and unreasonable manner. The superior man in such a case will turn round upon himself—"I must have been wanting in benevolence; I must have been wanting in propriety;—how should this have happened to me?"

5. He examines himself, and is specially benevolent. He turns round upon himself, and is specially observant of propriety. The perversity and unreasonableness of the other, however, are still the same. The superior man will again turn round on himself—"I must have been failing to do my utmost."

6. 'He turns round upon himself, and proceeds to do his utmost, but still the perversity and unreasonableness of the other are repeated. On this the superior man says, "This is a man utterly lost indeed! Since he conducts himself so, what is there to choose between him and a brute? Why should I go to contend with a brute?"

7. 'Thus it is that the superior man has a life-long anxiety and not one morning's calamity. As to what is matter of anxiety to him, that indeed be has.—He says, "Shun was a man, and I also am a man. But Shun became an example to all the kingdom, and his conduct was worthy to be handed down to after ages, while I am nothing better than a villager." This indeed is the proper matter of anxiety to him. And in what way is he anxious about it? Just that he maybe like Shun:—then only will he stop. As to what the superior man would feel to

be a calamity, there is no such thing. He does nothing which is not according to propriety. If there should befall him one morning's calamity, the superior man does not account it a calamity.'

CHAP. XXIX. 1. Yu and Chi, in an age when the world was being brought back to order, thrice passed their doors without entering them. Confucius praised them.

2. The disciple Yen, in an age of disorder, dwelt in a mean narrow lane, having his single bamboo-cup of rice, and his single gourd-dish of water; other men could not have endured the distress, but he did not allow his joy to be affected by it. Confucius praised him.

3. Mencius said, 'Yu, Chi, and Yen Hui agreed in the principle of their conduct.

4. 'Yu thought that if any one in the kingdom were drowned, it was as if he drowned him. Chi thought that if any one in the kingdom suffered hunger, it was as if he famished him. It was on this account that they were so earnest.

5. If Yu and Chi, and Yen-tsze, had exchanged places, each would have done what the other did.

6. 'Here now in the same apartment with you are people fighting:—you ought to part them. Though you part them with your cap simply tied over your unbound hair, your conduct will be allowable.

7. 'If the fighting be only in the village or neighbourhood, if you go to put an end to it with your cap tied over your hair unbound, you will be in error. Although you should shut your door in such a case, your conduct would be allowable.'

CHAP. XXX. 1. The disciple Kung-tu said, 'Throughout the whole kingdom everybody pronounces K'wang Chang unfilial. But you, Master, keep company with him, and moreover treat him with politeness. I venture to ask why you do so.'

2. Mencius replied, 'There are five things which are pronounced in the common usage of the age to be unfilial. The first is laziness in the use of one's four limbs, without attending to the nourishment of his parents. The second is gambling and chess-playing, and being fond of wine, without attending to the nourishment of his parents. The third is being fond of

goods and money, and selfishly attached to his wife and children, without attending to the nourishment of his parents. The fourth is following the desires of one's ears and eyes, so as to bring his parents to disgrace. The fifth is being fond of bravery, fighting and quarrelling so as to endanger his parents. Is Chang guilty of any one of these things?

3. 'Now between Chang and his father there arose disagreement, he, the son, reproving his father, to urge him to what was good.

4. 'To urge one another to what is good by reproofs is the way of friends. But such urging between father and son is the greatest injury to the kindness, which should prevail between them.

5. 'Moreover, did not Chang wish to have in his family the relationships of husband and wife, child and mother? But because he had offended his father, and was not permitted to approach him, he sent away his wife, and drove forth his son, and all his life receives no cherishing attention from them. He settled it in his mind that if he did not act in this way, his would be one of the greatest of crimes.—Such and nothing more is the case of Chang.'

CHAP. XXXI. 1. When the philosopher Tsang dwelt in Wu-ch'ang, there came a band from Yueh to plunder it. Someone said to him, 'The plunderers are coming:—why not leave this?' Tsang on this left the city, saying to the man in charge of the house, 'Do not lodge any persons in my house, lest they break and injure the plants and trees.' When the plunderers withdrew, he sent word to him, saying, 'Repair the walls of my house. I am about to return.' When the plunderers retired, the philosopher Tsang returned accordingly. His disciples said, 'Since our master was treated with so much sincerity and respect, for him to be the first to go away on the arrival of the plunderers, so as to be observed by the people, and then to return on their retiring, appears to us to be improper.' Ch'an-yu Hsing said, 'You do not understand this matter. Formerly, when Ch'an-yu was exposed to the outbreak of the grass-carriers, there were seventy disciples in our master's following, and none of them took part in the matter.'

2. When Tsze-sze was living in Wei, there came a band from Ch'i to plunder. Some one said to him, 'The plunderers are coming;—why not leave this?' Tsze-sze said, 'If I go away, whom will the prince have to guard the State with?'

3. Mencius said, 'The philosophers Tsang and Tsze-sze agreed in the principle of their conduct. Tsang was a teacher;—in the place of a father or elder brother. Tsze-sze was a minister;—in a meaner place. If the philosophers Tsang and Tsze-sze had exchanged places the one would have done what the other did.'

CHAP. XXXII. The officer Ch'u said to Mencius, 'Master, the king sent persons to spy out whether you were really different from other men.' Mencius said, 'How should I be different from other men? Yao and Shun were just the same as other men.'

CHAP. XXXIII. 1. A man of Ch'i had a wife and a concubine, and lived together with them in his house. When their husband went out, he would get himself well filled with wine and flesh, and then return, and, on his wife's asking him with whom he ate and drank, they were sure to be all wealthy and honourable people. The wife informed the concubine, saying, 'When our good man goes out, he is sure to come back having partaken plentifully of wine and flesh. I asked with whom he ate and drank, and they are all, it seems, wealthy and honourable people. And yet no people of distinction ever come here. I will spy out where our good man goes.' Accordingly, she got up early in the morning, and privately followed wherever her husband went. Throughout the whole city, there was no one who stood or talked with him. At last, he came to those who were sacrificing among the tombs beyond the outer wall on the east, and begged what they had over. Not being satisfied, he looked about, and went to another party;—and this was the way in which he got himself satiated. His wife returned, and informed the concubine, saying, 'It was to our husband that we looked up in hopeful contemplation, with whom our lot is cast for life;—and now these are his ways!' On this, along with the concubine she reviled their husband, and they wept together in the middle hall. In the meantime the husband, knowing nothing of all this, came in with a jaunty air, carrying himself proudly to his wife and concubine.

2. In the view of a superior man, as to the ways by which men seek for riches, honours, gain, and advancement, there are few of their wives and concubines who would not be ashamed and weep together on account of them.

BOOK V. WAN CHANG, PART I

CHAP. I. 1. Wan Chang asked Mencius, saying, 'When Shun went into the fields, he cried out and wept towards the pitying heavens. Why did he cry out and weep?' Mencius replied, 'He was dissatisfied, and full of earnest desire.'

2. Wan Chang said, 'When his parents love him, a son rejoices and forgets them not. When his parents hate him, though they punish him, he does not murmur. Was Shun then murmuring against his parents?' Mencius answered, 'Ch'ang Hsi asked Kung-ming Kao, saying, "As to Shun's going into the fields, I have received your instructions, but I do not know about his weeping and crying out to the pitying heavens and to his parents." Kung-ming Kao answered him, "You do not understand that matter." Now, Kung-ming Kao supposed that the heart of the filial son could not be so free of sorrow. Shun would say, "I exert my strength to cultivate the fields, but I am thereby only discharging my office as a son. What can there be in me that my parents do not love me?"

3. 'The Ti caused his own children, nine sons and two daughters, the various officers, oxen and sheep, storehouses and granaries, all to be prepared, to serve Shun amid the channelled fields. Of the scholars of the kingdom there were multitudes who flocked to him. The sovereign designed that Shun should superintend the kingdom along with him, and then to transfer it to him entirely. But because his parents were not in accord with him, he felt like a poor man who has nowhere to turn to.

4. 'To be delighted in by all the scholars of the kingdom, is what men desire, but it was not sufficient to remove the sorrow of Shun. The possession of beauty is what men desire, and Shun had for his wives the two daughters of the Ti, but this was not sufficient to remove his sorrow. Riches are what men desire, and the kingdom was the rich property of Shun, but this was not sufficient to remove his sorrow. Honours are what men desire, and Shun had the dignity of being sovereign, but this was not sufficient to remove his sorrow. The reason

why the being the object of men's delight, with the possession of beauty, riches, and honours were not sufficient to remove his sorrow, was that it could be removed only by his getting his parents to be in accord with him.

5. 'The desire of the child is towards his father and mother. When he becomes conscious of the attractions of beauty, his desire is towards young and beautiful women. When he comes to have a wife and children, his desire is towards them. When he obtains office, his desire is towards his sovereign:—if he cannot get the regard of his sovereign, he burns within. But the man of great filial piety, to the end of his life, has his desire towards his parents. In the great Shun I see the case of one whose desire at fifty year's was towards them.'

CHAP. II. 1. Wan Chang asked Mencius, saying, 'It is said in the Book of Poetry,

"In marrying a wife, how ought a man to proceed?

He must inform his parents."

If the rule be indeed as here expressed, no man ought to have illustrated it so well as Shun. How was it that Shun's marriage took place without his informing his parents?' Mencius replied, 'If he had informed them, he would not have been able to marry. That male and female should dwell together, is the greatest of human relations. If Shun had informed his parents, he must have made void this greatest of human relations, thereby incurring their resentment. On this account, he did not inform them!

2. Wan Chang said, 'As to Shun's marrying without informing his parents, I have heard your instructions; but how was it that the Ti Yao gave him his daughters as wives without informing Shun's parents?' Mencius said, 'The Ti also knew that if he informed them, he could not marry his daughters to him.'

3. Wan Chang said, 'His parents set Shun to repair a granary, to which, the ladder having been removed, Ku-sau set fire. They also made him dig a well. He got out, but they, not knowing that, proceeded to cover him up. Hsiang said, "Of the scheme to cover up the city-forming prince, the merit is all mine. Let my parents have his oxen and sheep. Let them have

229

his storehouses and granaries. His shield and spear shall be mine. His lute shall be mine. His bow shall be mine. His two wives I shall make attend for me to my bed." Hsiang then went away into Shun's palace, and there was Shun on his couch playing on his lute. Hsiang said, "I am come simply because I was thinking anxiously about you." At the same time, he blushed deeply. Shun said to him, "There are all my officers:— do you undertake the government of them for me." I do not know whether Shun was ignorant of Hsiang's wishing to kill him.' Mencius answered, 'How could he be ignorant of that? But when Hsiang was sorrowful, he was also sorrowful; when Hsiang was joyful, he was also joyful.'

4. Chang said, 'In that case, then, did not Shun rejoice hypocritically?' Mencius replied, 'No. Formerly, some one sent a present of a live fish to Tsze-ch'an of Chang. Tsze-ch'an ordered his pond-keeper to keep it in the pond, but that officer cooked it, and reported the execution of his commission, saying, "When I first let it go, it embarrassed. In a little while, it seemed to be somewhat at ease, then it swam away joyfully." Tsze-ch'an observed, "It had got into its element! It had got into its element!" The pond-keeper then went out and said, "Who calls Tsze-ch'an a wise man? After I had cooked and eaten the fish, he says,—It had got into its element! It had got into its element!" Thus a superior man may be imposed on by what seems to be as it ought to be, but he cannot be entrapped by what is contrary to right principle. Hsiang came in the way in which the love of his elder brother would have made him come; therefore Shun sincerely believed him, and rejoiced. What hypocrisy was there?'

CHAP. III. 1. Wan Chang said, 'Hsiang made it his daily business to slay Shun. When Shun was made sovereign, how was it that he only banished him?' Mencius said, 'He raised him to be a prince. Some supposed that it was banishing him?'

2. Wan Chang said, 'Shun banished the superintendent of works to Yu-chau; he sent away Hwan-tau to the mountain Ch'ung; he slew the prince of San-miao in San-wei; and he imprisoned Kwan on the mountain Yu. When the crimes of those four were thus punished, the whole kingdom

acquiesced:—it was a cutting off of men who were destitute of benevolence. But Hsiang was of all men the most destitute of benevolence, and Shun raised him to be the prince of Yu-pi;—of what crimes had the people of Yu-pi been guilty? Does a benevolent man really act thus? In the case of other men, he cut them off; in the case of his brother, he raised him to be a prince.' Mencius replied, 'A benevolent man does not lay up anger, nor cherish resentment against his brother, but only regards him with affection and love. Regarding him with affection, he wishes him to be honourable: regarding him with love, he wishes him to be rich. The appointment of Hsiang to be the prince of Yu-pi was to enrich and ennoble him. If while Shun himself was sovereign, his brother had been a common man, could he have been said to regard him with affection and love?'

3. Wan Chang said, 'I venture to ask what you mean by saying that some supposed that it was a banishing of Hsiang?' Mencius replied, 'Hsiang could do nothing in his State. The Son of Heaven appointed an officer to administer its government, and to pay over its revenues to him. This treatment of him led to its being said that he was banished. How indeed could he be allowed the means of oppressing the people? Nevertheless, Shun wished to be continually seeing him, and by this arrangement, he came incessantly to court, as is signified in that expression—"He did not wait for the rendering of tribute, or affairs of government, to receive the prince of Yu-pi."'

CHAP. IV. 1. Hsien-ch'iu Mang asked Mencius, saying, 'There is the saying, "A scholar of complete virtue may not be employed as a minister by his sovereign, nor treated as a son by his father. Shun stood with his face to the south, and Yao, at the head of all the princes, appeared before him at court with his face to the north. Ku-sau also did the same. When Shun saw Ku-sau, his countenance became discomposed. Confucius said, At this time, in what a perilous condition was the kingdom! Its state was indeed unsettled."—I do not know whether what is here said really took place.' Mencius replied, 'No. These are not the words of a superior man. They are the

231

sayings of an uncultivated person of the east of Ch'i. When Yao was old, Shun was associated with him in the government. It is said in the Canon of Yao, "After twenty and eight years, the Highly Meritorious one deceased. The people acted as if they were mourning for a father or mother for three years, and up to the borders of the four seas every sound of music was hushed." Confucius said, "There are not two suns in the sky, nor two sovereigns over the people." Shun having been sovereign, and, moreover, leading on all the princes to observe the three years' mourning for Yao, there would have been in this case two sovereigns.'

2. Hsien-ch'iu Mang said, 'On the point of Shun's not treating Yao as a minister, I have received your instructions. But it is said in the Book of Poetry,

"Under the whole heaven,
Every spot is the sovereign's ground;
To the borders of the land,
Every individual is the sovereign's minister;"

—and Shun had become sovereign. I venture to ask how it was that Ku-sau was not one of his ministers.' Mencius answered, 'That ode is not to be understood in that way:—it speaks of being laboriously engaged in the sovereign's business, so as not to be able to nourish one's parents, as if the author said, "This is all the sovereign's business, and how is it that I alone am supposed to have ability, and am made to toil in it?" Therefore, those who explain the odes, may not insist on one term so as to do violence to a sentence, nor on a sentence so as to do violence to the general scope. They must try with their thoughts to meet that scope, and then we shall apprehend it. If we simply take single sentences, there is that in the ode called "The Milky Way,"—

"Of the black-haired people of the remnant of Chau,
There is not half a one left."

If it had been really as thus expressed, then not an individual of the people of Chau was left.

3. 'Of all which a filial son can attain to, there is nothing greater than his honouring his parents. And of what can be attained to in the honouring one's parents, there is nothing

greater than the nourishing them with the whole kingdom. Ku-sau was the father of the sovereign;—this was the height of honour. Shun nourished him with the whole kingdom;—this was the height of nourishing. In this was verified the sentiment in the Book of Poetry,

"Ever cherishing filial thoughts,

Those filial thoughts became an example to after ages."

4. 'It is said in the Book of History, "Reverently performing his duties, he waited on Ku-sau, and was full of veneration and awe. Ku-sau also believed him and conformed to virtue."—This is the true case of the scholar of complete virtue not being treated as a son by his father.'

CHAP. V. 1. Wan Chang said, 'Was it the case that Yao gave the throne to Shun?' Mencius said, 'No. The sovereign cannot give the throne to another.'

2. 'Yes;—but Shun had the throne. Who gave it to him?' 'Heaven gave it to him,' was the answer.

3. '"Heaven gave it to him:"—did Heaven confer its appointment on him with specific injunctions?'

4. Mencius replied, 'No. Heaven does not speak. It simply showed its will by his personal conduct and his conduct of affairs.'

5. '"It showed its will by his personal conduct and his conduct of affairs:"—how was this?' Mencius's answer was, 'The sovereign can present a man to Heaven, but he cannot make Heaven give that man the throne. A prince can present a man to the sovereign, but he cannot cause the sovereign to make that man a prince. A great officer can present a man to his prince, but he cannot cause the prince to make that man a great officer. Yao presented Shun to Heaven, and Heaven accepted him. He presented him to the people, and the people accepted him. Therefore I say, "Heaven does not speak. It simply indicated its will by his personal conduct and his conduct of affairs."'

6. Chang said, 'I presume to ask how it was that Yao presented Shun to Heaven, and Heaven accepted him; and that he exhibited him to the people, and the people accepted him.' Mencius replied, 'He caused him to preside over the sacrifices,

and all the spirits were well pleased with them;—thus Heaven accepted him. He caused him to preside over the conduct of affairs, and affairs were well administered, so that the people reposed under him;—thus the people accepted him. Heaven gave the throne to him. The people gave it to him. Therefore I said, "The sovereign cannot give the throne to another."

7. 'Shun assisted Yao in the government for twenty and eight years;—this was more than man could have done, and was from Heaven. After the death of Yao, when the three years' mourning was completed, Shun withdrew from the son of Yao to the south of South river. The princes of the kingdom, however, repairing to court, went not to the son of Yao, but they went to Shun. Litigants went not to the son of Yao, but they went to Shun. Singers sang not the son of Yao, but they sang Shun. Therefore I said, "Heaven gave him the throne." It was after these things that he went to the Middle Kingdom, and occupied the seat of the Son of Heaven. If he had, before these things, taken up his residence in the palace of Yao, and had applied pressure to the son of Yao, it would have been an act of usurpation, and not the gift of Heaven.

8. 'This sentiment is expressed in the words of The Great Declaration,—"Heaven sees according as my people see; Heaven hears according as my people hear."'

CHAP. VI. 1. Wan Chang asked Mencius, saying, 'People say, "When the disposal of the kingdom came to Yu, his virtue was inferior to that of Yao and Shun, and he transmitted it not to the worthiest but to his son." Was it so?' Mencius replied, 'No; it was not so. When Heaven gave the kingdom to the worthiest, it was given to the worthiest. When Heaven gave it to the son of the preceding sovereign, it was given to him. Shun presented Yu to Heaven. Seventeen years elapsed, and Shun died. When the three years' mourning was expired, Yu withdrew from the son of Shun to Yang-ch'ang. The people of the kingdom followed him just as after the death of Yao, instead of following his son, they had followed Shun. Yu presented Yi to Heaven. Seven years elapsed, and Yu died. When the three years' mourning was expired, Yi withdrew from the son of Yu to the north of mount Ch'i. The princes, repairing to court, went not to Yi, but they went to Ch'i. Litigants did not go to Yi, but they went to Ch'i, saying, "He is the son of our sovereign;" the singers did not sing Yi, but they sang Ch'i, saying, "He is the son of our sovereign."

2. 'That Tan-chu was not equal to his father, and Shun's son not equal to his; that Shun assisted Yao, and Yu assisted Shun, for many years, conferring benefits on the people for a long time; that thus the length of time during which Shun, Yu, and Yi assisted in the government was so different; that Ch'i was able, as a man of talents and virtue, reverently to pursue the same course as Yu; that Yi assisted Yu only for a few years, and had not long conferred benefits on the people; that the periods of service of the three were so different; and that the sons were one superior, and the other superior:—all this was from Heaven, and what could not be brought about by man. That which is done without man's doing is from Heaven. That which happens without man's causing is from the ordinance of Heaven.

3. 'In the case of a private individual obtaining the throne, there must be in him virtue equal to that of Shun or Yu; and moreover there must be the presenting of him to Heaven by the preceding sovereign. It was on this account that Confucius did not obtain the throne.

4. 'When the kingdom is possessed by natural succession, the sovereign who is displaced by Heaven must be like Chieh or Chau. It was on this account that Yi, I Yin, and Chau-kung did not obtain the throne.

5. 'I Yin assisted T'ang so that he became sovereign over the kingdom. After the demise of T'ang, T'ai-ting having died before he could be appointed sovereign, Wa'i-ping reigned two years, and Chung-zin four. T'ai-chia was then turning upside down the statutes of T'ang, when I Yin placed him in T'ung for three years. There T'ai-chia repented of his errors, was contrite, and reformed himself. In T'ung be came to dwell in benevolence and walk in righteousness, during those three years, listening to the lessons given to him by I Yin. Then I Yin again returned with him to Po.

6. 'Chau-kung not getting the throne was like the case of Yi

and the throne of Hsia, or like that of I Yin and the throne of Yin.

7. 'Confucius said, "T'ang and Yu resigned the throne to their worthy ministers. The sovereign of Hsia and those of Yin and Chau transmitted it to their sons. The principle of righteousness was the same in all the cases."'

CHAP. VII. 1. Wan Chang asked Mencius, saying, 'People say that I Yin sought an introduction to T'ang by his knowledge of cookery. Was it so?'

2. Mencius replied, 'No, it was not so. I Yin was a farmer in the lands of the prince of Hsin, delighting in the principles of Yao and Shun. In any matter contrary to the righteousness which they prescribed, or contrary to their principles, though he had been offered the throne, he would not have regarded it; though there had been yoked for him a thousand teams of horses, he would not have looked at them. In any matter contrary to the righteousness which they prescribed, or contrary to their principles, he would neither have given nor taken a single straw.

3. 'T'ang sent persons with presents of silk to entreat him to enter his service. With an air of indifference and self-satisfaction he said, "What can I do with those silks with which T'ang invites me? Is it not best for me to abide in the channelled fields, and so delight myself with the principles of Yao and Shun?"

4. 'T'ang thrice sent messengers to invite him. After this, with the change of resolution displayed in his countenance, he spoke in a different style,—"Instead of abiding in the channelled fields and thereby delighting myself with the principles of Yao and Shun, had I not better make this prince a prince like Yao or Shun, and this people like the people of Yao or Shun? Had I not better in my own person see these things for myself?

5. "'Heaven's plan in the production of mankind is this:— that they who are first informed should instruct those who are later in being informed, and they who first apprehend principles should instruct those who are slower to do so. I am one of Heaven's people who have first apprehended;—I will

take these principles and instruct this people in them. If I do not instruct them, who will do so?"

6. 'He thought that among all the people of the kingdom, even the private men and women, if there were any who did not enjoy such benefits as Yao and Shun conferred, it was as if he himself pushed them into a ditch. He took upon himself the heavy charge of the kingdom in this way, and therefore he went to T'ang, and pressed upon him the subject of attacking Hsia and saving the people.

7. 'I have not heard of one who bent himself, and at the same time made others straight;—how much less could one disgrace himself, and thereby rectify the whole kingdom? The actions of the sages have been different. Some have kept remote from court, and some have drawn near to it; some have left their offices, and some have not done so:—that to which those different courses all agree is simply the keeping of their persons pure.

8. 'I have heard that I Yin sought an introduction to T'ang by the doctrines of Yao and Shun. I have not heard that he did so by his knowledge of cookery.

9. 'In the "Instructions of I," it is said, "Heaven destroying Chieh commenced attacking him in the palace of Mu. I commenced in Po."'

CHAP. VIII. 1. Wan Chang asked Mencius, saying, 'Some say that Confucius, when he was in Wei, lived with the ulcer-doctor, and when he was in Ch'i, with the attendant, Ch'i Hwan;—was it so?' Mencius replied, 'No; it was not so. Those are the inventions of men fond of strange things.

2. 'When he was in Wei, he lived with Yen Ch'au-yu. The wives of the officer Mi and Tsze-lu were sisters, and Mi told Tsze-lu, "If Confucius will lodge with me, he may attain to the dignity of a high noble of Wei." Tsze-lu informed Confucius of this, and he said, "That is as ordered by Heaven." Confucius went into office according to propriety, and retired from it according to righteousness. In regard to his obtaining office or not obtaining it, he said, "That is as ordered." But if he had lodged with the attendant Chi Hwan, that would neither have been according to righteousness, nor any ordering of Heaven.

3. 'When Confucius, being dissatisfied in Lu and Wei, had left those States, he met with the attempt of Hwan, the Master of the Horse, of Sung, to intercept and kill him. He assumed, however, the dress of a common man, and passed by Sung. At that time, though he was in circumstances of distress, he lodged with the city-master Ch'ang, who was then a minister of Chau, the marquis of Ch'an.

4. 'I have heard that the characters of ministers about court may be discerned from those whom they entertain, and those of stranger officers, from those with whom they lodge. If Confucius had lodged with the ulcer-doctor, and with the attendant Chi Hwan, how could he have been Confucius?'

CHAP. IX. 1. Wan Chang asked Mencius, 'Some say that Pai-li Hsi sold himself to a cattle-keeper of Ch'in for the skins of five rams, and fed his oxen, in order to find an introduction to the duke Mu of Ch'in;—was this the case?' Mencius said, 'No; it was not so. This story was invented by men fond of strange things.

2. 'Pai-li Hsi was a man of Yu. The people of Tsin, by the inducement of a round piece of jade from Ch'ui-chi, and four horses of the Ch'u breed, borrowed a passage through Yu to attack Kwo. On that occasion, Kung Chih-ch'i remonstrated against granting their request, and Pai-li Hsi did not remonstrate.

3. 'When he knew that the duke of Yu was not to be remonstrated with, and, leaving that State, went to Ch'in, he had reached the age of seventy. If by that time he did not know that it would be a mean thing to seek an introduction to the duke Mu of Ch'in by feeding oxen, could he be called wise? But not remonstrating where it was of no use to remonstrate, could he be said not to be wise? Knowing that the duke of Yu would be ruined, and leaving him before that event, he cannot be said not to have been wise. Being then advanced in Ch'in, he knew that the duke Mu was one with whom he would enjoy a field for action, and became minister to him;—could he, acting thus, be said not to be wise? Having become chief minister of Ch'in, he made his prince distinguished throughout the kingdom, and worthy of being handed down to future

ages;—could he have done this, if he had not been a man of talents and virtue? As to selling himself in order to accomplish all the aims of his prince, even a villager who had a regard for himself would not do such a thing; and shall we say that a man of talents and virtue did it?'

BOOK V. WAN CHANG, PART II

CHAP. I. 1. Mencius said, 'Po-i would not allow his eyes to look on a bad sight, nor his ears to listen to a bad sound. He would not serve a prince whom he did not approve, nor command a people whom he did not esteem. In a time of good government he took office, and on the occurrence of confusion he retired. He could not bear to dwell either in a court from which a lawless government emanated, or among lawless people. He considered his being in the same place with a villager, as if he were to sit amid mud and coals with his court robes and court cap. In the time of Chau he dwelt on the shores of the North sea, waiting the purification of the kingdom. Therefore when men now hear the character of Po-i, the corrupt become pure, and the weak acquire determination.

2. 'I Yin said, "Whom may I not serve? My serving him makes him my sovereign. What people may I not command? My commanding them makes them my people." In a time of good government he took office, and when confusion prevailed, he also took office. He said, "Heaven's plan in the production of mankind is this:—that they who are first informed should instruct those who are later in being informed, and they who first apprehend principles should instruct those who are slower in doing so. I am the one of Heaven's people who has first apprehended;—I will take these principles and instruct the people in them." He thought that among all the people of the kingdom, even the common men and women, if there were any who did not share in the enjoyment of such benefits as Yao and Shun conferred, it was as if he himself pushed them into a ditch;—for he took upon himself the heavy charge of the kingdom.

3. 'Hui of Liu-hsia was not ashamed to serve an impure prince, nor did he think it low to be an inferior officer. When advanced to employment, he did not conceal his virtue, but made it a point to carry out his principles. When dismissed and left without office, he did not murmur. When straitened by

poverty, he did not grieve. When thrown into the company of village people, he was quite at ease and could not bear to leave them. He had a saying, "You are you, and I am I. Although you stand by my side with breast and arms bare, or with your body naked, how can you defile me?" Therefore when men now hear the character of Hui of Liu-hsia, the mean become generous, and the niggardly become liberal.

4. 'When Confucius was leaving Ch'i, he strained off with his hand the water in which his rice was being rinsed, took the rice, and went away. When he left Lu, he said, "I will set out by-and-by:"—it was right he should leave the country of his parents in this way. When it was proper to go away quickly, he did so; when it was proper to delay, he did so; when it was proper to keep in retirement, he did so; when it was proper to go into office, he did so:—this was Confucius.'

5. Mencius said, 'Po-i among the sages was the pure one; I Yin was the one most inclined to take office; Hui of Liu-hsia was the accommodating one; and Confucius was the timeous one.

6. 'In Confucius we have what is called a complete concert. A complete concert is when the large bell proclaims the commencement of the music, and the ringing stone proclaims its close. The metal sound commences the blended harmony of all the instruments, and the winding up with the stone terminates that blended harmony. The commencing that harmony is the work of wisdom. The terminating it is the work of sageness.

7. 'As a comparison for wisdom, we may liken it to skill, and as a comparison for sageness, we may liken it to strength;—as in the case of shooting at a mark a hundred paces distant. That you reach it is owing to your strength, but that you hit the mark is not owing to your strength.'

CHAP. II. 1. Pei-kung I asked Mencius, saying, 'What was the arrangement of dignities and emoluments determined by the House of Chau?'

2. Mencius replied, 'The particulars of that arrangement cannot be learned, for the princes, disliking them as injurious to themselves, have all made away with the records of them.

241

Still I have learned the general outline of them.

3. 'The SON OF HEAVEN constituted one dignity; the KUNG one; the HAU one; the PAI one; and the TSZE and the NAN each one of equal rank:—altogether making five degrees of rank. The RULER again constituted one dignity; the CHIEF MINISTER one; the GREAT OFFICERS one; the SCHOLARS OF THE FIRST CLASS one; THOSE OF THE MIDDLE CLASS one; and THOSE OF THE LOWEST CLASS one:—altogether making six degrees of dignity.

4. 'To the Son of Heaven there was allotted a territory of a thousand li square. A Kung and a Hau had each a hundred li square. A Pai had seventy li, and a Tsze and a Nan had each fifty li. The assignments altogether were of four amounts. Where the territory did not amount to fifty li, the chief could not have access himself to the Son of Heaven. His land was attached to some Hau-ship, and was called a FU-YUNG.

5. 'The Chief ministers of the Son of Heaven received an amount of territory equal to that of a Hau; a Great officer received as much as a Pai; and a scholar of the first class as much as a Tsze or a Nan.

6. 'In a great State, where the territory was a hundred li square, the ruler had ten times as much income as his Chief ministers; a Chief minister four times as much as a Great officer; a Great officer twice as much as a scholar of the first class; a scholar of the first class twice as much as one of the middle; a scholar of the middle class twice as much as one of the lowest; the scholars of the lowest class, and such of the common people as were employed about the government offices, had for their emolument as much as was equal to what they would have made by tilling the fields.

7. 'In a State of the next order, where the territory was seventy li square, the ruler had ten times as much revenue as his Chief minister; a Chief minister three times as much as a Great officer; a Great officer twice as much as a scholar of the first class; a scholar of the first class twice as much as one of the middle; a scholar of the middle class twice as much as one of the lowest; the scholars of the lowest class, and such of the common people as were employed about the government

offices, had for their emolument as much as was equal to what they would have made by tilling the fields.

8. 'In a small State, where the territory was fifty li square, the ruler had ten times as much revenue as his Chief minister; a Chief minister had twice as much as a Great officer; a Great officer twice as much as a scholar of the highest class; a scholar of the highest class twice as much as one of the middle; a scholar of the middle class twice as much as one of the lowest; scholars of the lowest class, and such of the common people as were employed about the government offices, had the same emolument;—as much, namely, as was equal to what they would have made by tilling the fields.

9. 'As to those who tilled the fields, each husbandman received a hundred mau. When those mau were manured, the best husbandmen of the highest class supported nine individuals, and those ranking next to them supported eight. The best husbandmen of the second class supported seven individuals, and those ranking next to them supported six; while husbandmen of the lowest class only supported five. The salaries of the common people who were employed about the government offices were regulated according to these differences.'

CHAP. III. 1. Wan Chang asked Mencius, saying, 'I venture to ask the principles of friendship.' Mencius replied, 'Friendship should be maintained without any presumption on the ground of one's superior age, or station, or the circumstances of his relatives. Friendship with a man is friendship with his virtue, and does not admit of assumptions of superiority.

2. 'There was Mang Hsien, chief of a family of a hundred chariots. He had five friends, namely, Yo-chang Chiu, Mu Chung, and three others whose names I have forgotten. With those five men Hsien maintained a friendship, because they thought nothing about his family. If they had thought about his family, he would not have maintained his friendship with them.

3. 'Not only has the chief of a family of a hundred chariots acted thus. The same thing was exemplified by the sovereign

of a small State. The duke Hui of Pi said, "I treat Tsze-sze as my Teacher, and Yen Pan as my Friend. As to Wang Shun and Ch'ang Hsi, they serve me."

4. 'Not only has the sovereign of a small State acted thus. The same thing has been exemplified by the sovereign of a large State. There was the duke P'ing of Tsin with Hai T'ang:—when T'ang told him to come into his house, he came; when he told him to be seated, he sat; when he told him to eat, he ate. There might only be coarse rice and soup of vegetables, but he always ate his fill, not daring to do otherwise. Here, however, he stopped, and went no farther. He did not call him to share any of Heaven's places, or to govern any of Heaven's offices, or to partake of any of Heaven's emoluments. His conduct was but a scholar's honouring virtue and talents, not the honouring them proper to a king or a duke.

5. 'Shun went up to court and saw the sovereign, who lodged him as his son-in-law in the second palace. The sovereign also enjoyed there Shun's hospitality. Alternately he was host and guest. Here was the sovereign maintaining friendship with a private man.

6. Respect shown by inferiors to superiors is called giving to the noble the observance due to rank. Respect shown by superiors to inferiors is called giving honour to talents and virtue. The rightness in each case is the same.'

CHAP. IV. 1. Wan Chang asked Mencius, saying, 'I venture to ask what feeling of the mind is expressed in the presents of friendship?' Mencius replied, 'The feeling of respect.'

2. 'How is it,' pursued Chang, 'that the declining a present is accounted disrespectful?' The answer was, 'When one of honourable rank presents a gift, to say in the mind, "Was the way in which he got this righteous or not? I must know this before I can receive it;"—this is deemed disrespectful, and therefore presents are not declined.'

3. Wan Chang asked again, 'When one does not take on him in so many express words to refuse the gift, but having declined it in his heart, saying, "It was taken by him unrighteously from the people," and then assigns some other reason for not receiving it;—is not this a proper course?'

244

Mencius said, 'When the donor offers it on a ground of reason, and his manner of doing so is according to propriety;—in such a case Confucius would have received it.'

4. Wan Chang said, 'Here now is one who stops and robs people outside the gates of the city. He offers his gift on a ground of reason, and does so in a manner according to propriety;—would the reception of it so acquired by robbery be proper?' Mencius replied, 'It would not be proper. in "The Announcement to Kang" it is said, "When men kill others, and roll over their bodies to take their property, being reckless and fearless of death, among all the people there are none but detest them:"—thus, such characters are to be put to death, without waiting to give them warning. Yin received this rule from Hsia and Chau received it from Yin. It cannot be questioned, and to the present day is clearly acknowledged. How can the grift of a robber be received?'

5. Chang said, 'The princes of the present day take from their people just as a robber despoils his victim. Yet if they put a good face of propriety on their gifts, then the superior man receives them. I venture to ask how you explain this.' Mencius answered, 'Do you think that, if there should arise a truly royal sovereign, he would collect the princes of the present day, and put them all to death? Or would he admonish them, and then, on their not changing their ways, put them to death? Indeed, to call every one who takes what does not properly belong to him a robber, is pushing a point of resemblance to the utmost, and insisting on the most refined idea of righteousness. When Confucius was in office in Lu, the people struggled together for the game taken in hunting, and he also did the same. If that struggling for the captured game was proper, how much more may the gifts of the princes be received!'

6. Chang urged, 'Then are we to suppose that when Confucius held office, it was not with the view to carry his doctrines into practice?' 'It was with that view,' Mencius replied, and Chang rejoined, 'If the practice of his doctrines was his business, what had he to do with that struggling for the captured game?' Mencius said, 'Confucius first rectified his vessels of sacrifice according to the registers, and did not fill

them so rectified with food gathered from every quarter.' 'But why did he not go away?' He wished to make a trial of carrying his doctrines into practice. When that trial was sufficient to show that they could be practised and they were still not practised, then he went away, and thus it was that he never completed in any State a residence of three years.

7. 'Confucius took office when he saw that the practice of his doctrines was likely; he took office when his reception was proper; he took office when he was supported by the State. In the case of his relation to Chi Hwan, he took office, seeing that the practice of his doctrines was likely. With the duke Ling of Wei he took office, because his reception was proper. With the duke Hsiao of Wei he took office, because he was maintained by the State.'

CHAP. V. 1. Mencius said, 'Office is not sought on account of poverty, yet there are times when one seeks office on that account. Marriage is not entered into for the sake of being attended to by the wife, yet there are times when one marries on that account.

2. 'He who takes office on account of his poverty must decline an honourable situation and occupy a low one; he must decline riches and prefer to be poor.

3. 'What office will be in harmony with this declining an honourable situation and occupying a low one, this declining riches and preferring to be poor? Such an one as that of guarding the gates, or beating the watchman's stick.

4. 'Confucius was once keeper of stores, and he then said, "My calculations must be all right. That is all I have to care about." He was once in charge of the public fields, and he then said, "The oxen and sheep must be fat and strong, and superior. That is all I have to care about."

5. 'When one is in a low situation, to speak of high matters is a crime. When a scholar stands in a prince's court, and his principles are not carried into practice, it is a shame to him.'

CHAP. VI. 1. Wan Chang said, 'What is the reason that a scholar does not accept a stated support from a prince?' Mencius replied, 'He does not presume to do so. When a prince loses his State, and then accepts a stated support from another prince, this is in accordance with propriety. But for a scholar to accept such support from any of the princes is not in accordance with propriety.'

2. Wan Chang said, 'If the prince send him a present of grain, for instance, does he accept it?' 'He accepts it,' answered Mencius. 'On what principle of righteousness does he accept it?' 'Why—the prince ought to assist the people in their necessities.'

3. Chang pursued, 'Why is it that the scholar will thus accept the prince's help, but will not accept his pay?' The answer was, 'He does not presume to do so.' 'I venture to ask why he does not presume to do so.' 'Even the keepers of the gates, with their watchmen's sticks, have their regular offices for which they can take their support from the prince. He who without a regular office should receive the pay of the prince must be deemed disrespectful.'

4. Chang asked, 'If the prince sends a scholar a present, he accepts it;—I do not know whether this present may be constantly repeated.' Mencius answered, 'There was the conduct of the duke Mu to Tsze-sze—He made frequent inquiries after Tsze-sze's health, and sent him frequent presents of cooked meat. Tsze-sze was displeased; and at length, having motioned to the messenger to go outside the great door, he bowed his head to the ground with his face to the north, did obeisance twice, and declined the gift, saying, "From this time forth I shall know that the prince supports me as a dog or a horse." And so from that time a servant was no more sent with the presents. When a prince professes to be pleased with a man of talents and virtue, and can neither promote him to office, nor support him in the proper way, can he be said to be pleased with him?

5. Chang said, 'I venture to ask how the sovereign of a State, when he wishes to support a superior man, must proceed, that he may be said to do so in the proper way?' Mencius answered, 'At first, the present must be offered with the prince's commission, and the scholar, making obeisance twice with his head bowed to the ground, will receive it. But after this the storekeeper will continue to send grain, and the master of the

kitchen to send meat, presenting it as if without the prince's express commission. Tsze-sze considered that the meat from the prince's caldron, giving him the annoyance of constantly doing obeisance, was not the way to support a superior man.

6. 'There was Yao's conduct to Shun:—He caused his nine sons to serve him, and gave him his two daughters in marriage; he caused the various officers, oxen and sheep, storehouses and granaries, all to be prepared to support Shun amid the channelled fields, and then he raised him to the most exalted situation. From this we have the expression—"The honouring of virtue and talents proper to a king or a duke."'

CHAP. VII. 1. Wan Chang said, 'I venture to ask what principle of righteousness is involved in a scholar's not going to see the princes?' Mencius replied, 'A scholar residing in the city is called "a minister of the market-place and well," and one residing in the country is called "a minister of the grass and plants." In both cases he is a common man, and it is the rule of propriety that common men, who have not presented the introductory present and become ministers, should not presume to have interviews with the prince.'

2. Wan Chang said, 'If a common man is called to perform any service, he goes and performs it;—how is it that a scholar, when the prince, wishing to see him, calls him to his presence, refuses to go?' Mencius replied, 'It is right to go and perform the service; it would not be right to go and see the prince.'

3. 'And,' added Mencius, 'on what account is it that the prince wishes to see the scholar?' 'Because of his extensive information, or because of his talents and virtue,' was the reply. 'If because of his extensive information,' said Mencius, 'such a person is a teacher, and the sovereign would not call him;—how much less may any of the princes do so? If because of his talents and virtue, then I have not heard of any one wishing to see a person with those qualities, and calling him to his presence.

4. 'During the frequent interviews of the duke Mu with Tsze-sze, he one day said to him, "Anciently, princes of a thousand chariots have yet been on terms of friendship with scholars;—what do you think of such an intercourse?" Tsze-

sze was displeased, and said, "The ancients have said, 'The scholar should be served:' how should they have merely said that he should be made a friend of?" When Tsze-sze was thus displeased, did he not say within himself,—"With regard to our stations, you are sovereign, and I am subject. How can I presume to be on terms of friendship with my sovereign! With regard to our virtue, you ought to make me your master. How can you be on terms of friendship with me?" Thus, when a ruler of a thousand chariots sought to be on terms of friendship with a scholar, he could not obtain his wish:—how much less could he call him to his presence!

5. 'The duke Ching of Ch'i, once, when he was hunting, called his forester to him by a flag. The forester would not come, and the duke was going to kill him. With reference to this incident, Confucius said, "The determined officer never forgets that his end may be in a ditch or a stream; the brave officer never forgets that he may lose his head." What was it in the forester that Confucius thus approved? He approved his not going to the duke, when summoned by the article which was not appropriate to him.'

6. Chang said, 'May I ask with what a forester should be summoned?' Mencius replied, 'With a skin cap. A common man should be summoned with a plain banner; a scholar who has taken office, with one having dragons embroidered on it; and a Great officer, with one having feathers suspended from the top of the staff.

7. 'When the forester was summoned with the article appropriate to the summoning of a Great officer, he would have died rather than presume to go. If a common man were summoned with the article appropriate to the summoning of a scholar, how could he presume to go? How much more may we expect this refusal to go, when a man of talents and virtue is summoned in a way which is inappropriate to his character!

8. 'When a prince wishes to see a man of talents and virtue, and does not take the proper course to get his wish, it is as if he wished him to enter his palace, and shut the door against him. Now, righteousness is the way, and propriety is the door, but it is only the superior man who can follow this way, and

go out and in by this door. It is said in the Book of Poetry,
"The way to Chau is level like a whetstone,
And straight as an arrow.
The officers tread it,
And the lower people see it."'

9. Wan Chang said, 'When Confucius received the prince's message calling him, he went without waiting for his carriage. Doing so, did Confucius do wrong?' Mencius replied, 'Confucius was in office, and had to observe its appropriate duties. And moreover, he was summoned on the business of his office.'

CHAP. VIII. 1. Mencius said to Wan Chang, 'The scholar whose virtue is most distinguished in a village shall make friends of all the virtuous scholars in the village. The scholar whose virtue is most distinguished throughout a State shall make friends of all the virtuous scholars of that State. The scholar whose virtue is most distinguished throughout the kingdom shall make friends of all the virtuous scholars of the kingdom.

2. 'When a scholar feels that his friendship with all the virtuous scholars of the kingdom is not sufficient to satisfy him, he proceeds to ascend to consider the men of antiquity. He repeats their poems, and reads their books, and as he does not know what they were as men, to ascertain this, he considers their history. This is to ascend and make friends of the men of antiquity.'

CHAP. IX. 1. The king Hsuan of Ch'i asked about the office of high ministers. Mencius said, 'Which high ministers is your Majesty asking about?' 'Are there differences among them?' inquired the king. 'There are' was the reply. 'There are the high ministers who are noble and relatives of the prince, and there are those who are of a different surname.' The king said, 'I beg to ask about the high ministers who are noble and relatives of the prince.' Mencius answered, 'If the prince have great faults, they ought to remonstrate with him, and if he do not listen to them after they have done so again and again, they ought to dethrone him.'

2. The king on this looked moved, and changed

countenance.

3. Mencius said, 'Let not your Majesty be offended. You asked me, and I dare not answer but according to truth.'

4. The king's countenance became composed, and he then begged to ask about high ministers who were of a different surname from the prince. Mencius said, 'When the prince has faults, they ought to remonstrate with him; and if he do not listen to them after they have done this again and again, they ought to leave the State.'

BOOK VI. KAO TSZE, PART I

CHAP. I. 1. The philosopher Kao said, 'Man's nature is like the ch'i-willow, and righteousness is like a cup or a bowl. The fashioning benevolence and righteousness out of man's nature is like the making cups and bowls from the ch'i-willow.'

2. Mencius replied, 'Can you, leaving untouched the nature of the willow, make with it cups and bowls? You must do violence and injury to the willow, before you can make cups and bowls with it. If you must do violence and injury to the willow in order to make cups and bowls with it, on your principles you must in the same way do violence and injury to humanity in order to fashion from it benevolence and righteousness! Your words, alas! would certainly lead all men on to reckon benevolence and righteousness to be calamities.'

CHAP. II. 1. The philosopher Kao said, 'Man's nature is like water whirling round in a corner. Open a passage for it to the east, and it will flow to the east; open a passage for it to the west, and it will flow to the west. Man's nature is indifferent to good and evil, just as the water is indifferent to the east and west.'

2. Mencius replied, 'Water indeed will flow indifferently to the east or west, but will it flow indifferently up or down? The tendency of man's nature to good is like the tendency of water to flow downwards. There are none but have this tendency to good, just as all water flows downwards.

3. 'Now by striking water and causing it to leap up, you may make it go over your forehead, and, by damming and leading it you may force it up a hill;—but are such movements according to the nature of water? It is the force applied which causes them. When men are made to do what is not good, their nature is dealt with in this way.'

CHAP. III. 1. The philosopher Kao said, 'Life is what we call nature!'

2. Mencius asked him, 'Do you say that by nature you mean life, just as you say that white is white?' 'Yes, I do,' was the reply. Mencius added, 'Is the whiteness of a white feather like

that of white snow, and the whiteness of white snow like that of white jade?' Kao again said 'Yes.'

3. 'Very well,' pursued Mencius. 'Is the nature of a dog like the nature of an ox, and the nature of an ox like the nature of a man?'

CHAP. IV. 1. The philosopher Kao said, 'To enjoy food and delight in colours is nature. Benevolence is internal and not external; righteousness is external and not internal.'

2. Mencius asked him, 'What is the ground of your saying that benevolence is internal and righteousness external?' He replied, 'There is a man older than I, and I give honour to his age. It is not that there is first in me a principle of such reverence to age. It is just as when there is a white man, and I consider him white; according as he is so externally to me. On this account, I pronounce of righteousness that it is external.'

3. Mencius said, 'There is no difference between our pronouncing a white horse to be white and our pronouncing a white man to be white. But is there no difference between the regard with which we acknowledge the age of an old horse and that with which we acknowledge the age of an old man? And what is it which is called righteousness?—the fact of a man's being old? or the fact of our giving honour to his age?'

4. Kao said, 'There is my younger brother;—I love him. But the younger brother of a man of Ch'in I do not love: that is, the feeling is determined by myself, and therefore I say that benevolence is internal. On the other hand, I give honour to an old man of Ch'u, and I also give honour to an old man of my own people: that is, the feeling is determined by the age, and therefore I say that righteousness is external.'

5. Mencius answered him, 'Our enjoyment of meat roasted by a man of Ch'in does not differ from our enjoyment of meat roasted by ourselves. Thus, what you insist on takes place also in the case of such things, and will you say likewise that our enjoyment of a roast is external?'

CHAP. V. 1. The disciple Mang Chi asked Kung-tu, saying, 'On what ground is it said that righteousness is internal?'

2. Kung-tu replied, 'We therein act out our feeling of respect, and therefore it is said to be internal.'

3. The other objected, 'Suppose the case of a villager older than your elder brother by one year, to which of them would you show the greater respect?' 'To my brother,' was the reply. 'But for which of them would you first pour out wine at a feast?' 'For the villager.' Mang Chi argued, 'Now your feeling of reverence rests on the one, and now the honour due to age is rendered to the other;—this is certainly determined by what is without, and does not proceed from within.'

4. Kung-tu was unable to reply, and told the conversation to Mencius. Mencius said, 'You should ask him, "Which do you respect most,—your uncle, or your younger brother?" He will answer, "My uncle." Ask him again, "If your younger brother be personating a dead ancestor, to which do you show the greater respect,—to him or to your uncle?" He will say, "To my younger brother." You can go on, "But where is the respect due, as you said, to your uncle?" He will reply to this, "I show the respect to my younger brother, because of the position which he occupies," and you can likewise say, "So my respect to the villager is because of the position which he occupies. Ordinarily, my respect is rendered to my elder brother; for a brief season, on occasion, it is rendered to the villager."'

5. Mang Chi heard this and observed, 'When respect is due to my uncle, I respect him, and when respect is due to my younger brother, I respect him;—the thing is certainly determined by what is without, and does not proceed from within.' Kung-tu replied, 'In winter we drink things hot, in summer we drink things cold; and so, on your principle, eating and drinking also depend on what is external!'

CHAP. VI. 1. The disciple Kung-tu said, 'The philosopher Kao says, "Man's nature is neither good nor bad."

2. 'Some say, "Man's nature may be made to practise good, and it may be made to practise evil, and accordingly, under Wan and Wu, the people loved what was good, while under Yu and Li, they loved what was cruel."

3. 'Some say, "The nature of some is good, and the nature of others is bad." Hence it was that under such a sovereign as Yao there yet appeared Hsiang; that with such a father as Ku-

sau there yet appeared Shun; and that with Chau for their sovereign, and the son of their elder brother besides, there were found Ch'i, the viscount of Wei, and the prince Pi-Kan.

4. 'And now you say, "The nature is good." Then are all those wrong?'

5. Mencius said, 'From the feelings proper to it, it is constituted for the practice of what is good. This is what I mean in saying that the nature is good.

6. 'If men do what is not good, the blame cannot be imputed to their natural powers.

7. 'The feeling of commiseration belongs to all men; so does that of shame and dislike; and that of reverence and respect; and that of approving and disapproving. The feeling of commiseration implies the principle of benevolence; that of shame and dislike, the principle of righteousness; that of reverence and respect, the principle of propriety; and that of approving and disapproving, the principle of knowledge. Benevolence, righteousness, propriety, and knowledge are not infused into us from without. We are certainly furnished with them. And a different view is simply owing to want of reflection. Hence it is said, "Seek and you will find them. Neglect and you will lose them." Men differ from one another in regard to them;—some as much again as others, some five times as much, and some to an incalculable amount:—it is because they cannot carry out fully their natural powers.

8. 'It is said in the Book of Poetry,
"Heaven in producing mankind,
Gave them their various faculties and relations with their specific laws.
These are the invariable rules of nature for all to hold,
And all love this admirable virtue."
Confucius said, "The maker of this ode knew indeed the principle of our nature!" We may thus see that every faculty and relation must have its law, and since there are invariable rules for all to hold, they consequently love this admirable virtue.'

CHAP. VII. 1. Mencius said, 'In good years the children of the people are most of them good, while in bad years the most

255

of them abandon themselves to evil. It is not owing to any difference of their natural powers conferred by Heaven that they are thus different. The abandonment is owing to the circumstances through which they allow their minds to be ensnared and drowned in evil.

2. 'There now is barley.—Let it be sown and covered up; the ground being the same, and the time of sowing likewise the same, it grows rapidly up, and, when the full time is come, it is all found to be ripe. Although there may be inequalities of produce, that is owing to the difference of the soil, as rich or poor, to the unequal nourishment afforded by the rains and dews, and to the different ways in which man has performed his business in reference to it.

3. 'Thus all things which are the same in kind are like to one another;—why should we doubt in regard to man, as if he were a solitary exception to this? The sage and we are the same in kind.

4. 'In accordance with this the scholar Lung said, "If a man make hempen sandals without knowing the size of people's feet, yet I know that he will not make them like baskets." Sandals are all like one another, because all men's feet are like one another.

5. 'So with the mouth and flavours;—all mouths have the same relishes. Yi-ya only apprehended before me what my mouth relishes. Suppose that his mouth in its relish for flavours differed from that of other men, as is the case with dogs or horses which are not the same in kind with us, why should all men be found following Yi-ya in their relishes? In the matter of tastes all the people model themselves after Yi-ya; that is, the mouths of all men are like one another.

6. 'And so also it is with the ear. In the matter of sounds, the whole people model themselves after the music-master K'wang; that is, the ears of all men are like one another.

7. 'And so also it is with the eye. In the case of Tsze-tu, there is no man but would recognise that he was beautiful. Any one who would not recognise the beauty of Tsze-tu must have no eyes.

8. 'Therefore I say,—Men's mouths agree in having the

256

same relishes; their ears agree in enjoying the same sounds; their eyes agree in recognising the same beauty:—shall their minds alone be without that which the similarly approve? What is it then of which they similarly approve? It is, I say, the principles of our nature, and the determinations of righteousness. The sages only apprehended before me that of which my mind approves along with other men. Therefore the principles of our nature and the determinations of righteousness are agreeable to my mind, just as the flesh of grass and grain-fed animals is agreeable to my mouth.'

CHAP. VIII. 1. Mencius said, 'The trees of the Niu mountain were once beautiful. Being situated, however, in the borders of a large State, they were hewn down with axes and bills;—and could they retain their beauty? Still through the activity of the vegetative life day and night, and the nourishing influence of the rain and dew, they were not without buds and sprouts springing forth, but then came the cattle and goats and browsed upon them. To these things is owing the bare and stripped appearance of the mountain, and when people now see it, they think it was never finely wooded. But is this the nature of the mountain?

2. 'And so also of what properly belongs to man;—shall it be said that the mind of any man was without benevolence and righteousness? The way in which a man loses his proper goodness of mind is like the way in which the trees are denuded by axes and bills. Hewn down day after day, can it—the mind—retain its beauty? But there is a development of its life day and night, and in the calm air of the morning, just between night and day, the mind feels in a degree those desires and aversions which are proper to humanity, but the feeling is not strong, and it is fettered and destroyed by what takes place during the day. This fettering taking place again and again, the restorative influence of the night is not sufficient to preserve the proper goodness of the mind; and when this proves insufficient for that purpose, the nature becomes not much different from that of the irrational animals, and when people now see it, they think that it never had those powers which I assert. But does this condition represent the feelings proper to

humanity?

3. 'Therefore, if it receive its proper nourishment, there is nothing which will not grow. If it lose its proper nourishment, there is nothing which will not decay away.

4. 'Confucius said, "Hold it fast, and it remains with you. Let it go, and you lose it. Its outgoing and incoming cannot be defined as to time or place." It is the mind of which this is said!'

CHAP. IX. 1. Mencius said, 'It is not to be wondered at that the king is not wise!

2. 'Suppose the case of the most easily growing thing in the world;—if you let it have one day's genial heat, and then expose it for ten days to cold, it will not be able to grow. It is but seldom that I have an audience of the king, and when I retire, there come all those who act upon him like the cold. Though I succeed in bringing out some buds of goodness, of what avail is it?

3. 'Now chess-playing is but a small art, but without his whole mind being given, and his will bent, to it, a man cannot succeed at it. Chess Ch'iu is the best chess-player in all the kingdom. Suppose that he is teaching two men to play.—The one gives to the subject his whole mind and bends to it all his will, doing nothing but listening to Chess Ch'iu. The other, although he seems to be listening to him, has his whole mind running on a swan which he thinks is approaching, and wishes to bend his bow, adjust the string to the arrow, and shoot it. Although he is learning along with the other, he does not come up to him. Why?—because his intelligence is not equal? Not so.'

CHAP. X. 1. Mencius said, 'I like fish, and I also like bear's paws. If I cannot have the two together, I will let the fish go, and take the bear's paws. So, I like life, and I also like righteousness. If I cannot keep the two together, I will let life go, and choose righteousness.

2. 'I like life indeed, but there is that which I like more than life, and therefore, I will not seek to possess it by any improper ways. I dislike death indeed, but there is that which I dislike more than death, and therefore there are occasions when I will

not avoid danger.

3. 'If among the things which man likes there were nothing which he liked more than life, why should he not use every means by which he could preserve it? If among the things which man dislikes there were nothing which he disliked more than death, why should he not do everything by which he could avoid danger?

4. 'There are cases when men by a certain course might preserve life, and they do not employ it; when by certain things they might avoid danger, and they will not do them.

5. 'Therefore, men have that which they like more than life, and that which they dislike more than death. They are not men of distinguished talents and virtue only who have this mental nature. All men have it; what belongs to such men is simply that they do not lose it.

6. 'Here are a small basket of rice and a platter of soup, and the case is one in which the getting them will preserve life, and the want of them will be death;—if they are offered with an insulting voice, even a tramper will not receive them, or if you first tread upon them, even a beggar will not stoop to take them.

7. 'And yet a man will accept of ten thousand chung, without any consideration of propriety or righteousness. What can the ten thousand chung add to him? When he takes them, is it not that he may obtain beautiful mansions, that he may secure the services of wives and concubines, or that the poor and needy of his acquaintance may be helped by him?

8. 'In the former case the offered bounty was not received, though it would have saved from death, and now the emolument is taken for the sake of beautiful mansions. The bounty that would have preserved from death was not received, and the emolument is taken to get the service of wives and concubines. The bounty that would have saved from death was not received, and the emolument is taken that one's poor and needy acquaintance may be helped by him. Was it then not possible likewise to decline this? This is a case of what is called—"Losing the proper nature of one's mind."'

CHAP. XI. 1. Mencius said, 'Benevolence is man's mind, and

righteousness is man's path.

2. 'How lamentable is it to neglect the path and not pursue it, to lose this mind and not know to seek it again!

3. 'When men's fowls and dogs are lost, they know to seek for them again, but they lose their mind, and do not know to seek for it.

4. 'The great end of learning is nothing else but to seek for the lost mind.'

CHAP. XII. 1. Mencius said, 'Here is a man whose fourth finger is bent and cannot be stretched out straight. It is not painful, nor does it incommode his business, and yet if there be any one who can make it straight, he will not think the way from Ch'in to Ch'u far to go to him; because his finger is not like the finger of other people.

2. 'When a man's finger is not like those of other people, he knows to feel dissatisfied, but if his mind be not like that of other people, he does not know to feel dissatisfaction. This is called—"Ignorance of the relative importance of things."'

CHAP. XIII. Mencius said, 'Anybody who wishes to cultivate the t'ung or the tsze, which may be grasped with both hands, perhaps with one, knows by what means to nourish them. In the case of their own persons, men do not know by what means to nourish them. Is it to be supposed that their regard of their own persons is inferior to their regard for a t'ung or tsze? Their want of reflection is extreme.'

CHAP. XIV. 1. Mencius said, 'There is no part of himself which a man does not love, and as he loves all, so he must nourish all. There is not an inch of skin which he does not love, and so there is not an inch of skin which he will not nourish. For examining whether his way of nourishing be good or not, what other rule is there but this, that he determine by reflecting on himself where it should be applied?

2. 'Some parts of the body are noble, and some ignoble; some great, and some small. The great must not be injured for the small, nor the noble for the ignoble. He who nourishes the little belonging to him is a little man, and he who nourishes the great is a great man.

3. 'Here is a plantation-keeper, who neglects his wu and

chia, and cultivates his sour jujube-trees;—he is a poor plantation-keeper.

4. 'He who nourishes one of his fingers, neglecting his shoulders or his back, without knowing that he is doing so, is a man who resembles a hurried wolf.

5. 'A man who only eats and drinks is counted mean by others;—because he nourishes what is little to the neglect of what is great.

6. 'If a man, fond of his eating and drinking, were not to neglect what is of more importance, how should his mouth and belly be considered as no more than an inch of skin?'

CHAP. XV. 1. The disciple Kung-tu said, 'All are equally men, but some are great men, and some are little men;—how is this?' Mencius replied, 'Those who follow that part of themselves which is great are great men; those who follow that part which is little are little men.'

2. Kung-tu pursued, 'All are equally men, but some follow that part of themselves which is great, and some follow that part which is little;—how is this?' Mencius answered, 'The senses of hearing and seeing do not think, and are obscured by external things. When one thing comes into contact with another, as a matter of course it leads it away. To the mind belongs the office of thinking. By thinking, it gets the right view of things; by neglecting to think, it fails to do this. These—the senses and the mind—are what Heaven has given to us. Let a man first stand fast in the supremacy of the nobler part of his constitution, and the inferior part will not be able to take it from him. It is simply this which makes the great man.'

CHAP. XVI. 1. Mencius said, 'There is a nobility of Heaven, and there is a nobility of man. Benevolence, righteousness, self-consecration, and fidelity, with unwearied joy in these virtues;—these constitute the nobility of Heaven. To be a kung, a ch'ing, or a ta-fu;—this constitutes the nobility of man.

2. 'The men of antiquity cultivated their nobility of Heaven, and the nobility of man came to them in its train.

3. 'The men of the present day cultivate their nobility of Heaven in order to seek for the nobility of man, and when they

261

have obtained that, they throw away the other:—their delusion is extreme. The issue is simply this, that they must lose that nobility of man as well.'

CHAP. XVII. 1. Mencius said, 'To desire to be honoured is the common mind of men. And all men have in themselves that which is truly honourable. Only they do not think of it.

2. 'The honour which men confer is not good honour. Those whom Chao the Great ennobles he can make mean again.

3. 'It is said in the Book of Poetry,
"He has filled us with his wine,
He has satiated us with his goodness."
"Satiated us with his goodness," that is, satiated us with benevolence and righteousness, and he who is so satiated, consequently, does not wish for the fat meat and fine millet of men. A good reputation and far-reaching praise fall to him, and he does not desire the elegant embroidered garments of men.'

CHAP. XVIII. 1. Mencius said, 'Benevolence subdues its opposite just as water subdues fire. Those, however, who now-a-days practise benevolence do it as if with one cup of water they could save a whole waggon-load of fuel which was on fire, and when the flames were not extinguished, were to say that water cannot subdue fire. This conduct, moreover, greatly encourages those who are not benevolent.

2. 'The final issue will simply be this—the loss of that small amount of benevolence.'

CHAP. XIX. Mencius said, 'Of all seeds the best are the five kinds of grain, yet if they be not ripe, they are not equal to the t'i or the pai. So, the value of benevolence depends entirely on its being brought to maturity.'

CHAP. XX. 1. Mencius said, 'I, in teaching men to shoot, made it a rule to draw the bow to the full, and his pupils also did the same.

2. 'A master-workman, in teaching others, uses the compass and square, and his pupils do the same.'

BOOK VI. KAO TSZE, PART II

CHAP. I. 1. A man of Zan asked the disciple Wu-lu, saying, 'Is an observance of the rules of propriety in regard to eating, or eating merely, the more important?' The answer was, 'The observance of the rules of propriety is the more important.'

2. 'Is the gratifying the appetite of sex, or the doing so only according to the rules of propriety, the more important?' The answer again was, 'The observance of the rules of propriety in the matter is the more important.'

3. The man pursued, 'If the result of eating only according to the rules of propriety will be death by starvation, while by disregarding those rules we may get food, must they still be observed in such a case? If according to the rule that he shall go in person to meet his wife a man cannot get married, while by disregarding that rule he may get married, must he still observe the rule in such a case?'

4. Wu-lu was unable to reply to these questions, and the next day he went to Tsau, and told them to Mencius. Mencius said, 'What difficulty is there in answering these inquiries?'

5. 'If you do not adjust them at their lower extremities, but only put their tops on a level, a piece of wood an inch square may be made to be higher than the pointed peak of a high building.

6. 'Gold is heavier than feathers;—but does that saying have reference, on the one hand, to a single clasp of gold, and, on the other, to a waggon-load of feathers?

7. 'If you take a case where the eating is of the utmost importance and the observing the rules of propriety is of little importance, and compare the things together, why stop with saying merely that the eating is more important? So, taking the case where the gratifying the appetite of sex is of the utmost importance and the observing the rules of propriety is of little importance, why stop with merely saying that the gratifying the appetite is the more important?

8. 'Go and answer him thus, "If, by twisting your elder brother's arm, and snatching from him what he is eating, you

can get food for yourself, while, if you do not do so, you will not get anything to eat, will you so twist his arm? If by getting over your neighbour's wall, and dragging away his virgin daughter, you can get a wife, while if you do not do so, you will not be able to get a wife, will you so drag her away?"'

CHAP. II. 1. Chiao of Tsao asked Mencius, saying, 'It is said, "All men may be Yaos and Shuns;"—is it so?' Mencius replied, It is.'

2. Chiao went on, 'I have heard that king Wan was ten cubits high, and T'ang nine. Now I am nine cubits four inches in height. But I can do nothing but eat my millet. What am I to do to realize that saying?'

3. Mencius answered him, 'What has this—the question of size—to do with the matter? It all lies simply in acting as such. Here is a man, whose strength was not equal to lift a duckling:—he was then a man of no strength. But to-day he says, "I can lift 3,000 catties' weight," and he is a man of strength. And so, he who can lift the weight which Wu Hwo lifted is just another Wu Hwo. Why should a man make a want of ability the subject of his grief? It is only that he will not do the thing.

4. 'To walk slowly, keeping behind his elders, is to perform the part of a younger. To walk quickly and precede his elders, is to violate the duty of a younger brother. Now, is it what a man cannot do—to walk slowly? It is what he does not do. The course of Yao and Shun was simply that of filial piety and fraternal duty.

5. 'Wear the clothes of Yao, repeat the words of Yao, and do the actions of Yao, and you will just be a Yao. And, if you wear the clothes of Chieh, repeat the words of Chieh, and do the actions of Chieh, you will just be a Chieh.'

6. Chiao said, 'I shall be having an interview with the prince of Tsau, and can ask him to let me have a house to lodge in. I wish to remain here, and receive instruction at your gate.'

7. Mencius replied, 'The way of truth is like a great road. It is not difficult to know it. The evil is only that men will not seek it. Do you go home and search for it, and you will have abundance of teachers.'

CHAP. III. 1. Kung-sun Ch'au asked about an opinion of the scholar Kao, saying, 'Kao observed, "The Hsiao P'an is the ode of a little man."' Mencius asked, 'Why did he say so?' 'Because of the murmuring which it expresses,' was the reply.

2. Mencius answered, 'How stupid was that old Kao in dealing with the ode! There is a man here, and a native of Yueh bends his bow to shoot him. I will advise him not to do so, but speaking calmly and smilingly;—for no other reason but that he is not related to me. But if my own brother be bending his bow to shoot the man, then I will advise him not to do so, weeping and crying the while;—for no other reason than that he is related to me. The dissatisfaction expressed in the Hsiao P'an is the working of relative affection, and that affection shows benevolence. Stupid indeed was old Kao's criticism on the ode.'

3. Ch'au then said, 'How is it that there is no dissatisfaction expressed in the K'ai Fang?'

4. Mencius replied, 'The parent's fault referred to in the K'ai Fang is small; that referred to in the Hsiao P'an is great. Where the parent's fault was great, not to have murmured on account of it would have increased the want of natural affection. Where the parent's fault was small, to have murmured on account of it would have been to act like water which frets and foams about a stone that interrupts its course. To increase the want of natural affection would have been unfilial, and to fret and foam in such a manner would also have been unfilial.

5 'Confucius said, "Shun was indeed perfectly filial! And yet, when he was fifty, he was full of longing desire about his parents."'

CHAP. IV. 1. Sung K'ang being about to go to Ch'u, Mencius met him in Shih-ch'iu.

2. 'Master, where are you going?' asked Mencius.

3. K'ang replied, 'I have heard that Ch'in and Ch'u are fighting together, and I am going to see the king of Ch'u and persuade him to cease hostilities. If he shall not be pleased with my advice, I shall go to see the king of Ch'in, and persuade him in the same way. Of the two kings I shall surely find that I can succeed with one of them.'

4. Mencius said, 'I will not venture to ask about the particulars, but I should like to hear the scope of your plan. What course will you take to try to persuade them?' K'ang answered, 'I will tell them how unprofitable their course is to them.' 'Master,' said Mencius, 'your aim is great, but your argument is not good.

5. 'If you, starting from the point of profit, offer your persuasive counsels to the kings of Ch'in and Ch'u, and if those kings are pleased with the consideration of profit so as to stop the movements of their armies, then all belonging to those armies will rejoice in the cessation of war, and find their pleasure in the pursuit of profit. Ministers will serve their sovereign for the profit of which they cherish the thought; sons will serve their fathers, and younger brothers will serve their elder brothers, from the same consideration:—and the issue will be, that, abandoning benevolence and righteousness, sovereign and minister, father and son, younger brother and elder, will carry on all their intercourse with this thought of profit cherished in their breasts. But never has there been such a state of society, without ruin being the result of it.

6. 'If you, starting from the ground of benevolence and righteousness, offer your counsels to the kings of Ch'in and Ch'u, and if those kings are pleased with the consideration of benevolence and righteousness so as to stop the operations of their armies, then all belonging to those armies will rejoice in the stopping from war, and find their pleasure in benevolence and righteousness. Ministers will serve their sovereign, cherishing the principles of benevolence and righteousness; sons will serve their fathers, and younger brothers will serve their elder brothers, in the same way:—and so, sovereign and minister, father and son, elder brother and younger, abandoning the thought of profit, will cherish the principles of benevolence and righteousness, and carry on all their intercourse upon them. But never has there been such a state of society, without the State where it prevailed rising to the royal sway. Why must you use that word "profit."'

CHAP. V. 1. When Mencius was residing in Tsau, the younger brother of the chief of Zan, who was guardian of Zan

266

at the time, paid his respects to him by a present of silks, which Mencius received, not going to acknowledge it. When he was sojourning in P'ing-lu, Ch'u, who was prime minister of the State, sent him a similar present, which he received in the same way.

2. Subsequently, going from Tsau to Zan, he visited the guardian; but when he went from Ping-lu to the capital of Ch'i, he did not visit the minister Ch'u. The disciple Wu-lu was glad, and said, 'I have got an opportunity to obtain some instruction.'

3. He asked accordingly, 'Master, when you went to Zan, you visited the chief's brother; and when you went to Ch'i, you did not visit Ch'u. Was it not because he is only the minister?'

4. Mencius replied, 'No. It is said in the Book of History, "In presenting an offering to a superior, most depends on the demonstrations of respect. If those demonstrations are not equal to the things offered, we say there is no offering, that is, there is no act of the will presenting the offering."

5. 'This is because the things so offered do not constitute an offering to a superior.'

6. Wu-lu was pleased, and when some one asked him what Mencius meant, he said, 'The younger of Zan could not go to Tsau, but the minister Ch'u might have gone to P'ing-lu.'

CHAP. VI. 1. Shun-yu K'wan said, 'He who makes fame and meritorious services his first objects, acts with a regard to others. He who makes them only secondary objects, acts with a regard to himself. You, master, were ranked among the three chief ministers of the State, but before your fame and services had reached either to the prince or the people, you have left your place. Is this indeed the way of the benevolent?'

2. Mencius replied, 'There was Po'i;—he abode in an inferior situation, and would not, with his virtue, serve a degenerate prince. There was I Yin;—he five times went to T'ang, and five times went to Chieh. There was Hui of Liu-hsia;—he did not disdain to serve a vile prince, nor did he decline a small office. The courses pursued by those three worthies were different, but their aim was one. And what was their one aim? We must answer—"To be perfectly virtuous."

And so it is simply after this that superior men strive. Why must they all pursue the same course?'

3. K'wan pursued, 'In the time of the duke Mu of Lu, the government was in the hands of Kung-i, while Tsze-liu and Tsze-sze were ministers. And yet, the dismemberment of Lu then increased exceedingly. Such was the case, a specimen how your men of virtue are of no advantage to a kingdom!'

4. Mencius said, 'The prince of Yu did not use Pai-li Hsi, and thereby lost his State. The duke Mu of Chin used him, and became chief of all the princes. Ruin is the consequence of not employing men of virtue and talents;—how can it rest with dismemberment merely?'

5. K'wan urged again, 'Formerly, when Wang P'ao dwelt on the Ch'i, the people on the west of the Yellow River all became skilful at singing in his abrupt manner. When Mien Ch'u lived in Kao-t'ang, the people in the parts of Ch'i on the west became skilful at singing in his prolonged manner. The wives of Hwa Chau and Ch'i Liang bewailed their husbands so skilfully, that they changed the manners of the State. When there is the gift within, it manifests itself without. I have never seen the man who could do the deeds of a worthy, and did not realize the work of one. Therefore there are now no men of talents and virtue. If there were, I should know them.'

6. Mencius answered, 'When Confucius was chief minister of Justice in Lu, the prince came not to follow his counsels. Soon after there was the solstitial sacrifice, and when a part of the flesh presented in sacrifice was not sent to him, he went away even without taking off his cap of ceremony. Those who did not know him supposed it was on account of the flesh. Those who knew him supposed that it was on account of the neglect of the usual ceremony. The fact was, that Confucius wanted to go away on occasion of some small offence, not wishing to do so without some apparent cause. All men cannot be expected to understand the conduct of a superior man.'

CHAP. VII. 1. Mencius said, 'The five chiefs of the princes were sinners against the three kings. The princes of the present day are sinners against the five chiefs. The Great officers of the present day are sinners against the princes.

2. 'The sovereign visited the princes, which was called "A tour of Inspection." The princes attended at the court of the sovereign, which was called "Giving a report of office." It was a custom in the spring to examine the ploughing, and supply any deficiency of seed; and in autumn to examine the reaping, and assist where there was a deficiency of the crop. When the sovereign entered the boundaries of a State, if the new ground was being reclaimed, and the old fields well cultivated; if the old were nourished and the worthy honoured; and if men of distinguished talents were placed in office: then the prince was rewarded,—rewarded with an addition to his territory. On the other hand, if, on entering a State, the ground was found left wild or overrun with weeds; if the old were neglected and the worthy unhonoured; and if the offices were filled with hard tax gatherers: then the prince was reprimanded. If a prince once omitted his attendance at court, he was punished by degradation of rank; if he did so a second time, be was deprived of a portion of his territory; if he did so a third time, the royal forces were set in motion, and he was removed from his government. Thus the sovereign commanded the punishment, but did not himself inflict it, while the princes inflicted the punishment, but did not command it. The five chiefs, however, dragged the princes to punish other princes, and hence I say that they were sinners against the three kings.

3. 'Of the five chiefs the most powerful was the duke Hwan. At the assembly of the princes in K'wei-ch'iu, he bound the victim and placed the writing upon it, but did not slay it to smear their mouths with the blood. The first injunction in their agreement was,—"Slay the unfilial; change not the son who has been appointed heir; exalt not a concubine to be the wife." The second was,—"Honour the worthy, and maintain the talented, to give distinction to the virtuous." The third was,— "Respect the old, and be kind to the young. Be not forgetful of strangers and travellers." The fourth was, "Let not offices be hereditary, nor let officers be pluralists. In the selection of officers let the object be to get the proper men. Let not a ruler take it on himself to put to death a Great officer." The fifth was,—"Follow no crooked policy in making embankments.

Impose no restrictions on the sale of grain. Let there be no promotions without first announcing them to the sovereign." It was then said, "All we who have united in this agreement shall hereafter maintain amicable relations." The princes of the present day all violate these five prohibitions, and therefore I say that the princes of the present day are sinners against the five chiefs.

4. 'The crime of him who connives at, and aids, the wickedness of his prince is small, but the crime of him who anticipates and excites that wickedness is great. The officers of the present day all go to meet their sovereigns' wickedness, and therefore I say that the Great officers of the present day are sinners against the princes.'

CHAP. VIII. 1. The prince of Lu wanted to make the minister Shan commander of his army.

2. Mencius said, 'To employ an uninstructed people in war may be said to be destroying the people. A destroyer of the people would not have been tolerated in the times of Yao and Shun.

3. 'Though by a single battle you should subdue Ch'i, and get possession of Nan-yang, the thing ought not to be done.'

4. Shan changed countenance, and said in displeasure, 'This is what I, Ku-Li, do not understand.'

5. Mencius said, 'I will lay the case plainly before you. The territory appropriated to the sovereign is 1,000 li square. Without a thousand li, he would not have sufficient for his entertainment of the princes. The territory appropriated to a Hau is 100 li square. Without 100 li, he would not have sufficient wherewith to observe the statutes kept in his ancestral temple.

6. 'When Chau-kung was invested with the principality of Lu, it was a hundred li square. The territory was indeed enough, but it was not more than 100 li. When T'ai-kung was invested with the principality of Ch'i, it was 100 li square. The territory was indeed enough, but it was not more than 100 li.

7. 'Now Lu is five times 100 li square. If a true royal ruler were to arise, whether do you think that Lu would be diminished or increased by him?

270

8. 'If it were merely taking the place from the one State to give it to the other, a benevolent man would not do it;—how much less will he do so, when the end is to be sought by the slaughter of men!

9. 'The way in which a superior man serves his prince contemplates simply the leading him in the right path, and directing his mind to benevolence.'

CHAP. IX. 1. Mencius said, 'Those who now-a-days serve their sovereigns say, "We can for our sovereign enlarge the limits of the cultivated ground, and fill his treasuries and arsenals." Such persons are now-a-days called "Good ministers," but anciently they were called "Robbers of the people." If a sovereign follows not the right way, nor has his mind bent on benevolence, to seek to enrich him is to enrich a Chieh.

2. 'Or they will say, "We can for our sovereign form alliances with other States, so that our battles must be successful." Such persons are now-a-days called "Good ministers," but anciently they were called "Robbers of the people." If a sovereign follows not the right way, nor has his mind directed to benevolence, to seek to enrich him is to enrich a Chieh.

3. 'Although a prince, pursuing the path of the present day, and not changing its practices, were to have the throne given to him, he could not retain it for a single morning.'

CHAP. X. 1. Pai Kwei said, 'I want to take a twentieth of the produce only as the tax. What do you think of it?'

2. Mencius said, 'Your way would be that of the Mo.

3. 'In a country of ten thousand families, would it do to have only one potter?' Kwei replied, 'No. The vessels would not be enough to use.'

4. Mencius went on, 'In Mo all the five kinds of grain are not grown; it only produces the millet. There are no fortified cities, no edifices, no ancestral temples, no ceremonies of sacrifice; there are no princes requiring presents and entertainments; there is no system of officers with their various subordinates. On these accounts a tax of one-twentieth of the produce is sufficient there.

271

5. 'But now it is the Middle Kingdom that we live in. To banish the relationships of men, and have no superior men;—how can such a state of things be thought of?

6. 'With but few potters a kingdom cannot subsist;—how much less can it subsist without men of a higher rank than others?

7. 'If we wish to make the taxation lighter than the system of Yao and Shun, we shall just have a great Mo and a small Mo. If we wish to make it heavier, we shall just have the great Chieh and the small Chieh.'

CHAP. XI. 1. Pai Kwei said, 'My management of the waters is superior to that of Yu.'

2. Mencius replied, 'You are wrong, Sir. Yu's regulation of the waters was according to the laws of water.

3. 'He therefore made the four seas their receptacle, while you make the neighbouring States their receptacle.

4. 'Water flowing out of its channels is called an inundation. Inundating waters are a vast waste of water, and what a benevolent man detests. You are wrong, my good Sir.'

CHAP. XII. Mencius said, 'If a scholar have not faith, how shall he take a firm hold of things?'

CHAP. XIII. 1. The prince of Lu wanting to commit the administration of his government to the disciple Yo-chang, Mencius said, 'When I heard of it, I was so glad that I could not sleep.'

2. Kung-sun Ch'au asked, 'Is Yo-chang a man of vigour?' and was answered, 'No.' 'Is he wise in council?' 'No.' 'Is he possessed of much information?' 'No.'

3. 'What then made you so glad that you could not sleep?'

4. 'He is a man who loves what is good.'

5. 'Is the love of what is good sufficient?'

6. 'The love of what is good is more than a sufficient qualification for the government of the kingdom;—how much more is it so for the State of Lu!

7. 'If a minister love what is good, all within the four seas will count 1000 li but a small distance, and will come and lay their good thoughts before him.

8. If he do not love what is good, men will say, "How self-

conceited he looks? He is saying to himself, I know it." The language and looks of that self-conceit will keep men off at a distance of 1,000 li. When good men stop 1,000 li off, calumniators, flatterers, and sycophants will make their appearance. When a minister lives among calumniators, flatterers, and sycophants, though he may wish the State to be well governed, is it possible for it to be so?'

CHAP. XIV. 1. The disciple Ch'an said, 'What were the principles on which superior men of old took office?' Mencius replied, 'There were three cases in which they accepted office, and three in which they left it.

2. 'If received with the utmost respect and all polite observances, and they could say to themselves that the prince would carry their words into practice, then they took office with him. Afterwards, although there might be no remission in the polite demeanour of the prince, if their words were not carried into practice, they would leave him.

3. 'The second case was that in which, though the prince could not be expected at once to carry their words into practice, yet being received by him with the utmost respect, they took office with him. But afterwards, if there was a remission in his polite demeanour, they would leave him.

4. 'The last case was that of the superior man who had nothing to eat, either morning or evening, and was so famished that he could not move out of his door. If the prince, on hearing of his state, said, "I must fail in the great point,—that of carrying his doctrines into practice, neither am I able to follow his words, but I am ashamed to allow him to die of want in my country;" the assistance offered in such a case might be received, but not beyond what was sufficient to avert death.'

CHAP. XV. 1. Mencius said, 'Shun rose from among the channelled fields. Fu Yueh was called to office from the midst of his building frames; Chiao-ko from his fish and salt; Kwan I-wu from the hands of his gaoler; Sun-shu Ao from his hiding by the sea-shore; and Pai-li Hsi from the market-place.

2. 'Thus, when Heaven is about to confer a great office on any man, it first exercises his mind with suffering, and his sinews and bones with toil. It exposes his body to hunger, and

subjects him to extreme poverty. It confounds his undertakings. By all these methods it stimulates his mind, hardens his nature, and supplies his incompetencies.

3. 'Men for the most part err, and are afterwards able to reform. They are distressed in mind and perplexed in their thoughts, and then they arise to vigorous reformation. When things have been evidenced in men's looks, and set forth in their words, then they understand them.

4. 'If a prince have not about his court families attached to the laws and worthy counsellors, and if abroad there are not hostile States or other external calamities, his kingdom will generally come to ruin.

5. 'From these things we see how life springs from sorrow and calamity, and death from ease and pleasure.'

CHAP. XVI. Mencius said, 'There are many arts in teaching. I refuse, as inconsistent with my character, to teach a man, but I am only thereby still teaching him.'

BOOK VII. TSIN SIN, PART I

CHAP. I. 1. Mencius said, 'He who has exhausted all his mental constitution knows his nature. Knowing his nature, he knows Heaven.

2. 'To preserve one's mental constitution, and nourish one's nature, is the way to serve Heaven.

3. 'When neither a premature death nor long life causes a man any double-mindedness, but he waits in the cultivation of his personal character for whatever issue;—this is the way in which he establishes his Heaven-ordained being.'

CHAP. II. 1. Mencius said, 'There is an appointment for everything. A man should receive submissively what may be correctly ascribed thereto.

2. 'Therefore, he who has the true idea of what is Heaven's appointment will not stand beneath a precipitous wall.

3. 'Death sustained in the discharge of one's duties may correctly be ascribed to the appointment of Heaven.

4. 'Death under handcuffs and fetters cannot correctly be so ascribed.'

CHAP. III. 1. Mencius said, 'When we get by our seeking and lose by our neglecting;—in that case seeking is of use to getting, and the things sought for are those which are in ourselves.

2. 'When the seeking is according to the proper course, and the getting is only as appointed;—in that case the seeking is of no use to getting, and the things sought are without ourselves.'

CHAP. IV. 1. Mencius said, 'All things are already complete in us.

2. 'There is no greater delight than to be conscious of sincerity on self-examination.

3. 'If one acts with a vigorous effort at the law of reciprocity, when he seeks for the realization of perfect virtue, nothing can be closer than his approximation to it.'

CHAP. V. Mencius said, 'To act without understanding, and to do so habitually without examination, pursuing the proper path all the life without knowing its nature;—this is the way of multitudes.'

CHAP. VI. Mencius said, 'A man may not be without shame. When one is ashamed of having been without shame, he will afterwards not have occasion to be ashamed.'

CHAP. VII. 1. Mencius said, 'The sense of shame is to a man of great importance.

2. 'Those who form contrivances and versatile schemes distinguished for their artfulness, do not allow their sense of shame to come into action.

3. 'When one differs from other men in not having this sense of shame, what will he have in common with them?'

CHAP. VIII. Mencius said, 'The able and virtuous monarchs of antiquity loved virtue and forgot their power. And shall an exception be made of the able and virtuous scholars of antiquity, that they did not do the same? They delighted in their own principles, and were oblivious of the power of princes. Therefore, if kings and dukes did not show the utmost respect, and observe all forms of ceremony, they were not permitted to come frequently and visit them. If they thus found it not in their power to pay them frequent visits, how much less could they get to employ them as ministers?'

CHAP. IX. 1. Mencius said to Sung Kau-ch'ien, 'Are you fond, Sir, of travelling to the different courts? I will tell you about such travelling.

2. 'If a prince acknowledge you and follow your counsels, be perfectly satisfied. If no one do so, be the same.'

3. Kau-ch'ien said, 'What is to be done to secure this perfect satisfaction?' Mencius replied, 'Honour virtue and delight in righteousness, and so you may always be perfectly satisfied.

4. 'Therefore, a scholar, though poor, does not let go his righteousness; though prosperous, he does not leave his own path.

5. 'Poor and not letting righteousness go;—it is thus that the scholar holds possession of himself. Prosperous and not leaving the proper path;—it is thus that the expectations of the people from him are not disappointed.

6. 'When the men of antiquity realized their wishes, benefits were conferred by them on the people. If they did not realize

their wishes, they cultivated their personal character, and became illustrious in the world. If poor, they attended to their own virtue in solitude; if advanced to dignity, they made the whole kingdom virtuous as well.'

CHAP. X. Mencius said, 'The mass of men wait for a king Wan, and then they will receive a rousing impulse. Scholars distinguished from the mass, without a king Wan, rouse themselves.'

CHAP. XI. Mencius said, 'Add to a man the families of Han and Wei. If he then look upon himself without being elated, he is far beyond the mass of men.'

CHAP. XII. Mencius said, 'Let the people be employed in the way which is intended to secure their ease, and though they be toiled, they will not murmur. Let them be put to death in the way which is intended to preserve their lives, and though they die, they will not murmur at him who puts them to death.'

CHAP. XIII. 1. Mencius said, 'Under a chief, leading all the princes, the people look brisk and cheerful. Under a true sovereign, they have an air of deep contentment.

2. 'Though he slay them, they do not murmur. When he benefits them, they do not think of his merit. From day to day they make progress towards what is good, without knowing who makes them do so.

3. 'Wherever the superior man passes through, transformation follows; wherever he abides, his influence is of a spiritual nature. It flows abroad, above and beneath, like that of Heaven and Earth. How can it be said that he mends society but in a small way!'

CHAP. XIV. 1. Mencius said, 'Kindly words do not enter so deeply into men as a reputation for kindness.

2. 'Good government does not lay hold of the people so much as good instructions.

3. 'Good government is feared by the people, while good instructions are loved by them. Good government gets the people's wealth, while good instructions get their hearts.'

CHAP. XV. 1. Mencius said, 'The ability possessed by men without having been acquired by learning is intuitive ability, and the knowledge possessed by them without the exercise of thought is their intuitive knowledge.

2. 'Children carried in the arms all know to love their parents, and when they are grown a little, they all know to love their elder brothers.

3. 'Filial affection for parents is the working of benevolence. Respect for elders is the working of righteousness. There is no other reason for those feelings;—they belong to all under heaven.'

CHAP. XVI. Mencius said, 'When Shun was living amid the deep retired mountains, dwelling with the trees and rocks, and wandering among the deer and swine, the difference between him and the rude inhabitants of those remote hills appeared very small. But when he heard a single good word, or saw a single good action, he was like a stream or a river bursting its banks, and flowing out in an irresistible flood.'

CHAP. XVII. Mencius said, 'Let a man not do what his own sense of righteousness tells him not to do, and let him not desire what his sense of righteousness tells him not to desire;—to act thus is all he has to do.'

CHAP. XVIII. 1. Mencius said, 'Men who are possessed of intelligent virtue and prudence in affairs will generally be found to have been in sickness and troubles.

2. 'They are the friendless minister and concubine's son, who keep their hearts under a sense of peril, and use deep precautions against calamity. On this account they become distinguished for their intelligence.'

CHAP. XIX. 1. Mencius said, 'There are persons who serve the prince;—they serve the prince, that is, for the sake of his countenance and favour.

2. 'There are ministers who seek the tranquillity of the State, and find their pleasure in securing that tranquillity.

3. 'There are those who are the people of Heaven. They, judging that, if they were in office, they could carry out their principles, throughout the kingdom, proceed so to carry them out.

4. 'There are those who are great men. They rectify themselves and others are rectified.'

CHAP. XX. 1. Mencius said, 'The superior man has three

things in which he delights, and to be ruler over the kingdom is not one of them.

2. 'That his father and mother are both alive, and that the condition of his brothers affords no cause for anxiety;—this is one delight.

3. 'That, when looking up, he has no occasion for shame before Heaven, and, below, he has no occasion to blush before men;—this is a second delight.

4. 'That he can get from the whole kingdom the most talented individuals, and teach and nourish them;—this is the third delight.

5. 'The superior man has three things in which he delights, and to be ruler over the kingdom is not one of them.'

CHAP. XXI. 1. Mencius said, 'Wide territory and a numerous people are desired by the superior man, but what he delights in is not here.

2. 'To stand in the centre of the kingdom, and tranquillize the people within the four seas;—the superior man delights in this, but the highest enjoyment of his nature is not here.

3. What belongs by his nature to the superior man cannot be increased by the largeness of his sphere of action, nor diminished by his dwelling in poverty and retirement;—for this reason that it is determinately apportioned to him by Heaven.

4. 'What belongs by his nature to the superior man are benevolence, righteousness, propriety, and knowledge. These are rooted in his heart; their growth and manifestation are a mild harmony appearing in the countenance, a rich fullness in the back, and the character imparted to the four limbs. Those limbs understand to arrange themselves, without being told.'

CHAP. XXII. 1. Mencius said, 'Po-i, that he might avoid Chau, was dwelling on the coast of the northern sea when he heard of the rise of king Wan. He roused himself and said, "Why should I not go and follow him? I have heard that the chief of the West knows well how to nourish the old." T'ai-kung, to avoid Chau, was dwelling on the coast of the eastern sea. When he heard of the rise of king Wan, he said, "Why should I not go and follow him? I have heard that the chief if the West knows well how to nourish the old." If there were a prince in the kingdom, who knew well how to nourish the old, all men of virtue would feel that he was the proper object for them to gather to.

2. 'Around the homestead with its five mau, the space beneath the walls was planted with mulberry trees, with which the women nourished silkworms, and thus the old were able to have silk to wear. Each family had five brood hens and two brood sows, which were kept to their breeding seasons, and thus the old were able to have flesh to eat. The husbandmen cultivated their farms of 100 mau, and thus their families of eight mouths were secured against want.

3. 'The expression, "The chief of the West knows well how to nourish the old," refers to his regulation of the fields and dwellings, his teaching them to plant the mulberry and nourish those animals, and his instructing the wives and children, so as to make them nourish their aged. At fifty, warmth cannot be maintained without silks, and at seventy flesh is necessary to satisfy the appetite. Persons not kept warm nor supplied with food are said to be starved and famished, but among the people of king Wan, there were no aged who were starved or famished. This is the meaning of the expression in question.'

CHAP. XXIII. 1. Mencius said, 'Let it be seen to that their fields of grain and hemp are well cultivated, and make the taxes on them light;—so the people may be made rich.

2. 'Let it be seen to that the people use their resources of food seasonably, and expend their wealth only on the prescribed ceremonies:—so their wealth will be more than can be consumed.

3. 'The people cannot live without water and fire, yet if you knock at a man's door in the dusk of the evening, and ask for water and fire, there is no man who will not give them, such is the abundance of these things. A sage governs the kingdom so as to cause pulse and grain to be as abundant as water and fire. When pulse and grain are as abundant as water and fire, how shall the people be other than virtuous?'

CHAP. XXIV. 1. Mencius said, 'Confucius ascended the eastern hill, and Lu appeared to him small. He ascended the

T'ai mountain, and all beneath the heavens appeared to him small. So he who has contemplated the sea, finds it difficult to think anything of other waters, and he who has wandered in the gate of the sage, finds it difficult to think anything of the words of others.

2. 'There is an art in the contemplation of water.—It is necessary to look at it as foaming in waves. The sun and moon being possessed of brilliancy, their light admitted even through an orifice illuminates.

3. 'Flowing water is a thing which does not proceed till it has filled the hollows in its course. The student who has set his mind on the doctrines of the sage, does not advance to them but by completing one lesson after another.'

CHAP. XXV. 1. Mencius said, 'He who rises at cock-crowing and addresses himself earnestly to the practice of virtue, is a disciple of Shun.

2. 'He who rises at cock-crowing, and addresses himself earnestly to the pursuit of gain, is a disciple of Chih.

3. 'If you want to know what separates Shun from Chih, it is simply this,—the interval between the thought of gain and the thought of virtue.'

CHAP. XXVI. 1. Mencius said, 'The principle of the philosopher Yang was—"Each one for himself." Though he might have benefited the whole kingdom by plucking out a single hair, he would not have done it.

2. 'The philosopher Mo loves all equally. If by rubbing smooth his whole body from the crown to the heel, he could have benefited the kingdom, he would have done it.

3. 'Tsze-mo holds a medium between these. By holding that medium, he is nearer the right. But by holding it without leaving room for the exigency of circumstances, it becomes like their holding their one point.

4. 'The reason why I hate that holding to one point is the injury it does to the way of right principle. It takes up one point and disregards a hundred others.'

CHAP. XXVII. 1. Mencius said, 'The hungry think any food sweet, and the thirsty think the same of any drink, and thus they do not get the right taste of what they eat and drink. The

281

hunger and thirst, in fact, injure their palate. And is it only the mouth and belly which are injured by hunger and thirst? Men's minds are also injured by them.

2. 'If a man can prevent the evils of hunger and thirst from being any evils to his mind, he need not have any sorrow about not being equal to other men.'

CHAP. XXVIII. Mencius said, 'Hui of Liu-Hsia would not for the three highest offices of State have changed his firm purpose of life.'

CHAP. XXIX. Mencius said, 'A man with definite aims to be accomplished may be compared to one digging a well. To dig the well to a depth of seventy-two cubits, and stop without reaching the spring, is after all throwing away the well.'

CHAP. XXX. 1. Mencius said, 'Benevolence and righteousness were natural to Yao and Shun. T'ang and Wu made them their own. The five chiefs of the princes feigned them.

2. 'Having borrowed them long and not returned them, how could it be known they did not own them?'

CHAP. XXXI. 1. Kung-sun Ch'au said, 'I Yin said, "I cannot be near and see him so disobedient to reason," and therewith he banished T'a-chia to T'ung. The people were much pleased. When T'a-chia became virtuous, he brought him back, and the people were again much pleased.

2. 'When worthies are ministers, may they indeed banish their sovereigns in this way when they are not virtuous?'

3. Mencius replied, 'If they have the same purpose as I Yin, they may. If they have not the same purpose, it would be usurpation.'

CHAP. XXXII. Kung-sun Ch'au said, 'It is said, in the Book of Poetry,

"He will not eat the bread of idleness!"

How is it that we see superior men eating without labouring?' Mencius replied, 'When a superior man resides in a country, if its sovereign employ his counsels, he comes to tranquillity, wealth and glory. If the young in it follow his instructions, they become filial, obedient to their elders, true-hearted, and faithful. What greater example can there be than this of not eating the bread of idleness?'

CHAP. XXXIII. 1. The king's son, Tien, asked Mencius, saying, 'What is the business of the unemployed scholar?'

2. Mencius replied, 'To exalt his aim.'

3. Tien asked again, 'What do you mean by exalting the aim?' The answer was, 'Setting it simply on benevolence and righteousness. He thinks how to put a single innocent person to death is contrary to benevolence; how to take what one has not a right to is contrary to righteousness; that one's dwelling should be benevolence; and one's path should be righteousness. Where else should he dwell? What other path should he pursue? When benevolence is the dwelling-place of the heart, and righteousness the path of the life, the business of a great man is complete.'

CHAP. XXXIV. Mencius said, 'Supposing that the kingdom of Ch'i were offered, contrary to righteousness, to Ch'an Chung, he would not receive it, and all people believe in him, as a man of the highest worth. But this is only the righteousness which declines a dish of rice or a plate of soup. A man can have no greater crimes than to disown his parents and relatives, and the relations of sovereign and minister, superiors and inferiors. How can it be allowed to give a man credit for the great excellences because he possesses a small one?'

CHAP. XXXV. 1. T'ao Ying asked, saying, 'Shun being sovereign, and Kao-yao chief minister of justice, if Ku-sau had murdered a man, what would have been done in the case?'

2. Mencius said, 'Kao-yao would simply have apprehended him.'

3. 'But would not Shun have forbidden such a thing?'

4. 'Indeed, how could Shun have forbidden it? Kao-yao had received the law from a proper source.'

5. 'In that case what would Shun have done?'

6. 'Shun would have regarded abandoning the kingdom as throwing away a worn-out sandal. He would privately have taken his father on his back, and retired into concealment, living some where along the sea-coast. There he would have been all his life, cheerful and happy, forgetting the kingdom.'

CHAP. XXXVI. 1. Mencius, going from Fan to Ch'i, saw the king of Ch'i's son at a distance, and said with a deep sigh, 'One's position alters the air, just as the nurture affects the body. Great is the influence of position! Are we not all men's sons in this respect?'

2. Mencius said, 'The residence, the carriages and horses, and the dress of the king's son, are mostly the same as those of other men. That he looks so is occasioned by his position. How much more should a peculiar air distinguish him whose position is in the wide house of the world!

3. 'When the prince of Lu went to Sung, he called out at the T'ieh-chai gate, and the keeper said, "This is not our prince. How is it that his voice is so like that of our prince?" This was occasioned by nothing but the correspondence of their positions.'

CHAP. XXXVII. 1. Mencius said, 'To feed a scholar and not love him, is to treat him as a pig. To love him and not respect him, is to keep him as a domestic animal.

2. 'Honouring and respecting are what exist before any offering of gifts.

3. 'If there be honouring and respecting without the reality of them, a superior man may not be retained by such empty demonstrations.'

CHAP. XXXVIII. Mencius said, 'The bodily organs with their functions belong to our Heaven-conferred nature. But a man must be a sage before he can satisfy the design of his bodily organization.'

CHAP. XXXIX. 1. The king Hsuan of Ch'i wanted to shorten the period of mourning. Kung-sun Ch'au said, 'To have one whole year's mourning is better than doing away with it altogether.'

2. Mencius said, 'That is just as if there were one twisting the arm of his elder brother, and you were merely to say to him "Gently, gently, if you please." Your only course should be to teach such an one filial piety and fraternal duty.'

3. At that time, the mother of one of the king's sons had died, and his tutor asked for him that he might be allowed to observe a few months' mourning. Kung-sun Ch'au asked,

'What do you say of this?'

4. Mencius replied, 'This is a case where the party wishes to complete the whole period, but finds it impossible to do so. The addition of even a single day is better than not mourning at all. I spoke of the case where there was no hindrance, and the party neglected the thing itself.'

CHAP. XL. 1. Mencius said, 'There are five ways in which the superior man effects his teaching.

2. 'There are some on whom his influence descends like seasonable rain.

3. 'There are some whose virtue he perfects, and some of whose talents he assists the development.

4. 'There are some whose inquiries he answers.

5. 'There are some who privately cultivate and correct themselves.

6. These five ways are the methods in which the superior man effects his teaching.'

CHAP. XLI. 1. Kung-sun Ch'au said, 'Lofty are your principles and admirable, but to learn them may well be likened to ascending the heavens,—something which cannot be reached. Why not adapt your teaching so as to cause learners to consider them attainable, and so daily exert themselves!'

2. Mencius said, 'A great artificer does not, for the sake of a stupid workman, alter or do away with the marking-line. I did not, for the sake of a stupid archer, charge his rule for drawing the bow.

3. 'The superior man draws the bow, but does not discharge the arrow, having seemed to leap with it to the mark; and he there stands exactly in the middle of the path. Those who are able, follow him.'

CHAP. XLII. 1. Mencius said, 'When right principles prevail throughout the kingdom, one's principles must appear along with one's person. When right principles disappear from the kingdom, one's person must vanish along with one's principles.

2. 'I have not heard of one's principles being dependent for their manifestation on other men.'

CHAP. XLIII. 1. The disciple Kung-tu said, 'When Kang of

T'ang made his appearance in your school, it seemed proper that a polite consideration should be paid to him, and yet you did not answer him. Why was that?'

2. Mencius replied, 'I do not answer him who questions me presuming on his nobility, nor him who presumes on his talents, nor him who presumes on his age, nor him who presumes on services performed to me, nor him who presumes on old acquaintance. Two of those things were chargeable on Kang of T'ang.'

CHAP. XLIV. 1. Mencius said, 'He who stops short where stopping is acknowledged to be not allowable, will stop short in everything. He who behaves shabbily to those whom he ought to treat well, will behave shabbily to all.

2. 'He who advances with precipitation will retire with speed.'

CHAP. XLV. Mencius said, 'In regard to inferior creatures, the superior man is kind to them, but not loving. In regard to people generally, he is loving to them, but not affectionate. He is affectionate to his parents, and lovingly disposed to people generally. He is lovingly disposed to people generally, and kind to creatures.'

CHAP. XLVI. 1. Mencius said, 'The wise embrace all knowledge, but they are most earnest about what is of the greatest importance. The benevolent embrace all in their love, but what they consider of the greatest importance is to cultivate an earnest affection for the virtuous. Even the wisdom of Yao and Shun did not extend to everything, but they attended earnestly to what was important. Their benevolence did not show itself in acts of kindness to every man, but they earnestly cultivated an affection for the virtuous.

2. 'Not to be able to keep the three years' mourning, and to be very particular about that of three months, or that of five months; to eat immoderately and swill down the soup, and at the same time to inquire about the precept not to tear the meat with the teeth;—such things show what I call an ignorance of what is most important.

BOOK VII. TSIN SIN, PART II

CHAP. I. 1. Mencius said, 'The opposite indeed of benevolent was the king Hui of Liang! The benevolent, beginning with what they care for, proceed to what they do not care for. Those who are the opposite of benevolent, beginning with what they do not care for, proceed to what they care for.'

2. 'Kung-sun Ch'au said, 'What do you mean?' Mencius answered, 'The king Hui of Liang, for the matter of territory, tore and destroyed his people, leading them to battle. Sustaining a great defeat, he would engage again, and afraid lest they should not be able to secure the victory, urged his son whom he loved till he sacrificed him with them. This is what I call—"beginning with what they do not care for, and proceeding to what they care for."'

CHAP. II. 1. Mencius said, 'In the "Spring and Autumn" there are no righteous wars. Instances indeed there are of one war better than another.

2. '"Correction" is when the supreme authority punishes its subjects by force of arms. Hostile States do not correct one another.'

CHAP. III. 1. Mencius said, 'It would be better to be without the Book of History than to give entire credit to it.

2. 'In the "Completion of the War," I select two or three passages only, which I believe.

3. '"The benevolent man has no enemy under heaven. When the prince the most benevolent was engaged against him who was the most the opposite, how could the blood of the people have flowed till it floated the pestles of the mortars?"'

CHAP. IV. 1. Mencius said, 'There are men who say—"I am skilful at marshalling troops, I am skilful at conducting a battle!"—They are great criminals.

2. 'If the ruler of a State love benevolence, he will have no enemy in the kingdom.

3. When T'ang was executing his work of correction in the south, the rude tribes on the north murmured. When he was

executing it in the east, the rude tribes on the west murmured. Their cry was—"Why does he make us last?"

4. 'When king Wu punished Yin, he had only three hundred chariots of war, and three thousand life-guards.

5. 'The king said, "Do not fear. Let me give you repose. I am no enemy to the people!" On this, they bowed their heads to the earth, like the horns of animals falling off.

6. '"Royal correction" is but another word for rectifying. Each State wishing itself to be corrected, what need is there for fighting?'

CHAP. V. Mencius said, 'A carpenter or a carriage-maker may give a man the circle and square, but cannot make him skilful in the use of them.'

CHAP. VI. Mencius said, 'Shun's manner of eating his parched grain and herbs was as if he were to be doing so all his life. When he became sovereign, and had the embroidered robes to wear, the lute to play, and the two daughters of Yao to wait on him, he was as if those things belonged to him as a matter of course.'

CHAP. VII. Mencius said, 'From this time forth I know the heavy consequences of killing a man's near relations. When a man kills another's father, that other will kill his father; when a man kills another's elder brother, that other will kill his elder brother. So he does not himself indeed do the act, but there is only an interval between him and it.'

CHAP. VIII. 1. Mencius said, 'Anciently, the establishment of the frontier-gates was to guard against violence.

2. 'Nowadays, it is to exercise violence.'

CHAP. IX. Mencius said, 'If a man himself do not walk in the right path, it will not be walked in even by his wife and children. If he order men according to what is not the right way, he will not be able to get the obedience of even his wife and children.'

CHAP. X. Mencius said, 'A bad year cannot prove the cause of death to him whose stores of gain are large; an age of corruption cannot confound him whose equipment of virtue is complete.'

CHAP. XI. Mencius said, 'A man who loves fame may be

able to decline a State of a thousand chariots; but if he be not really the man to do such a thing, it will appear in his countenance, in the matter of a dish of rice or a platter of soup.'

CHAP. XII. 1. Mencius said, 'If men of virtue and ability be not confided in, a State will become empty and void.

2. 'Without the rules of propriety and distinctions of right, the high and the low will be thrown into confusion.

3. 'Without the great principles of government and their various business, there will not be wealth sufficient for the expenditure.'

CHAP. XIII. Mencius said, 'There are instances of individuals without benevolence, who have got possession of a single State, but there has been no instance of the throne's being got by one without benevolence.'

CHAP. XIV. 1. Mencius said, 'The people are the most important element in a nation; the spirits of the land and grain are the next; the sovereign is the lightest.

2. 'Therefore to gain the peasantry is the way to become sovereign; to gain the sovereign is the way to become a prince of a State; to gain the prince of a State is the way to become a great officer.

3. 'When a prince endangers the altars of the spirits of the land and grain, he is changed, and another appointed in his place.

4. 'When the sacrificial victims have been perfect, the millet in its vessels all pure, and the sacrifices offered at their proper seasons, if yet there ensue drought, or the waters overflow, the spirits of the land and grain are changed, and others appointed in their place.'

CHAP. XV. Mencius said, 'A sage is the teacher of a hundred generations:—this is true of Po-i and Hui of Liu-Hsia. Therefore when men now bear the character of Po-i, the corrupt become pure, and the weak acquire determination. When they hear the character of Hui of Liu-Hsia, the mean become generous, and the niggardly become liberal. Those two made themselves distinguished a hundred generations ago, and after a hundred generations, those who hear of them, are all aroused in this manner. Could such effects be produced by them, if they had not been sages? And how much more did they affect those who were in contiguity with them, and felt their inspiring influence!'

CHAP. XVI. Mencius said, 'Benevolence is the distinguishing characteristic of man. As embodied in man's conduct, it is called the path of duty.'

CHAP. XVII. Mencius said, 'When Confucius was leaving Lu, he said, "I will set out by-and-by;"—this was the way in which to leave the State of his parents. When he was leaving Ch'i, he strained off with his hand the water in which his rice was being rinsed, took the rice, and went away;—this was the way in which to leave a strange State.'

CHAP. XVIII. Mencius said, 'The reason why the superior man was reduced to straits between Ch'an and Ts'ai was because neither the princes of the time nor their ministers sympathized or communicated with him.'

CHAP. XIX. 1. Mo Ch'i said, 'Greatly am I from anything to depend upon from the mouths of men.'

2. Mencius observed, 'There is no harm in that. Scholars are more exposed than others to suffer from the mouths of men.

3. 'It is said, in the Book of Poetry,
"My heart is disquieted and grieved,
I am hated by the crowd of mean creatures."
This might have been said by Confucius. And again,
"Though he did not remove their wrath,
He did not let fall his own fame."
This might be said of king Wan.'

CHAP. XX. Mencius said, 'Anciently, men of virtue and talents by means of their own enlightenment made others enlightened. Nowadays, it is tried, while they are themselves in darkness, and by means of that darkness, to make others enlightened.'

CHAP. XXI. Mencius said to the disciple Kao, 'There are the footpaths along the hills;—if suddenly they be used, they become roads; and if, as suddenly they are not used, the wild grass fills them up. Now, the wild grass fills up your mind.'

CHAP. XXII. 1. The disciple Kao said, 'The music of Yu

was better than that of king Wan.'

2. Mencius observed, 'On what ground do you say so?' and the other replied, 'Because at the pivot the knob of Yu's bells is nearly worn through.'

3. Mencius said, 'How can that be a sufficient proof? Are the ruts at the gate of a city made by a single two-horsed chariot?'

CHAP. XXIII. 1. When Ch'i was suffering from famine, Ch'an Tsin said to Mencius, 'The people are all thinking that you, Master, will again ask that the granary of T'ang be opened for them. I apprehend you will not do so a second time.'

2. Mencius said, 'To do it would be to act like Fang Fu. There was a man of that name in Tsin, famous for his skill in seizing tigers. Afterwards he became a scholar of reputation, and going once out to the wild country, he found the people all in pursuit of a tiger. The tiger took refuge in a corner of a hill, where no one dared to attack him, but when they saw Fang Fu, they ran and met him. Fang Fu immediately bared his arms, and descended from the carriage. The multitude were pleased with him, but those who were scholars laughed at him.'

CHAP. XXIV. 1. Mencius said, 'For the mouth to desire sweet tastes, the eye to desire beautiful colours, the ear to desire pleasant sounds, the nose to desire fragrant odours, and the four limbs to desire ease and rest;—these things are natural. But there is the appointment of Heaven in connexion with them, and the superior man does not say of his pursuit of them, "It is my nature."

2. 'The exercise of love between father and son, the observance of righteousness between sovereign and minister, the rules of ceremony between guest and host, the display of knowledge in recognising the talented, and the fulfilling the heavenly course by the sage;—these are the appointment of Heaven. But there is an adaptation of our nature for them. The superior man does not say, in reference to them, "It is the appointment of Heaven."'

CHAP. XXV. 1. Hao-shang Pu-hai asked, saying, 'What sort of man is Yo-chang?' Mencius replied, 'He is a good man, a real man.'

2. 'What do you mean by "A good man," "A real man?"'

3. The reply was, 'A man who commands our liking is what is called a good man.

4. 'He whose goodness is part of himself is what is called real man.

5. 'He whose goodness has been filled up is what is called beautiful man.

6. He whose completed goodness is brightly displayed is what is called a great man.

7. 'When this great man exercises a transforming influence, he is what is called a sage.

8. 'When the sage is beyond our knowledge, he is what is called a spirit-man.

9. 'Yo-chang is between the two first characters, and below the four last.'

CHAP. XXVI. 1. Mencius said, 'Those who are fleeing from the errors of Mo naturally turn to Yang, and those who are fleeing from the errors of Yang naturally turn to orthodoxy. When they so turn, they should at once and simply be received.

2. 'Those who nowadays dispute with the followers of Yang and Mo do so as if they were pursuing a stray pig, the leg of which, after they have got it to enter the pen, they proceed to tie.'

CHAP. XXVII. Mencius said, 'There are the exactions of hempen-cloth and silk, of grain, and of personal service. The prince requires but one of these at once, deferring the other two. If he require two of them at once, then the people die of hunger. If he require the three at once, then fathers and sons are separated.'

CHAP. XXVIII. Mencius said, 'The precious things of a prince are three;—the territory, the people, the government and its business. If one value as most precious pearls and jade, calamity is sure to befall him.'

CHAP. XXIX. Pan-ch'ang Kwo having obtained an official situation in Ch'i, Mencius said, 'He is a dead man, that Pan-ch'ang Kwo!' Pan-ch'ang Kwo being put to death, the disciples asked, saying, 'How did you know, Master, that he would meet with death?' Mencius replied, 'He was a man, who had a little ability, but had not learned the great doctrines of the superior man. He was just qualified to bring death upon himself, but for nothing more.'

CHAP. XXX. 1. When Mencius went to T'ang, he was lodged in the Upper palace. A sandal in the process of making had been placed there in a window, and when the keeper of the place came to look for it, he could not find it.

2. On this, some one asked Mencius, saying, 'Is it thus that your followers pilfer?' Mencius replied, 'Do you think that they came here to pilfer the sandal?' The man said, 'I apprehend not. But you, Master, having arranged to give lessons, do not go back to inquire into the past, and you do not reject those who come to you. If they come with the mind to learn, you receive them without any more ado.'

CHAP. XXXI. 1. Mencius said, 'All men have some things which they cannot bear;—extend that feeling to what they can bear, and benevolence will be the result. All men have some things which they will not do;—extend that feeling to the things which they do, and righteousness will be the result.

2. 'If a man can give full development to the feeling which makes him shrink from injuring others, his benevolence will be more than can be called into practice. If he can give full development to the feeling which refuses to break through, or jump over, a wall, his righteousness will be more than can be called into practice.

3. 'If he can give full development to the real feeling of dislike with which he receives the salutation, "Thou," "Thou," he will act righteously in all places and circumstances.

4. 'When a scholar speaks what he ought not to speak, by guile of speech seeking to gain some end; and when he does not speak what he ought to speak, by guile of silence seeking to gain some end;—both these cases are of a piece with breaking through a neighbour's wall.'

CHAP. XXXII. 1. Mencius said, 'Words which are simple, while their meaning is far-reaching, are good words. Principles which, as held, are compendious, while their application is extensive, are good principles. The words of the superior man do not go below the girdle, but great principles are contained in them.

2. 'The principle which the superior man holds is that of personal cultivation, but the kingdom is thereby tranquillized.

3. 'The disease of men is this:—that they neglect their own fields, and go to weed the fields of others, and that what they require from others is great, while what they lay upon themselves is light.'

CHAP. XXXIII. 1. Mencius said, 'Yao and Shun were what they were by nature; T'ang and Wu were so by returning to natural virtue.

2. 'When all the movements, in the countenance and every turn of the body, are exactly what is proper, that shows the extreme degree of the complete virtue. Weeping for the dead should be from real sorrow, and not because of the living. The regular path of virtue is to be pursued without any bend, and from no view to emolument. The words should all be necessarily sincere, not with any desire to do what is right.

3. 'The superior man performs the law of right, and thereby waits simply for what has been appointed.'

CHAP. XXXIV. 1. Mencius said, 'Those who give counsel to the great should despise them, and not look at their pomp and display.

2. 'Halls several times eight cubits high, with beams projecting several cubits;—these, if my wishes were to be realized, I would not have. Food spread before me over ten cubits square, and attendants and concubines to the amount of hundreds;—these, though my wishes were realized, I would not have. Pleasure and wine, and the dash of hunting, with thousands of chariots following after me;—these, though my wishes were realized, I would not have. What they esteem are what I would have nothing to do with; what I esteem are the rules of the ancients.—Why should I stand in awe of them?'

CHAP. XXXV. Mencius said, 'To nourish the mind there is nothing better than to make the desires few. Here is a man whose desires are few:—in some things he may not be able to keep his heart, but they will be few. Here is a man whose desires are many:—in some things he may be able to keep his heart, but they will be few.'

CHAP. XXXVI. 1. Mencius said, 'Tsang Hsi was fond of sheep-dates, and his son, the philosopher Tsang, could not bear to eat sheep-dates.'

2. Kung-sun Ch'au asked, saying, 'Which is best,—minced meat and broiled meat, or sheep-dates?' Mencius said, 'Mince and broiled meat, to be sure.' Kung-sun Ch'au went on, 'Then why did the philosopher Tsang eat mince and broiled meat, and would not eat sheep-dates?' Mencius answered, 'For mince and broiled meat there is a common liking, while that for sheep-dates was peculiar. We avoid the name, but do not avoid the surname. The surname is common; the name is peculiar.'

CHAP. XXXVII. 1. Wan Chang asked, saying, 'Confucius, when he was in Ch'an, said: "Let me return. The scholars of my school are ambitious, but hasty. They are for advancing and seizing their object, but cannot forget their early ways." Why did Confucius, when he was in Ch'an, think of the ambitious scholars of Lu?'

2. Mencius replied, 'Confucius not getting men pursuing the true medium, to whom he might communicate his instructions, determined to take the ardent and the cautiously-decided. The ardent would advance to seize their object; the cautiously-decided would keep themselves from certain things. It is not to be thought that Confucius did not wish to get men pursuing the true medium, but being unable to assure himself of finding such, he therefore thought of the next class.'

3. 'I venture to ask what sort of men they were who could be styled "The ambitious?"'

4. 'Such,' replied Mencius, 'as Ch'in Chang, Tsang Hsi, and Mu P'ei, were those whom Confucius styled "ambitious."'

5. 'Why were they styled "ambitious?"'

6. The reply was, 'Their aim led them to talk magniloquently, saying, "The ancients!" "The ancients!" But their actions, where we fairly compare them with their words, did not correspond with them.

7. 'When he found also that he could not get such as were thus ambitious, he wanted to get scholars who would consider anything impure as beneath them. Those were the cautiously-

decided, a class next to the former.'

8. Chang pursued his questioning, 'Confucius said, "They are only your good careful people of the villages at whom I feel no indignation, when they pass my door without entering my house. Your good careful people of the villages are the thieves of virtue." What sort of people were they who could be styled "Your good careful people of the villages?"'

9. Mencius replied, 'They are those who say, "Why are they so magniloquent? Their words have not respect to their actions and their actions have not respect to their words, but they say, "The ancients! The ancients! Why do they act so peculiarly, and are so cold and distant? Born in this age, we should be of this age, to be good is all that is needed." Eunuch-like, flattering their generation;—such are your good careful men of the villages.'

10. Wan Chang said, 'Their whole village styles those men good and careful. In all their conduct they are so. How was it that Confucius considered them the thieves of virtue?'

11. Mencius replied, 'If you would blame them, you find nothing to allege. If you would criticise them, you have nothing to criticise. They agree with the current customs. They consent with an impure age. Their principles have a semblance of right-heartedness and truth. Their conduct has a semblance of disinterestedness and purity. All men are pleased with them, and they think themselves right, so that it is impossible to proceed with them to the principles of Yao and Shun. On this account they are called "The thieves of virtue."

12. 'Confucius said, "I hate a semblance which is not the reality. I hate the darnel, lest it be confounded with the corn. I hate glib-tonguedness, lest it be confounded with righteousness. I hate sharpness of tongue, lest it be confounded with sincerity. I hate the music of Chang, lest it be confounded with the true music. I hate the reddish blue, lest it be confounded with vermilion. I hate your good careful men of the villages, lest they be confounded with the truly virtuous."

13. 'The superior man seeks simply to bring back the unchanging standard, and, that being correct, the masses are

roused to virtue. When they are so aroused, forthwith perversities and glossed wickedness disappear.'

CHAP. XXXVIII. 1. Mencius said, 'From Yao and Shun down to T'ang were 500 years and more. As to Yu and Kao Yao, they saw those earliest sages, and so knew their doctrines, while T'ang heard their doctrines as transmitted, and so knew them.

2. 'From T'ang to king Wan were 500 years and more. As to I Yin, and Lai Chu, they saw T'ang and knew his doctrines, while king Wan heard them as transmitted, and so knew them.

3. 'From king Wan to Confucius were 500 years and more. As to T'ai-kung Wang and San I-shang, they saw Wan, and so knew his doctrines, while Confucius heard them as transmitted, and so knew them.

4. 'From Confucius downwards until now, there are only 100 years and somewhat more. The distance in time from the sage is so far from being remote, and so very near at hand was the sage's residence. In these circumstances, is there no one to transmit his doctrines? Yea, is there no one to do so?

Printed in Great Britain
by Amazon

40061200R00172